HOW TO BE

THE
STARTUP
HERO

*A Guide and Textbook for
Entrepreneurs and Aspiring
Entrepreneurs*

TIM DRAPER

BETA 0.91

TABLE OF CONTENTS

PREFACE

DEDICATION

TO MY FATHER, BILL DRAPER, MY SPIRIT.

Dad is living an extraordinary life with great gusto and enthusiasm. He was a pioneer in venture capital, beginning his career in 1958, the year I was born. He was Chairman of the Export Import Bank, Administrator of the United Nations Development Programme (UNDP), and the first venture capitalist in India. He started the first social venture fund and supports an extended family that goes well beyond his nuclear one …and he wrote an awesome book called "The Startup Game." I recommend that you read that one too. It will lift your spirits. His optimism is contagious. He is my Startup Hero.

People just love my dad. He shows a real interest in everyone he meets. His judgment is extraordinary, he sees the good in everyone he meets, and he can tell in a short interview what someone's motivation and potential is. It is his gift. He has given me a lot of good advice over the years, for example, he said, "Put in that extra 10%," "Make deals so everyone is happy with it," "Leave your wallet and keys in the same place every day," "Back winners". But perhaps the best piece of advice he has given me was when he wanted me to sell a few tables to a fundraising event for the then soon-to-be Vice President George H.W. Bush: "Son, I am going to tell you something your grandfather told me. It doesn't matter who is doing the buying and who is doing the selling. It is the human connection that matters the most." This is terrific advice. Since that moment, I have never hesitated to ask for donations, make offers that might be a stretch, or raise money for my venture capital funds. It is all about the human connection. I have made some of my best friends and business connections by making an ask.

TO MY MOTHER, PHYLLIS DRAPER, MY GUIDE.

Mom made sure I minded my manners, read the classics, and learned to touch type. She kept me alive, fed me, taught me grammar, created an environment for me to explore and create, put me to work in the garden, and opened my eyes to the possibility of going to prep school. And she listens whenever I need her.

She is also the toughest person I know. When I asked her, "Isn't it awful?" regarding her Parkinson's disease, she said, "It is just another of life's challenges." She continues to walk a mile each day and go out to events that her children and grandchildren are involved in, even though her disease is horribly debilitating. When she falls, as she does often because of the disease, her first words are always, "I am fine." Her determination and perseverance is a model for everyone she meets. She is my Startup Hero.

TO MY WIFE, MELISSA. MY LOVE.

Melissa has been my solid ground. She has been my moral compass and my guiding light whenever I ran into a fork in the road. She sets me free and reels me in. She introduces me to a world I never would have seen without her, one full of the arts, and flowers, and interior design, and city living. Her cut-to-the-chase understanding of people and their motivations, her thoughtfulness, her clear sense of right and wrong, her unusually fun and wacky sense of humor, and her love and belief in me have made my life amazing-and made this book possible. She is my shelter from the storm. People ask me what drives me on. The answer is Melissa. Melissa drives me on to be my best self.

Together, we raised our four children to be Startup Heroes. She is my Startup Hero.

TO MY ASSISTANT, KAREN MOSTES-WITHROW. MY ALLY.

Karen has been my rock for the last 30 years. Throughout these years, no matter what happens, I know Karen has my back. I couldn't have done half of the things I have done without her. She knows what I need at work before I realize I need it. Her faith in me is unwavering. Her loyalty is unmatched. She has worked by my side, through thick and thin. I remember one time in particular, we used a low-end mover called Starving Students to take us from one office to another. The mover quit his job in the middle of the move, and we had to do it ourselves. Karen stayed with me until 1:30 in the morning, moving all that furniture into and out of the truck. When I ask her to do something, no matter how outrageous, she just does it, on what must be a glimmer of hope that there may be method to my madness. She is my Startup Hero.

TO MY BUDDY, CREE EDWARDS. MY FRIEND.

Cree has been my oldest and dearest friend since we shared a crib together as babies. Cree came up with the original idea for the pledge that I have organized this book around, and he has been a true friend through thick and thin. I backed both of his companies and he made them hugely successful. Now he serves on the board of Draper University. We love to compete in everything, pushing each other to excel and cheering each other on. Naturally, Cree is writing a book too. So, Cree, game on, Startup Hero!

TO ALL OTHERS.

Special thanks to Google, BrainyQuote, and Wikipedia for providing information and answers I required to write this book. I hope they are accurate. If they are not, I am sure I will get feedback. Special thanks also go to all the people I mention in this book. I understand that your recollections of events and mine may differ, but I did my best to lay out each story and I hope you appreciate the spirit of the book. Fortunately, I can change the online version of this book and don't have to wait for a new printing. If you do have a different recollection, please let me know, and I may make updates accordingly. If I don't, just think of this as fake news ;).

ORIGINS

DRAPER HISTORY

My grandfather, General William H. Draper Jr., was a dynamo. He led the economic portion of the Marshall Plan for Japan and Germany after World War II. He was the first Undersecretary of the Army and the first US Ambassador to NATO. He started Planned Parenthood, and as delegate to the United Nations Population Commission, he worked with Mao Zedong on the Family Planning Policy in China in 1970, which led to China's one child policy in 1979. He financed the San Francisco Bay Bridge while working at Dillon Read & Co. He worked his way through college by being "The Motorcycle Magician." But, perhaps his greatest contribution to the world was that he was the first Silicon Valley venture capitalist, founding Draper Gaither and Anderson in 1957.

My grandfather on my mother's side, William Culbertson was a networker. He was chairman of Merrill Lynch International, growing their remote offices overseas. Seeing an opportunity to spread the ability for people to more easily invest in the stock market, he set up brokerage offices for Merrill Lynch all over the world.

My father, William H. Draper III, is a trailblazer. He was a pioneer in venture capital, funding the first-ever software company, Activision; the first floppy disk manufacturers, Quantum and Priam; the first agricultural DNA company Hybritech; and the first Silicon Valley Chinese Immigrant entrepreneur, David Lee, who founded Qume, the first daisy wheel computer printer.

In 1981, he was appointed chairman of the US Export-Import Bank by President Ronald Reagan, where he led the various export-import banks from around the world to make their loans at market rates, saving all the countries billions of dollars. In 1986, he became administrator of the UNDP (second in ranking only to the Secretary General of the United Nations), where he visited leaders of 110 countries, promoting free markets, women in the work force, and democracy. He regularly told country despots that they were "life presidents" to get them thinking of legacy and secession planning. I remember going with Dad on a mission to Uganda, where we met President Museveni, and I watched as Dad guided Museveni to free market thinking by discussing minestrone soup. Museveni argued that they could serve tourists minestrone soup made from local vegetables, and Dad explained that the customer would be a better judge of how the minestrone soup should be made.

In 1994, at age 66, Dad started Draper International, the first cross-border Indian venture capital fund, where he made his investors 17 times their money with an infinite internal rate of return (IRR), since he got their commitments before he called their money and personally bankrolled an investment that returned the fund before he collected their investment dollars. In 2001, at age 73, he started Draper Richards Foundation, which brought his understanding of startups to the non-profit world. He made companies focus on sustainability and helped start innovative non-profit companies like Kiva, Room to Read and hundreds of others.

Driving progress is in my blood.

My mother kept the home fires burning and made sure my sisters and I were all kind and polite, well presented, spoke with good grammar, read great books, always thought the best of everyone and every situation, and willing to laugh at ourselves to keep our egos in check. When she was asked by my high school headmaster what she hoped for me to become, she said, "I want him to become a renaissance man."

My two older sisters, Becky and Polly, were instrumental in my development. Becky and I loved games, puzzles and math challenges. We loved the competitions, but fought each other like wild animals. She would regularly root out my weaknesses, both physical and psychological, and exploit and expose them. I remember her carrying around a photograph of me sitting naked on the toilet threatening to expose me if I didn't do her bidding. She was also my biggest supporter and a surrogate mother when Mom was away. She went to cheer me on at the Andover-Deerfield football game where Cree and I were pitted against each other on the line, defensive end to wide receiver. Cree threw an elbow and broke my nose and Becky shrieked at him and took me to the hospital. To this day, Cree is afraid of Becky.

Polly spurred on my imagination. She built forts, wrote plays and movies for us to perform, created forts in her room out of cardboard, and had a pet alligator. She once gave me a magic tree with hundreds of candy leaves, saying that it would grow new candy every day with the one stipulation that only one piece could be eaten per day for the tree to continue its magic power. The first day I ate a Snickers Bar, and a Milky Way appeared in its place. The second day, Cree came over and convinced me to take one piece and give one to him. The following day, the tree was barren. The fantasy became dark magic overnight. Polly is a gifted actor, writer and director today—she has retained her magic touch.

My formal education came from traditional schools and universities, Hillview Elementary School (public) for K-8, Phillips Academy Andover for high school, Stanford University for college, and the Harvard Business School for graduate school. Perhaps my more important education came from playing team and individual sports, exploring with friends while avoiding authorities, painting trailers, weeding the garden, mowing the lawn, selling apples, collecting baseball cards, hiking and camping under the stars, distributing oysters, creating Stanford: The Game, working on oil wells, traveling solo through Europe, negotiating with my sisters, and watching and learning from my father and mother.

I met my wife, Melissa, at Polly's graduation party. She was a friend to both of my sisters, this gorgeous, smart, funny girl wearing a polka dotted dress that she made herself. I asked her to dance, and she handed me a banana and said I was very ap-peel-ing. I was still 14 and she was 18. When I asked her to go out on our first date, she had to drive because I was too young (she still does, but now it is for safety reasons). I fell in love with her, but she had to go back to Smith College and I to Andover, so we let it be. Ten years later, we reconnected and got married in August of 1982, just before I went to business school and we started our life together in Boston. During our honeymoon, in preparation for business school, I had to learn the HP 12-C business calculator, so (as she occasionally reminds me) I was not the perfect romantic honeymooner. We had our first child, Jesse, while I was in business school. Fatherhood totally rocked my world. I was the first of any of my friends or siblings to have a child and I was clueless on how to manage. Luckily, Melissa seemed to know everything. We lived in a small apartment in Soldiers Field

Park, where Jesse slept in a chest drawer.

After business school, I took a half venture capital, half investment banking job with Alex. Brown & Sons, a boutique investment bank in San Francisco (with regular trips to Baltimore). Under the tutelage of Steven Brooks and Don Dixon for banking and Bruns Grayson for venture capital, I got some good training, but I mostly calculated discounted cash flow projections on spreadsheets, and I lasted about one year.

ORIGIN STORY

In July of 1985, I was 27 years old, just a year out of Harvard Business School, when I informed Melissa that I was going to start my own venture capital firm. She was very concerned. We had a child then and one on the way, and taking this kind of a risk with their future was scary for her. For me, it was exhilarating!

My father had left a registered Small Business Investment Company (SBIC) in a blind trust when he went to work for the US Export-Import Bank. He was moving over to the job at the United Nations. He suggested that I take over the family SBIC and see what I could do with it. It had about $2 million worth of illiquid private stocks in it. If I was going to invest anything, I would have to wait until there was a liquidity event, but the opportunity still sounded exciting to me. Burt McMurtry at Technology Venture Investors generously let me have an office there since I was good friends with Dave Marquardt and Bob Kagle, who were both young associates at the company. To find entrepreneurs, I started to knock on doors of companies who were working out of new real estate developments that had "software" in their name.

In studying the SBIC program, I discovered that I could borrow up to three times the assets in the fund as long as I followed some small business guidelines. I contacted Marvin Klapp, who was the sole administrator of the SBIC program (now there are 600 people in the same program, managing the same number of SBICs as Marvin handled alone), and I asked him if I could restructure the fund and borrow $6 million, the maximum leverage allowed. With that new $6 million, I would invest primarily in technology companies and would repay the money over a predetermined schedule.

Marvin went over a short checklist with me. At one point, he stopped and said, "You need to have 10 years of investment experience." I said, "No problem, I have been investing since I was about 10." Marvin must have liked me, because after a moment, he looked me in the eye and said, "Check!"

Having somehow convinced Marvin at the SBIC division of the Small Business Administration (SBA) that I should be able to take over my father's SBIC and borrow $6 million from the US government, I was in business. I will never forget the SBIC team of one. Thank you, Marvin!

I invested that borrowed money in a wide variety of companies over the next few years. Three of my first investments were in Home Security Center, Parenting Magazine and SPG Consulting. Home Security Center was run by Mike Leahy, an ambitious young entrepreneur who wanted to create a one-stop shop for all your security needs. The idea was to sell everything from fire extinguishers to security cameras. I invested $200,000 for 25% of the business. We opened the first store on Burlingame Avenue in Burlingame, California. We invited everyone we knew to the "Grand Opening," but almost no one came. The store was a little sparse and dark, so we brightened it up a little, and tried to add more items. Before the 12-month lease ran out, Home Security Center was out of business.

Robin Wolaner started Parenting Magazine. The idea of this new magazine was to compete with Parents Magazine, which had grown out of touch with the modern parent. I invested $250,000 in Parenting for 15% of the business. Robin had some real editorial chops, and she was also strong with experience in circulation. And she hit it just right. Her first few issues were very popular, and advertisers were starting to come on board. Six months into the business, Time Magazine came and offered us $5 million to buy us out. Robin would stay on board and run the business inside Time and I would get $750,000. It was validating that I was able to actually get a return on one of my early investments. I remember John Glynn, of Glynn Ventures, saying, "Three times in six months! That is the best venture return anyone has seen in years."

But Parenting would be my only liquidity event for quite a while.

I worked for Apollo Computer as the assistant to the president, Charlie Specter, in my summer between years at business school. I had made several friends there, one of whom was Ian Edmonds, who I worked with on a market research project. When I started Draper Associates, I called Ian and asked him, "What are the top software products that will run on Apollo?" Ian responded that SPG Consulting was one of them. I flew to Boston to meet with SPG Consulting's president. Sam Geisberg was a Russian immigrant with a heavy accent. I could hardly understand him. But he showed me something that was like sleight of hand to me. He was able to take a series of 2D drawings and turn them into a 3D rendering, and then he could turn a 3D drawing into its component 2D drawings. This "reflexive" technology had never been done before.

In my search for a job coming out of business school, I had met Don Fedderson, a veteran entrepreneur and recently minted venture capitalist with Charles River Ventures. Don had run Applicon, a 2D computer aided design company, and I thought Don would be a good fit for Sam. I needed him to help me make an offer that would be large enough to resonate with Sam. Don brought in Steve Walske and Dick Harrison, two young guys who had been in the software business before. I flew back to meet them to see if I also thought they would be a good fit for the business and with Sam.

I arrived a little late and they were all seated for lunch at an outside table with lots of people around. I sat down to join them, and we all heard the loudest "rrrrriiiiiiiiip." I had put on a few pounds and my pants ripped from my back belt to my crotch. It was loud and embarrassing, and although I had some fleeting hope that none of them had heard it, in reading their faces, I could tell that there was no denying it. Then Richard said, "Did you just rip your pants?" I said, "I think I will just stay seated," and I did the whole interview with my tight whites blaring in the sun for all to see. We all had a good laugh and bonded at that lunch. I was thrilled with the team and their spirit, and I gave Don the go ahead. Don led the deal and cut me in for $175,000 with an option to put in another $125,000 at a later date and at a higher price if they hit their milestones. The company changed its name to Parametric Technology Corporation

(PTC), and it was off to the races. This investment would be a fund maker for Charles River and would put Draper Associates on the map. "Thank you Don, thank you Sam, thank you Ian, thank you Apollo Computer, and thank you Steve and Dick."

But before any of us knew that PTC would be the big winner it was, I nearly lost it all. It was 1989 and the SBIC group (now about 10 people) called me to say I was now on their "watch" list. I wasn't in trouble yet, but in another six months, if the asset ratios were not in line, they would be calling the loan. And, sure enough, after six months went by, I got another call. I was now on their "dirt" list. The loan was about to be called and my venture capital career was about to end.

I got on the soonest possible plane to Washington, DC, and headed out to meet with the team at SBIC. I spent an hour and a half working to convince them to bear with me, telling them that lemons ripen early and pearls take a long time to cultivate. I explained that what they were seeing was typical in early-stage venture capital and that there were many good companies in there that just hadn't had enough time to show their worth.

Whether it was my persuasive argument or that the people at the SBIC really didn't want to call the loan, since that would mean they would have to manage out the portfolio, the SBIC team gave me a break, saying that as long as I kept making the loan payments, they would ignore the issues with the asset ratio. Phew!

Fortunately, in 1991, before I missed a loan payment, the public market window opened and five of my portfolio companies went public. My small investment in SPG Consulting (now PTC) made 175x on the investment for my fund. With just one-third of the winnings from PTC, I was able to pay the SBIC program back completely and send enough cash to all the shareholders (who were all family members) so that they got all their money back and a 15% compounded return. With all the winnings, the investors' annual IRR under my management was calculated at approximately 40%. Family gatherings would be easier now that I was playing with house money, and now I had a real track record! PTC is still the largest software company in New England.

Meanwhile, back in Washington, I eased off the SBIC dirt list and my image magically appeared on the wall of the SBA lobby, where they had my picture framed as "SBIC Venture Capitalist of the Year."

Now, six years after founding Draper Associates, I had a good enough story to raise a venture capital fund from outside (non-family) investors. All I needed to do was find some good partners.

I recruited John Fisher and Larry Kubal to join me. I knew Larry through my sister Becky, who went to Stanford's Graduate School of Business with him. He had occasionally coinvested with me while I managed the SBIC. Larry agreed to work part time with me because he also was running a family office. Having a wealthy family office connected to us was helpful because we could commit to larger investments than we could make alone, and "wrestle above our weight class." Larry had a great sense of humor, which would keep us laughing through our successes and our pitfalls.

John Fisher was brilliant, ambitious and hardworking. His education included Phillips Exeter Academy, Harvard University and Harvard Business School. We had worked together at Alex. Brown & Sons for a year, and we got along famously. When I left to start Draper Associates, I remember our boss, Don Dixon, saying with a threatening tone in his voice, "Don't you dare take Fisher with you." The panic in Don's voice cemented in my mind that I would eventually bring John in as a partner.

John and I looked at the world differently, which might have come from our families' circumstances. I had watched as my father's optimistic efforts grew great wealth for him and the people around him, and John had watched as his father had made a fortune in the advertising business only to be sued into bankruptcy in one bad deal.

Our differences helped us build the business, with my aggression and optimism and his intellect and caution. I tended to think about how big a startup could get, and he tended to watch out for pitfalls. I focused on the entrepreneur and supported them at all costs, and John focused on our investors and made sure we were fulfilling our fiduciary obligations. For venture capital, we pretty much spoke two different languages, but we learned over time that both languages are mission critical to creating a great venture capital firm.

Note: I highly recommend bringing on co-founders that have very different backgrounds and different wirings. The discourse may give you frustration, but the outcome will likely be a good one and you will have a much more extraordinary journey. We can now laugh about our differences and our poor communication connection, but we learned a lot from each other as the business went through its fits and starts.

THE RHUBARB INVESTMENT CLUB STORY

With my newly-granted honor of being the SBIC venture capitalist of the year, John's experience in investment banking and venture capital, and our fresh-faced enthusiasm, we set out to raise our first outside fund. On our road show, we visited some investors in Chicago and then we had to get to Detroit, where we would meet up with one of John's contacts, the Rhubarb Investment Club. Due to bad weather, we couldn't fly, so we drove most of the night. We determined that if we took a quick catnap, we could just make it to Detroit for our lunch meeting. At 2 am, we stopped and got a room to sleep for a few hours at a Motel 6 in Battle Creek, Michigan, home of Kellogg's Cereals. We got back on the road at 6 am. We made it just in time to pitch a group of retired automobile execs on the virtues of venture capital, and why we might be a good place to invest some of their retirement money. They were a tough crowd, but we left hoping that we had convinced them.

Right after our meeting, we had to catch a plane back to San Francisco. It was going to be a tight connection. We had about an hour to spare. We didn't think about the fact that our rental car had already gone from Chicago to Detroit without stopping for gas, and we ran out of gas on the way to the airport.

I suggested that I run to the next exit, get some gas and run back. John agreed, and I took off for the gas station. Fortunately, the gas station was no more than a mile or two down the road, and they had a five-gallon tank to sell me. I ran back with the gas in hand, but when I got to the top of the hill where I left John and the car, they were gone.

It turned out that while John waited for me, he had an idea. The car was on the top of a hill when it ran out of gas, and if he just gave it a little push, he could get it to roll down the hill for quite some ways. He figured that he could cut my running distance by about one-half mile. But on my run back, I had taken a short cut, not staying on the highway.

In a panic, I took off down the road, trying to figure out what had happened. When I caught up with him about a mile down the road, we both looked at each other a little confused at what the other had done.

We gassed up the car and floored it to the airport. By the time we got there, the plane was due to take off in five minutes, so we left the car right in front of United departures, called Hertz to let them know where it was, and ran to the terminal. We have been running ever since, but not necessarily in the same direction. But I think we needed to go in different directions so that the business could really spread its wings. And it did.

Incidentally, this adventure continued. We made it onto the plane as the flight attendant was closing the door. We took our seats in the back row next to another big guy, and the plane took off. Being in the middle seat and still a little wired from our race to the plane, I got up and started walking the aisle to give more room to the other two. I struck up a conversation with the flight attendants.

John got tired of sitting too, and joined the conversation in the back of the plane. When the flight attendants said they needed to pass out hot towels, we offered to help. John and I finished our first road trip walking up and down the aisles of the Boeing 707 with a tray saying, "Hot towel…hot towel…hot towel."

The Rhubarb Investment Club declined, and missed out on our first fund, which would have far outperformed anything they would have invested in in the automotive industry, but they came in for our next fund, which ended up giving them an enormous multiple on their money.

For the duration of our first fund together, John and I had some very tough discussions. We often disagreed on investment decisions and used Larry Kubal as our tiebreaker. But Larry wanted to run his own fund and started Labrador Ventures, leaving John and I without our tiebreaker. If we were going to build a great business, we would have to figure out how best to make decisions when we disagreed. Our dilemma was solved when we met Steve Jurvetson.

I got an unsolicited resume in the mail that looked almost too good to be true. Steve Jurvetson had graduated in two and half years and was number one in his class in electrical engineering from Stanford. He then got a master's degree, again graduating as the top student. He had written a patent and seven of his chip designs were manufactured by HP before he left the engineering school at Stanford. He was an Arjay Miller Scholar at Stanford's Graduate School of Business, and he was the winner of the prestigious Ernest C. Arbuckle Award, as voted by his fellow students When we met him, we loved him too.

We recruited Steve hard. He liked ultimate Frisbee, so we went out to play a game with him at Stanford. We liked his competitive spirit. Melissa and I took him and his then wife, Karla, out to a tennis tournament to see Andre Agassi play Michael Chang. I slid down the stair bannister to get down through the crowd quickly after the game, and Steve, who was being heavily recruited by many other venture firms, decided to go with us because of that slide.

With Steve on board, we easily raised what was now Draper Fisher Associates Fund III, and we were off to the races again. The triad worked so well, that we made Jurvetson a partner in just over six months of working with him. We had a big exit with Hotmail and several other companies, and we were on a roll.

We raised fund after fund and recruited awesome partner after awesome partner. Warren Packard, Jennifer Fonstad, and Andreas Stavropoulos were all top students and great people, and for the much of the next decade we were at the top of the heap. Our results were astronomical, and we were raising money at will. In one fund, we made 25 investments and I think 19 of them were acquired for big returns or went public!

I decided that venture capital didn't have to be just in Silicon Valley (with some activity in Boston), and I worked to build out venture offices and funds all over the US. The funds became known as the DFJ Network (now the Draper Venture Network). And we even worked with some people to go global with a new revolutionary fund called DFJ ePlanet.

Then the market collapsed. We, along with the rest of the venture capital industry, went from heroes to zeroes. Our investors (called limited partners), who until this time were thrilled with us, were now desperately looking to get liquidity (cash). The valuations of our portfolio companies (the ones that could even stay in business) were falling by as much as 90% or more. We had an investor who was so desperate for liquidity that he sued us, so we had to go through a lawsuit that we ultimately settled on the courthouse steps. While our annual investor meetings were great celebrations through the 1990s, where we got to show off all the exciting technologies with a view to the amazing future, now we faced frustrated and angry investors and the meetings made us feel like hockey goalies without protection.

The next 10 years were the worst ever for the venture capital business. From 2000-2004, the "post-bubble period" the business was in free fall. It seemed to be recovering from 2004-2008, but then we were hit with the global meltdown from 2008-2010. The industry went from being a powerful rising tide to one that clearly had a downside and looked to be cyclical, being no different from any other industry. Worse, investors in venture capital had grown to expect the kind of returns we had made through the booming Internet years, and now it looked like it would be years before we even got them their money back.

To our credit, we became the top of the bottom. The whole industry was in turmoil. John used to say our industry committed "venture fratricide" because so much money had been invested in venture capital that too many of the same kind of companies got funded, so they drove each other out of business. Our domestic funds raised during the post-bubble period were lackluster performers and when the government piled on Sarbanes Oxley Act regulations to public companies, our best form of financial exit was sabotaged. Our international investments through DFJ ePlanet were our saving grace, since they included Baidu and Skype, but overall, this post-bubble period was the worst we have ever experienced. My dad says, "Don't confuse brains with a bull market," but the corollary didn't seem so relevant. We all felt pretty stupid. Meanwhile, our international fund, DFJ ePlanet was an outstanding success. Our investments in Skype and Baidu propelled our firm to the top of the heap, but it was indeed a heap. No one was interested in hearing about venture capital. After the global meltdown, our various teams struggled to raise money and keep their portfolio businesses rolling while venture capital became the tar baby of financial instruments. To this day, the venture capital industry suffers in the institutional investor marketplace, where they believe it is not an asset class, but an anomaly, with just a handful of firms that through some alchemy are able to consistently produce strong results.

It took years for the venture industry to recover. And when it did, John, Steve and I made some significant money through our profits interest (called "carried interest") from our success with DFJ ePlanet. With our newfound wealth, we each discussed what we would like to do going forward. We decided to peel off into what we would call the three rockets. John Fisher decided to focus on late-stage investing and created and helped build DFJ Growth with Barry Schuler, former CEO of AOL, and Mark Bailey, who previously worked at KPCB, Symantec and WebMD. Later they were joined by a former venture capitalist from the Tribune Group, Randy Glein, who became a major workhorse for the fund. Steve Jurvetson, Andreas Stavropoulos and our new star partner, Josh Stein, stayed the course and drove DFJ Venture. I raised a new early-stage fund with my son Billy, reclaiming the original name Draper Associates. I also created an ecosystem around Draper University and relaunched the Draper Venture Network with Gabe Turner. Our other partners felt their independence too. Jennifer Fonstad started a new independent venture firm with Theresia Gouw called Access Ventures. And Warren Packard started a new company around sports highlights called Thuuz.

Our support team had some growing pains with the new triad direction. CFO Mark Greenstein tried to balance the interests of the three rockets so that we all felt fairly treated. Our IT expert, Gil Lubetsky, was stretched very thin handling networks for all three groups in three different locations; and we had to split up a very homogeneous and very efficient team to make it work for everyone. Fortunately, star controllers Desiree Omran and Rose Yip came with me.

I think our three rockets plan played out well. Today, DFJ Growth manages over $1.3 billion. The DFJ Venture team has continued to find and fund interesting companies with great potential, and I raised a new fund, started a school and created a whole ecosystem that I believe will be the model for the future of entrepreneurship and venture capital. I got an early window on Bitcoin and the blockchain, and I became a bellwether in crypto financings. The school, Draper University of Heroes, has shaken up the education establishment by offering team-based learning, project-oriented experiences and survival training, and has transformed the lives of 1000 young people who have come from 68 different countries and started about 300 companies at this writing, one of which is a unicorn already.

Since deciding to invest through my new vehicle, Draper Associates, I have had a few early successes. Twitch.TV, a company that created a platform for fans to watch people play video games, was sold to Amazon for $1 billion; Cruise Automation, the first independent self-driving car company was sold to General Motors for $1 billion; and my son Billy sourced a company that simplifies investing in the public markets called Robinhood, which just completed a venture round at a valuation over $1 billion. Billy and I were able to raise a $190 million fund and we are enjoying working together.

The Draper Venture Network now boasts 16 relationships covering 40 cities around the world and several billion dollars under management. The team has created systems to have member venture capitalists leapfrog their competition through CEO Summits, limited partner events, corporate mixers and best practices events.

Hero City, which is the name we call our ecosystem offices, seems to have had a big impact on the City of San Mateo. It is about three blocks from the train station and 10 minutes from San Francisco International airport. Roughly 80 new startups run through Hero City every six months. Once they grow out of Hero City, the startups often move nearby, helping grow the local economy.

My children have all gotten into the game. Billy works with me at Draper Associates; Jesse runs Halogen Ventures, the first venture fund dedicated to funding only women; and Adam runs Boost, the leading accelerator for advanced technologies, starting with Bit-coin/Blockchain, Virtual Reality and Augmented Reality (VR/AR), and moving to anything that gets us closer to having commercially available Ironman suits. My youngest daughter, Eleanor, is the first employee at a startup called Bulletin that segments retail space for artisans who want to become entrepreneurs.

If I were to do it all over again, I would.

LEADERS GO FIRST

The more you try new things, the more chances you have to suc-ceed.

When I started in the venture capital business, many of the firms were 20 years older than we were. In order to be noticed, I had to do things differently. It is amazing to note that, at that time, no venture firm had ever advertised. When I negotiated for a page in Upside Magazine, it was the first venture capital advertisement in history. Naturally, many followed suit, but not before Draper Associates was the dominant name in early-stage venture capital.

When we discovered the Internet in 1995, we told all our in-vestors that our next fund would be 100% Internet. We lost a lot of good investors because of our boldness as we went into the great unknown, but we got the fund closed and it became number one of that vintage.

And there were no venture firms outside the US. We had already set up multiple funds in the US, but we decided to go global and build out a network of venture capitalists all over the world. This was unheard of in 1999, but we went ahead with it anyway, and became the first Silicon Valley venture capital firm with offices overseas. The 10% of our investment dollars dedicated for international invest-ments yielded 70% of our gains.

What I learned is that there are advantages to going first. Since we had so many firsts in the venture capital business, our competitors often had to play catch up. In many geographies, we were the only one the entrepreneurs would think to go to, so we had no competi-tion there.

If you are first in your industry, you can also define that industry, leading to better long-term positioning and network effects that give you an edge. Be a leader.

DECISION MAKING

I learned a lot about group decision making. As we grew the team at Draper Fisher Jurvetson (DFJ), we found that it became harder and harder to make decisions to invest in unusual and innovative companies because what one partner saw, other partners may not envision. Without support for the outliers, the investments might end up being too "safe." In the venture capital business, investors can't keep making the safe investments and achieve the best returns, because while they may not lose as much money on their investments, they are less likely to get the big bonanza. As a pioneering entrepreneur, it is more efficient and effective to keep control over the decisions that guide direction of your firm while still, of course, getting as much input from your team as you can.

INTRODUCTION

Here's to the crazy ones. The misfits. The rebels. The troublemakers. The round pegs in the square holes. The ones who see things differently. They're not fond of rules. And they have no respect for the status quo. You can quote them, disagree with them, glorify or vilify them. About the only thing you can't do is ignore them. Because they change things. They push the human race forward. And while some may see them as the crazy ones, we see genius. Because the people who are crazy enough to think they can change the world, are the ones who do.

ROB SILTANEN FROM THE APPLE AD CAMPAIGN

This book is for those crazy ones. I call them Startup Heroes. I have spent more than half of my life supporting them, driving them, coaching them, counseling them and funding them. They have helped make my life full, and while many have failed, some have made an enormous impact on our world. In this book, you will read about some of them and how they represent the value system that makes up the structure of this book, which I have organized as two "books."

THE STARTUP HERO'S PLEDGE

The first book I call "The Startup Hero's Pledge." The pledge can be your compass when you are lost in the storm. If you are going to be a successful entrepreneur, a revolutionary, an artist, a change agent, or even someone who thinks a little differently, you will want to understand the pledge. I will encourage you to memorize it, to know it and to understand, even "grok" each line of it. I felt that when I created Draper University of Heroes, it would be important for the students who went through Startup Hero training to have a "code" to live by. It is not just a guide for the launching of a business, but it is a life guide that I hope you will refer to periodically when you come to a fork in the road or a big life decision or a difficult negotiation. I want the pledge to be your business guide, and maybe even your life guide.

I hope you will refer to the pledge when you come up against a difficult choice or a challenging dilemma. I want you to know the pledge inside and out so that the right line comes to you when you need it most. To make it stick with you, I employ famous quotes, tell a few stories, and throw in a few surprises to help you remember the lines of the pledge from many sides of your brain so that you can recall them when the going gets tough for you.

THE STARTUP HERO'S WORKBOOK

The second book I call "The Startup Hero's Workbook," because in it I give you some activities and tips of ways to think about your business as a Startup Hero. I challenge you to hammer out the technical challenges of your business, understanding how to ideate, plan, finance, market and pursue your business. I encourage you to screw your mind around to test your ideas thoroughly, to think about your customer, and to understand how you will be paid for the service you provide. I give you a box of tools to help you think about what makes a good business, what I might fund, and what might be needed in the world today. I encourage you to plot and measure your progress, to understand your goals and your direction. And I finish with a fun test that I wrote (with no scientific research at all) that might help you think about what some Startup Heroes think about before starting a business.

As a whole, this book can help you on your journey to becoming a Startup Hero. Take your time with it. Apply each concept to your own business, your own life, and your own mission. The writing is varied so that you expect the unexpected. After all, if you are going to be a Startup Hero, you need to be prepared for anything.

And just for fun, anyone who sends me their solutions to all the puzzles in this book to tim@draperuniversity.com will be given one more puzzle, and the first person with a correct answer to that puzzle will get one Bitcoin. Other winners might get a surprise too, but no promises.

Just know that anything is possible. And you can be the one who makes it so.

WHO SHOULD READ THIS BOOK?

It is not the critic who counts; not the man who points out how the strong man stumbles, or where the doer of deeds could have done them better. The credit belongs to the man who is actually in the arena, whose face is marred by dust and sweat and blood; who strives valiantly; who errs, who comes short again and again, because there is no effort without error and shortcoming; but who does actually strive to do the deeds; who knows great enthusiasms, the great devotions; who spends himself in a worthy cause; who at the best knows in the end the triumph of high achievement, and who at the worst, if he fails, at least fails while daring greatly, so that his place shall never be with those cold and timid souls who neither know victory nor defeat.

TEDDY ROOSEVELT

This book is not for everyone. This book is for those of you who have a spark in your eye, energy in your soul, and a drive to see a mission through. This book is for those of you in the arena, or who want to get there, or who want to help others get there.

For those of you who like the world as it is, this book is dangerous.

But for would-be Startup Heroes, those who are compelled to make an impact in this world, this book is for you. If you have vision of a better future and don't just want to change the world but believe that you have to change the world just as you have to breathe, this book will guide you to make that change.

For those who want to help Startup Heroes achieve their visions, this book might help you think about what a Startup Hero is thinking and feeling. I expect you will have an interesting journey as you read, and you might become (as I am) a supporter of Startup Heroes and all that they do: the chances they take, the visions they believe in and fight for, and the hope and optimism that they bring to the world. And you might just find that you are a Startup Hero yourself!

It is in the spirit of helping Startup Heroes go into action that I write this book. I hope this book becomes a handbook for you as you live and build your business. Inside this book is a wealth of opportunity. There are ideas for new businesses to start, there are stories from which to learn, and there are tools that you can use as you transform industries, save lives, improve government, and help people.

And for those of you who are up to the challenge, I make this commitment. Start a company around some idea you found in this book or came up with while reading this book, send your plan to www.draper.vc, and I will enter you into the Startup Hero competition I am planning for 2019. The winner will get $1 million in funding at a $5 million (or negotiated) valuation.

I hope you enjoy reading this book as much as I enjoyed writing it.

DON'T DO IT!

Stop! Take Elon Musk's advice. "Don't do it!"

Most people are not cut out for being an entrepreneur. They are content living out their lives by not making waves, not obsessing about rules, drawing inside the lines, and staying inside the box. But you bought this book, or at least you are reading it, so it is possible that you are different. With a little training, you might become an entrepreneur, a revolutionary, a Startup Hero. Read on and you might be the one making the waves, making the rules, drawing the lines, and asking, "What box?"

I took a Draper University group of students (who we call "heroes in training" or "HITS"—we dropped the "Super" or "S" part of the acronym for obvious reasons) to the Tesla factory in Fremont, California, to watch as Elon Musk, Tesla's CEO and one of the most extraordinary and successful entrepreneurs in history, launched the Model S. The plant is enormous. It seems to go for miles in all directions. Robots as big as elephants move around connecting car parts, fastening attachments, and painting the body.

The launch was to great fanfare. The Governor of California came and cut the ribbon, the first 10 cars were rolled off the assembly line for us lucky early "Founder Series" buyers, and all 1000 Tesla employees shared a proud moment as they watched all their amazing labor and efforts come to life.

Elon made some time for us before his big event and answered a few questions. The first question was from one of the HITS. She said, "Mr. Musk, what would you recommend to an entrepreneur who is just starting who wants to become a successful Startup Hero like you?" Elon hesitated. His hair a little disheveled and he looked exhausted, his hair a little disheveled and his demeanor exhausted. After all, he had just orchestrated one of the most amazing launches of one of the most revolutionary vehicles the world had ever seen. After a deep breath and an uncomfortably long pause, he said, "Don't do it!"

He went on to say that that was the best advice he could give to an aspiring entrepreneur, because if you accepted that advice, you really aren't ready to be an entrepreneur and he would have just saved you from going through a brutal, extraordinary effort when your heart isn't really in it. And if you didn't, well then...send me a business plan.

I can only imagine what Elon was going through that day. He was notably sweating, looked very thin, had circles under his eyes and was firing up for his proud moment. Entrepreneurship isn't easy. But Elon Musk has brought us PayPal, SpaceX and Tesla, so all that work that he puts in has shown amazing results and generated real change. After all, he is on a mission. He has a swirling desire in his gut telling him that he must save our planet.

Anyway, if you accept Elon's advice, so be it. You can drop this book off with a friend, stick with the safe choices and remain an upstanding member of the status quo. BUT, if you didn't accept his advice, perhaps you are a true entrepreneur after all and nothing anyone says will keep you from your mission. In fact, many of the best entrepreneurs are those who have to be told, "It will never work," or "Don't do it." In many cases, it makes them want to do it even more to prove the status quo wrong.

Having said that, before you build your business plan, there are some fundamental questions you will need to ask and be honest with yourself.

- Really?
- Do you really want to do this? Why? Why do you care?
- Is your business really that important to you?
- Are you going to regret it if you don't do it?
- Is this all you really care about?
- Is your product going to really be that much better than what exists out there today?
- Will it still be better 15 years from now?
- Are you prepared?
- Are you prepared to make sacrifices?
- Are you prepared to be ridiculed?
- Are you prepared to go personally broke
- Are you prepared to have to fire your best friend?

- Are you prepared to face lawsuits, press attacks, and predatory practices from the status quo incumbents in your field?

- Are you prepared to dedicate yourself completely to the cause when even your family and your friends say, "Enough!"?

When I picked up my new Tesla at this phenomenal event, I took several groups of Tesla employees for test drives. I asked what each of them worked on. On the whole, they showed (well warranted) pride in what they had accomplished.

"I worked on the brakes," said one. "The brakes work like they do in other cars, but as you take your foot off the accelerator, the car slows down and charges up the battery, so there were some innovations there."

"The frunk," said another. "There is no engine, so we had all this extra space that we made into a front trunk, or frunk."

"Software," said a third. We have controllers and sensors on every movable part in the car, and we can constantly update them. Your car will continue to update as we design in new features and replace old ones."

"The key," said a fourth. "See how it looks like a car. You press here and the doors unlock, press here and the rear opens, and press here to open the frunk."

I was so glad I volunteered my car to give people test drives. I had no idea at the revolution in automotive that I was witnessing. So much innovation. So many hardworking, proud employees.

I hope this book helps you start something that brings to life a business that serves to design a product as awesome and important as the Tesla Model S car.

Entrepreneurship is often thankless, and when an entrepreneur fails it can be tragic. But maybe I can help you think about your journey in a new way. To better help you think about what a Startup Hero does and the impact he or she creates, whether in a success or a failure. I provide you here with a story.

THE TESLA STORY

Ian Wright came to pitch his new business, Wright Motors. We met at DFJ's offices on Sand Hill Road in Menlo Park, California. He brought with him an invention that was strung together with tires, PVC pipes, some fabric, and magic Lithium Ion batteries. It was a new kind of electric car. He asked me to sit in the machine and get strapped in with a five-point harness. I asked why I needed to be strapped in since the only electric cars I had seen were golf carts and the original Chevy Volt that George Schultz drove, and none of them had much in the way of scary pickup. He explained that golf carts used Nickel Cadmium batteries, and this battery was the Lithium Ion battery like the one you had in your computer. He told me it was much stronger, and the torque was awesome. I let him strap me in, and I am glad I did.

When he got into the driver's seat and strapped in next to me, he put his foot down on the pedal, and I experienced a g-force I had only previously felt on a roller coaster. He took me out to Interstate 280 and showed me how the car could go from 0 to 60 MPH in about three seconds, and then, as we were coming back, he said, "and watch this." He was going 60 and we were getting dangerously close to running a red light. He hit the brake and the car stopped dead in its tracks. A new world opened up for me right there. There was going to be a point in the not so distant future when the price performance of an electric car would be better than that for a gas-powered car!

That experience got me fascinated with electric cars. I decided to go out and meet as many electric car inventors and hobbyists as I could. I visited an electric car show and interviewed almost everyone there, and every one of them mentioned this company called Tesla. I arranged to meet Martin Eberhard, the then founder and president of Tesla. He explained that these magic Lithium Ion batteries occasionally exploded and were a dangerous fire hazard, so he decided to link together a bunch of small ones in parallel, so if one blew up, there would be no fire and the car could still run as the drivetrain could route around the bad battery. This parallel linking had the added advantage of providing even more torque. Tesla was the clear winner in this field, so I decided to make an investment in the company.

But, when I pushed my partners to invest in Tesla, there was some understandable discomfort in the idea, since the startup junkyard was full of failed car companies from the DeLorean to the Packard. Many had tried to start a car company to compete with the oligopolistic Big Three, but all of them had failed for lack of capital. I did have some strong support though. My partner, Steve Jurvetson, was also particularly excited about investing in Tesla, since he too got a test drive from Ian Wright that first day, but the rest of the partners made a very strong case. By the end of the discussion, we all knew that it would be difficult for our partnership to support the company alone. Success would require too much capital. We decided to make a smaller investment ourselves, but to work with other venture capitalists to "syndicate" the investment so that we could share the capital risk. By making a smaller investment, we figured we could keep some "dry powder" for future rounds of funding that would almost certainly come up in the future.

And we were lucky we did. Tesla ran out of money just over one year later and was having a hard time finding a bold enough investor to take the car forward. Martin was still working on the first prototype and the well was dry.

Enter Elon Musk. Elon was an early and very active investor in the company and sat on its board. He believed that Tesla was going to help save the world from the greenhouse effect created by carbon emissions. He also had a shrewd business mind. He offered to save the company with a $10 million investment as long as he would run it from here on out. The board, which Steve Jurvetson would eventually join, supported the idea, and the rest is history. Elon got people to pay for their cars in advance, engineered a clean technology loan from the US government for $400 million, bought the NUMI plant at a deep discount, and redesigned the car with the attitude of "delighting the customer."

And he did delight the customer. His first car, the Roadster, was indeed amazing, faster and quieter than anything near its price point, but it was handicapped by having a Lotus body that didn't take full advantage of technologies that were newly available. But it gave the company market credibility and was exciting enough to encourage customers to prepay for the cars.

But the crown jewel of the company came when Tesla launched the S-Car, [My daughter Jesse interviewed Elon on the Valley Girl Show, and they shared escargot saying, "look at that S-car go," in honor of an old car industry joke.] The S-Car had it all. An intuitive remotely programmable dashboard, a tracking system via the Internet, car balance that allowed the car to turn a corner without slowing down, a sunroof that could be opened or closed with buttons on a touch screen, and a key that was shaped like the car. The car would change the automotive industry forever. And it did. It broke all safety records, won Car of the Year in almost every car magazine, and its customers are more passionate than almost any I've ever encountered.

All three of these entrepreneurs, Ian Wright, Martin Eberhard and Elon Musk, are Startup Heroes. All three took long odds at extraordinary outcomes. We all know that Elon is the one who came out the public hero that we all celebrate, and we should. What Elon has done is extraordinary. Nevertheless, both Ian Wright and Martin Eberhard were also instrumental in the success of Tesla. Without all of them, there might be no Tesla. But there is, and it is awesome!

So yes, being an entrepreneur is a thankless, difficult job. It is emotionally, mentally, and sometimes physically strenuous. An entrepreneur takes on a challenge that is truly risky. An entrepreneurial journey is a financial, career, and social risk, among others. An entrepreneur often gives up a secure career that he or she may never be able to return to, a salary that may never come back, and social status--since an entrepreneur's friends are usually confused by the decision until they are able to see the same vision. An entrepreneur also has far less time for his or her friends and family, so there is less emotional support for someone who is willing to step out and be a Startup Hero.

But every entrepreneur moves human progress forward. Every entrepreneur, win or lose, makes technology advance, spurs on competitors and rivals, and drives improvements in the world. Whether you become Ian Wright, Martin Eberhard or Elon Musk, if you start a business with an extraordinary outcome in mind, you are a Startup Hero.

After Tesla became a public company and the cars were well known, I was asked to come speak at David Kirkpatrick's Techonomy conference in Detroit. After my speech, the first question I got was, "What do you recommend we people of Detroit do to get the kind of prosperity we hear about from the Silicon Valley?" I answered, "Well, you have been living off the automotive teat for more than three generations. That is long enough! I recommend that you do something else."

Then she followed up with, "But if we want to stay in automotive, what then?" I said, "Well, you have lost the electric car game to Tesla, so you better make 'em fly."

The press took that message to the car companies, and the quotes I saw from the CEOs of the Big Three were understandably a little angry. Two of them went on the attack, saying in effect, "Who is this jerk from the Silicon Valley coming to Detroit to tell us how the auto industry should work?" The President of Ford, to his credit, did say something to the effect that they were not as up on the new technologies as they would like to be, but it was clear that I had lit a fuse. And that fuse went boom in a way that was completely unexpected.

It was several years later when I invested in Kyle Vogt at Cruise Automation. I had backed Kyle before. He had previously been one of the four founders of JustinTV, which became Twitch.tv, a company that let people watch other people play video games and had sold for $1.1 billion to Amazon, making us, his investors, many times on our money. Kyle pitched me on Cruise. He said that Cruise was creating software and hardware so cars could be self-driving. He would start by designing a device into his Audi, and then make it a standard add-in for all cars everywhere.

Kyle took me for a ride to show off the technology, and while the car was in the lane, it was working pretty well, but as soon as we reached an intersection, the car took a sharp left into what might have been oncoming traffic. Argh! We could have died. Well, demos rarely work the way you want them to, so I was forgiving. At the end of the ride, I turned to him and said, "OK, I will back you again."

45

After that horrendous but still impressive demo, I became an investor in Cruise Automation. I had a lot of faith in Kyle. He is very creative and capable, and he has hero's blood. He and his previous team had made me money in the past, and I liked that this would be a large market with technology that I believed would advance quickly. And I thought it would be an interesting ride.

Just over two years later, the technology was working pretty well. I heard reports of many miles of road traveled without a driver. It wasn't ready for primetime, but it was making great strides. The future president of GM might have had my words ringing in her ears because she jumped in and bought the company for about $1 billion. If a "unicorn" is a company that achieves $1 billion in value, I guess that makes Kyle a "duicorn." Having done it twice makes him so much more unusual and whimsical than a unicorn.

It seems that as angry as the CEOs of the Big Three auto companies were at me, at least this GM exec was paying attention. She made the first bold move to "make them fly" autonomously.

Kyle is a Startup Hero. He took the first step and all the steps after that. He was willing to take long odds at the extraordinary outcome. So is the CEO of GM, who stuck her neck and professional reputation on the line to leap into the great unknown and invest in a self-driving car.

THE STARTUP HERO'S PLEDGE

This book is written to help make you a Startup Hero. A Startup Hero needs a guide for when life gets complicated. I have written this pledge to help Startup Heroes get centered. A Startup Hero must also be flexible and willing to continue marching forward when things are not predictable. I have written this book not to be predictable. Your mind will have to switch from left to right brain, from creative thought to memory to ambition and back to fully absorb it.

Book One centers around the Startup Pledge. Each line of the pledge is a new chapter. Each chapter starts with some famous quotes that somehow align with the pledge. Then I tell a story or two that exemplify each given line of the pledge. At the end of each chapter, I give you exercises and problems that I call "quexercises" to help you think, apply what you read to your business and just generally keep you on your toes. After all, as a Startup Hero, you will be faced with all sorts of problems, concerns, thoughts, issues and actions that you will need to work through in your journey, and you need to be able to make decisions under great uncertainty.

I have written a poem for each chapter. Poetry often brings out truths that prose can't. Each poem is written in a different form that identifies it with the appropriate line of the pledge.

If you are going to be a Startup Hero, you need a guide, a way of thinking that will direct you through your life as a Startup Hero. If you have a spark and desire to build something delightful, I wrote this pledge for you. You, who wants to change the world. You, who has ambitions for a better life for people. You, who has decided to become an entrepreneur or has stumbled upon Draper University or just feel compelled to be something extraordinary. Here is the pledge in its entirety. Memorize it. Make it your own. These are words to live by. Sign it, and honor it.

THE STARTUP HERO PLEDGE

I WILL PROMOTE FREEDOM AT ALL COSTS.

I WILL DO EVERYTHING IN MY POWER TO DRIVE, BUILD AND PURSUE PROGRESS AND CHANGE.

MY BRAND, MY NETWORK AND MY REPUTATION ARE PARAMOUNT.

I WILL SET POSITIVE EXAMPLES FOR OTHERS TO EMULATE.

I WILL INSTILL GOOD HABITS IN MYSELF. I WILL TAKE CARE OF MYSELF.

I WILL FAIL AND FAIL AGAIN UNTIL I SUCCEED.

I WILL EXPLORE THE WORLD WITH GUSTO AND ENTHUSIASM.

I WILL TREAT PEOPLE WELL.

I WILL MAKE SHORT-TERM SACRIFICES FOR LONG-TERM SUCCESS.

I WILL PURSUE FAIRNESS, OPENNESS, HEALTH AND FUN WITH ALL THAT I ENCOUNTER…MOSTLY FUN.

I WILL KEEP MY WORD.

I WILL TRY MY BEST TO MAKE REPARATIONS FOR MY DIGRESSIONS.

THE SUPERHERO CLAUSE: I WILL ACCEPT THE LIFELONG OBLIGATION TO HONE MY SUPERHERO POWERS, AND APPLY THOSE SUPERHERO POWERS TO THE GOOD OF THE UNIVERSES.

THE EVANGELISM CLAUSE: I WILL PROMOTE AND ADD TO THE ONGOING SUCCESS OF DRAPER UNIVERSITY, ITS STUDENTS, ITS FACULTY, ITS ADMINISTRATION, AND ITS FACILITIES. I WILL HELP PREPARE THE NEXT GENERATION OF SUPERHEROES. (THE EVANGELISM CLAUSE IS NOT A REQUIREMENT UNLESS YOU ARE AN ALUM, OR JUST WANT TO SUPPORT US.)

THE BLACK SWAN CLAUSE: I AM BOUND TO THIS OATH UNLESS, IN MY TRAVELS, I DETERMINE THAT THE OATH HAS SOMEHOW MISSED SOMETHING IMPORTANT AND EXTRAORDINARY.

SWORN TO BY: _____

(SIGN YOUR NAME HERE)

I WILL PROMOTE FREEDOM AT ALL COSTS.

Give me liberty or give me death.

PATRICK HENRY

A hero is someone who understands the responsibility that comes with his freedom.

BOB DYLAN

Liberty, when it begins to take root, is a plant of rapid growth.

GEORGE WASHINGTON

Conformity is the jailer of freedom and the enemy of growth.

JOHN F. KENNEDY

If you're not ready to die for it, put the word 'freedom' out of your vocabulary.

MALCOLM X

I would like to be remembered as a person who wanted to be free so other people would be also free.

ROSA PARKS

Money won't create success, the freedom to make it will.

NELSON MANDELA

Some people get rich first.

DENG XIAOPING

Freedom is never more than one generation away from extinction. We didn't pass it to our children in the bloodstream. It must be fought for, protected, and handed on for them to do the same.

RONALD REAGAN

FREEDOM MATTERS MOST

The more I live, the more I travel, and the more people I meet, the more I realize that freedom matters most. Free people are capable of anything. Free countries outgrow government controlled countries, and the freer they are, the faster they grow. And free products spread faster. Here are my favorite stories about freedom.

THE HOTMAIL STORY

Sabeer Bhatia and Jack Smith were two 26-year olds. Sabeer was a confident Indian who commanded certainty with his every word. Jack was a focused engineer who believed that he could make anything work. They came to DFJ through Dev Purkayastha, a fellow venture capitalist from Idanta Partners, who told John Fisher that he liked these two young guys, but their company was too young for Idanta to fund. Jack and Sabeer's original plan was not particularly exciting to us, but Steve Jurvetson, seeing a couple of strong co-founders, asked if they had another idea. They came forth with an unusual idea to give people web-based email. It would be so inexpensive to provide that they wanted to give it away for free! We were all stoked about this company because it was so novel, but we had no idea how the company would ultimately make money by providing free email for everyone.

Their messaging was clear, "Free everything!" In addition to providing free email, their offices were on Freedom Blvd. in Fremont, California. And they launched their product, Hotmail, on Independence Day.

Steve Jurvetson and I were sitting in the first Hotmail board meeting, when Jack said, "It is up." He meant that they had just launched free web-based email. After a short demo, I asked, "How are you going to market this amazing product?" Sabeer answered, "We will put billboards on Highway 101 and get TV ads."

I responded that with the funding we provided, $150,000, they could get about a nanosecond of TV time and a postage stamp on a billboard for a day. But before Sabeer had a chance to respond, I asked, "Hey, can't you just send an email to everyone on the Internet?" At that time, the Internet was mostly visited only by academics and military personnel, but I figured that audience could be early customers. Jack responded that sending out a blast email would be "spam," and that was against the spirit of the Internet.

Then I thought, "Words spread. If I send emails to my friends, then they send emails to their friends, and them to their friends, we would eventually reach everyone." I said, "You are giving this away for free. What if you put a message at the bottom of everyone's emails that says, 'P.S. I love you. Get your free email at Hotmail.' It will go from one user to the next. From me to you to your friends and to their friends." It reminded me of the Tupperware case we studied at business school, where anyone who wanted to buy Tupperware would have to throw a Tupperware party, making the customers its salesforce. As I spoke, I got more and more excited.

It was a very contentious idea at the time, Sabeer kept saying, "No." So I focused on Jack and his technical chops. I said, "But Jack, can you technically do it?" Jack responded that yes, he could technically do it, so I pleaded with them, "Just try it!" Eventually, Sabeer came back to me and said, "We are going to try it, but there will be no 'P.S. I love you.' It will just say, "Get your free email at Hotmail."

Now, with the benefit of 20/20 hindsight, I joke, "If they had kept the "P.S. I love you," we would have a much more peaceful and loving world. But either way, the company did extraordinary things for global communication. Hotmail spread to 11 million users in 18 months. Sabeer sent one email to his friend in India, and within three weeks we had 100,000 Hotmail users in India. (This was extraordinary because it is likely that there were not even 100,000 computers in India at that time.). Hotmail became the fastest growing consumer product of all time.

Steve and I called my invention "viral marketing" because it was a new method for marketing that spread like a virus from person to person, and we thought that the name viral marketing was catchy. We were a little concerned that computer viruses had become a real problem around then and it might have a negative connotation, but we went with viral marketing anyway, since a little controversy might even be to our advantage.

Incidentally, I decided not to patent but instead give away my invention—for free—to everyone. I thought about the long-term impact that this kind of marketing would have on the world and I didn't want to add friction to it. I was also extremely caught up in the venture capital business and didn't want to waste a lot of effort on legal work.

Hotmail spread throughout the world. People were communicating with their long-lost relatives and making new friends online. The company was growing its user base at 10,000 new users every week.

All this spreading became a problem and, ultimately, an opportunity. Every time Hotmail gave away a new email account, it cost us a few cents in compute power and bandwidth as people sent and received emails on our servers. We were able to raise some money from Doug Carlisle at Menlo Ventures, but with our new-found method of spreading our product through viral marketing, the user base was growing exponentially, and the wheels were starting to come off the business. The company blew through the Menlo Ventures' investment in a matter of months. The team there started to worry. Doug told his partners, "They are handing out dollar bills. What are those guys at Hotmail smoking?"

I cobbled together another small round of funding by stretching my own investment and by convincing a few other investors to support Hotmail. We put together a creative financial term sheet that covered both our upside and our downside, but the money we invested would only last the company another month or two. We got a little hopeful when we got a term sheet from GE Ventures to invest $10 million at a $120 million valuation, but when they learned about how fast we were burning through money, they backed away. Then we got an offer from Yahoo! to buy the whole company for $40 million. Before we even got back to them, Microsoft came in with a $90 million offer. The bidding war began. Eventually, it came down to Microsoft offering $350 million in all cash, and us being non-committal. After hearing that offer, Doug Carlisle came to me, told me what he had said to his partners, and then jokingly said, "What are you guys smoking? We want some!"

Microsoft set up a meeting with us and brought about 20 people, including CFO Greg Maffei, down from Redmond, Washington, to negotiate the deal. We met in an enormous board room provided by the Microsoft law firm. Sabeer and I sat on one end of the table and the Microsoft CFO sat at the other end flanked by his extensive entourage. Jack Smith and his father Rex sat next to Sabeer and my partners, John Fisher and Steve Jurvetson, sat next to me. Greg spoke first, saying, "We like your company and we will pay you $350 million cash for it. That is our final offer." After consulting with Sabeer and Jack, I responded with as much bravado as I could muster, "We like the company too. It is worth $2 billion, but we will take $400 million in Microsoft stock."

The Microsoft team hemmed and hawed. Greg mumbled something like, "This is all we are authorized to pay." The team's nervousness and what seemed like the closeness of their offer to our counter, made me think that maybe the Microsoft stock was worth more than the market said it was worth, and these guys didn't want to give it up, so we stuck to our guns.

Greg said, "Well then, we have nothing more to talk about." Sabeer and I said, "OK," and we left the room with tension and bravado lingering like fog. Rather than allowing us to leave, the Microsoft lawyer escorted us both into a small conference room where we were expected to rethink our decision. It was a little weird. We thought we were walking out, but our team didn't follow. John, Steve, Rex and Jack stayed behind. None of them wanted the deal to die.

Meanwhile back in the big boardroom, John Fisher took over masterfully. He said to the Microsoft team, "What is the problem? You only have to pay $50 million more and to make it in stock rather than cash, and then you get the prize." John said "prize" with a lilt and an emphasis on the "I," sending a strong message to the Microsoft team that a small change would be all that it took to win the day.

Greg told John that he would no longer deal with Sabeer, Steve or me in the negotiation. I guess we seemed irrational. John and Greg continued to negotiate. Finally, a few days before Christmas, as John was about to board a plane to the Bahamas where he explained that there was no phone service, so the deal would have to wait until after January 1st, Greg shouted, "Goddammit! ALRIGHT! I will pay it," and continued to curse a blue streak. John cleared it with Sabeer and boarded the plane just before the door shut.

We agreed not to say what Microsoft paid for the company, but it was in stock. Sabeer and I were still a little steamed from the drama, but we were also a little relieved that the deal came together. In looking back, I realize that those 20 Microsoft big wigs were not going to leave empty-handed, so we might have been able to hold out for more, but lucky for us, the Microsoft stock quadrupled over the next year. Holding out for stock turned out to be the right decision for our investors. And it worked out well for Microsoft too. Bill Gates has said that the best purchase he ever made was Hotmail, which reached 500 million users around the world and helped Microsoft market its other products to all the new free email users. And we helped make freedom ring around the world.

Viral marketing and the implied endorsement spread Hotmail broadly. Many companies followed suit. Yahoo Mail, Gmail, and many others have spread web-based email to reach over three billion people (nearly half the world). The free product made an enormous impact on the world. People became closer, better connected, and had more freedom because they could now email anyone anywhere for free. Communications around the world was now free. Hotmail even helped several countries free their people.

Viral marketing provided companies like Facebook, Twitter and Skype the ability to spread global communication too. Nearly the entire world is connected, and I believe that a new chapter of freedom and prosperity around the world is happening. When communications are combined with all the shared information we get from search engines like Google and Baidu, all the people of the world will have similar footing when they look to become productive. An entrepreneur in Tel Aviv will have access to similar information and communications tools available to an entrepreneur in Silicon Valley, or Jakarta, or Accra.

I have made it a part of my practice to apply viral techniques to help companies spread their products, and I believe that it gives those companies a competitive edge in attracting and acquiring customers cheaply and rapidly. If a product is spread more quickly and easily, the entropy of a great product happens faster, and we all benefit from the new way of life the product offers. Ultimately, viral marketing has the effect of leveling the playing field, because when there is a breakthrough, it spreads so fast that anyone with a computing device gets it.

For the Startup Hero, this new fast-spreading virus of information and products creates both an opportunity and a dilemma. If word spreads so quickly around the world, the startup needs to get its product out before the competitors do. But it also means the Startup Hero needs to be more innovative than the other people in his or her industry. New product ideas are transitory. People create new modifications to whatever is the state-of-the-art of the times. Since they all have access to the same information, they can all innovate from there.

Hundreds of companies now use viral marketing to distribute a wide variety of product categories. Any product that is communications based uses viral marketing. The AT&T Friends and Family marketing program, the LinkedIn network and the Twitter hashtag are some obvious examples. Facebook and Snapchat use viral marketing to share photos. The founders of Skype implemented several viral elements in growing their audio business and even more when Skype video was introduced.

THE SKYPE VIDEO STORY

I was fascinated by the new peer-to-peer technology that allowed people to share files. I met with Napster, Streamcast, and Grokster as I researched the industry. I had gotten the distinct impression that the file-sharing business was pretty much crushed by a powerful and litigious music industry, but I was pretty sure there would be other applications to this revolutionary technology.

I read in the paper that the guys from Kazaa, another file-sharing music business, were selling the business and looking to do something new with file-sharing technology. I put it in my head to make sure I found out what they were up to. I registered that Niklas Zennstrom was from Sweden and Janus Fries was from Denmark, so I would have to make sure I connected with them when I was next in Northern Europe. Later, I heard the company was starting in London.

My dad hired Howard Hartenbaum to scout for companies in Europe for his venture business. I first met Howard at an ETRE conference in Seville, where we discussed the venture business generally while we were on a bus going from one venue to another. He had just joined Dad and wanted to get a feel for what I looked for when I invested. I gave him some advice and suggested that he run down a few business leads I had seen at the conference. And then, knowing that he was regularly traveling throughout Europe, I said, "Hey Howard, will you also go see the guys who started Kazaa? I think they are working in London now." Howard said that he would.

About three months later, Howard called me and said, "Tim, I think you should come and check this out. The founders of Kazaa who you asked me to visit have something called Skyper and I think they are on to something."

I flew out to London to meet with Niklas. He is about my height, 6'4", and has a commanding presence. We met in a London pub and started discussing his new idea. The idea was that Skyper would use peer-to-peer file-sharing technology to allow people to share Wi-Fi signals. I was so excited, I committed on the spot. I negotiated out a term sheet with Niklas to invest in Skyper, where DFJ and Dad's fund would share the investment.

Then Niklas called me and said, "Tim, before you invest, we have to tell you something. Instead of doing shared Wi-Fi, we have decided to take on the phone companies and make these peer-to-peer packets into a vehicle to transport voice calls." I said, "I didn't realize that was possible, but of course we are still in."

I came back to my partnership to plead my case and was shot down. There was talk about piracy and liability from their previous company. The final nail in the coffin came from one partner who said, "Those guys are outlaws." Instead of sharing the deal, that first round went exclusively to Dad.

The team changed the name to Skype and the peer-to-peer free calls were a hit. The company would give free calls to anyone who had signed up for Skype and charge for calls, both incoming and outgoing, that came from outside the network. The service was taking off. It had over three million users and was running about 100,000 simultaneous audio calls. Skype was now a hot ticket. The company decided to raise more money from venture capitalists, and our partnership was now ready to go in big. It was competitive, because by now many venture capitalists knew about Skype's newfound ubiquity, but we were lucky that Howard was on our side. He fought hard for us and we invested through our international fund, DFJ ePlanet. I joined the company's board of directors and we had a tiger by the tail.

The first board meeting was to take place in Tallinn, Estonia, but the date they chose, July 18, 2005, conflicted with a commitment I had to speak at Tony Perkins' conference in Palo Alto, California. Tony was a good friend of mine and I didn't want to let him down. I racked my brain to think of a way I could be in two places at one time, and I came up with the idea of a video conference.

Video conference systems at that time were bulky, expensive and of very poor quality. Sometimes they would have very shaky audio, sometimes the video would freeze, and sometimes they would just cut off. For me to suggest that Tony use video conferencing for his big conference was a little unfair. And the idea that we would do a video conference from a place as remote as Tallinn made the whole thing seem like a disaster waiting to happen.

To his credit, Tony said, "Sure, and I have heard of Skype. Can you get Niklas to be on the video conference with you?" I said, "I will check," and called Niklas. He was happy to oblige. Then I asked him if he could get his hands on a video conference system in Tallinn, and to my surprise, he said after a slight hesitation, "Sure, no problem."

We were a "go," and we figured that if it didn't turn out well, Tony could just put our images up on the screen and we could do a voice call.

When Jesse and I got to the Skype office in Tallinn, they were all set up for us. Niklas and I sat down on some plastic chairs and got ready to go on air. Just after we sat down, Niklas looked over my shoulder and shouted, "OK, throw the switch!" I asked Niklas, "What switch? What is happening?" and he said something nebulous like, "It is interesting that we have been working on something around video in the lab here."

We did the video conference and it worked well. In fact, Tony said that he had never seen a clearer picture. "We could see the pores on your skin and the voices were crystal clear."

Niklas started chuckling with extreme pride. I asked him, "What is so funny?" He said, "That was the first ever Skype video call. It is our new VSkype product." Once I realized what had just happened, I responded with excitement. "Niklas, we have a huge winner here! That is awesome. You mean we can have free video calls that are crystal clear for everyone?"

Niklas said, "Not so fast, Tim. We cut off 100,000 simultaneous audio calls to get the bandwidth we needed to operate that video call. We will have to send out an apology for being down for that hour." The best Startup Heroes will do whatever it takes to make a company successful!

Jesse can also claim to have been on the first Skype video call. She is a good friend of Tony's daughter and when she heard Tony's voice, she poked her head in and said, "Hi." Neither of us knew how big Skype video would become, and how great a communications tool it would be, and how much freer the world would be because of it, but we knew that the world would never be the same.

Skype became the largest telecommunications company in the world by most metrics. In 2009, Skype sold out to eBay for $4 billion in cash and eBay shares, and after being briefly held by a private equity firm, was sold to Microsoft for $8.5 billion. There have been more than one billion downloads of Skype, over 300 million daily active users, and users have been on Skype for more than one trillion minutes. Skype has had a lasting effect on us all. Estonia became a new entrepreneurial hotspot since the engineers came from there, and that in turn brought on e-Governance there (more on that later).

From viral marketing evolved Skype audio calls, video calls, social media, email blasting, marketing magnets, gaming customer rankings on search engines, growth hacking, crowdsourcing, and collaborative marketplaces. When we are all connected, progress accelerates faster.

Every piece of software, website, program, app, and novel new product, whether digital or physical is, will be or should be using viral marketing. Your goal as a Startup Hero should be to best figure out how to market products liberally throughout the world with little or no cost of distribution. Now, when I look to evaluate new company proposals, one of the things I look for as a potential investor is how a company will spread from customer to customer. How the customer will become the company's salesforce. How they will promote freedom at all costs.

Hotmail and Skype created a new platform for freedom. Possibilities opened up for people. People everywhere could now freely and for free communicate amongst themselves. Physical borders would be less important because people could befriend others from anywhere in the world. People would learn about what opportunities exist around the world. Cultures would blend. Globalism would trump patriotism. People could now decide whether they could find a better life in another place, and adjust accordingly.

Countries too would have to reinvent themselves and their thinking. Countries from this point on would have to think about how best to compete for their citizens. Geographic borders would now start to dissolve, and the world would really open up. The tribal world that has held the planet's people since before the dark ages might finally be overthrown by a free market for governance. If people could freely move around the world, the governments of the world would now need to attract those with the brainpower, the money, the businesses and the entrepreneurial spirit to help them succeed. Governments would now have to make their services attractive for potential citizens, or they would lose them to a more attractive government. "International" would now be a term of the past. "Global" would be the term to drive the next century.

THE UKRAINE STORY

I took my daughter Jesse with me to Kiev, Ukraine. I like taking my children on business trips so they can learn about my work and see where I go. I heard about a potential investment in an outsourcing company in Ukraine called USC, and I wanted to go check it out. The promoter of the company was a fast-talking man called Roman Kyzyk, who knew (then) Ukraine President Yuschenko, and he arranged for us to meet him. Roman told me about the Orange Revolution, where the revolutionaries kept the heat on the capital by using instant messaging to organize the supply chain of food and flowers for the rebels. The food was to keep people pressing the capital to overthrow the government. The flowers were for the pretty girls to put in the guns of the men guarding the capital to melt away from the front line. The revolution succeeded, but not without at least one casualty. President Yuschenko was poisoned. He lived through it, but the poison left him weakened and his face blotchy.

We went through a maze of buildings and a variety of security guards to eventually get to the president's office. He met us in a beautiful room with a great tapestry. He pointed to it and explained that it was a historic tapestry that showed Ukraine was the first democracy, and he said he planned to bring Ukraine back to its roots and become a democracy once again. Then he told me to invest in his country. I said, "Why would I invest in your country? I heard that it takes 6 months and 23 bureaucrats to even incorporate here."

He said, rising above his illness and with great authority, "That will be one bureaucrat, one week!" This was a man who had fought for his country's freedom, and he planned to make bold moves to make that country free. We left hopeful that he would be successful in bringing freedom and free markets to Ukraine.

Still caught up in the excitement of just having met the president, we went to see the outsourcing company. Unbeknownst to me, they had staged 40 engineers to sit and look like they were working in order to get me to invest. And it worked. Against the better judgment of my daughter who thought the entrepreneur was "creepy," I invested in the company. Roman then set up a huge, standing room only press conference around the investment. I don't think I have ever seen so many cameras in one place. We then left Ukraine feeling excited about all the entrepreneurial goodwill we had left there.

As it turned out, the entrepreneur failed, and he couldn't account for where the money went. Interestingly, this is one of only three times in my 30 years as an investor where I believe I was cheated. Entrepreneurs are by and large driven by their mission, and the money is just a conduit to their road to unfurling their visions.

What I learned was that Ukraine has a long way to go to building an honest entrepreneurial society, but I also saw that Ukraine was trying to change. Through the technology of texting, Ukraine put in motion a new way of thinking. And even though Yuschenko lost the next election and the country went back to its corrupt past, the nation was exposed to the potential of democracy and capitalism. It is likely that, eventually, competition and accountability will permeate Ukraine, and the country will have a chance at prosperity. Corrupt government leads to corrupt people which leads to poverty. Honest open government leads to honest open people, freedom and wealth.

Ukraine's revolution built around texting led to other revolutions. After the Orange Revolution, Facebook and Twitter were instrumental to the successful overthrowing of corrupt governments in Tunisia and Egypt, in the so-called Arab Spring. Freedom and openness are spreading through viral marketing. The countries of the world are all connected now, and they have been put on notice that they need to perform for their constituents or they may have a viral revolution on their hands.

ESTONIA'S E-GOVERNANCE STORY

President Toomas Hendrik and Prime Minister Taavi Roivas of Estonia took this new opportunity to heart. They made it their mission to virtualize government and compete for real and virtual citizens around the world, just as businesses must compete for their customers. The two leaders coined their mission e-government, and because of their pioneering work, I suspect that the world will never be governed by geographic territory alone again.

The Prime Minister came to speak at Draper University's Hero City. He said, "Just by instituting digital signatures, we saved 2% of our GDP," and "by digitizing our voting, all the young people started voting." Apparently, young people would rather check boxes on their mobile phones than go into some antiquated creepy booth.

He went on to discuss Estonia's digital identity program, which lowered the crime rate and improved the business climate in his country. He bestowed on me the third virtual residency of Estonia. Now, without even setting foot in Estonia, I can open a European bank account in less than 24 hours (I did this), buy European real estate, and do business digitally anywhere in Europe.

I recently completed a financing with Kaidi Ruusalep of Funderbeam, a company that provides liquidity to private companies in Estonia. We sealed the deal with a remote smart contract electronically signed on the Estonian blockchain. This process freed us from having to be on site or even from having lawyers physically present for the signing. The contract is permanent and easily accessible for each of us to see.

Other countries are following Estonia's lead. Singapore's government has been working on its own form of e-governing, since it has historically led the way with digitizing and automating government services. The British Parliament has begun to automate and encourage crowdfunding and Bitcoin. And both Singapore and Switzerland have innovated by leading the world with legal systems for smart contracts and blockchain initial coin offerings (ICOs). I will discuss more on that later. Japan announced that they are accepting Bitcoin as legal tender in their country. Governments are recognizing that they are in competition for the great minds and capital of the world, and they are being held accountable to their citizenry—a citizenry that is armed with information, communications and community.

The Prime Minister of Kazakhstan came to meet me and to see Draper University and Hero City to try to understand what the magic of the Draper ecosystem is. He invited me back to Astana, Kazakhstan, to come speak to some of his advisors and staff. He is trying to change Kazakhstan.

I suggested that he take a page out of Estonia's book and create a competitive e-residency system. I said, "Estonia only has 20,000 e-residents four years after launching. You can do much better. You can do something to spread your message to billions around the globe." I suggested that instead of asking everyone for a visa, he should have nice people greet visitors with e-residency cards saying, "Welcome to Kazakhstan. This is your e-residency card. Swipe this the next time you are here and you will skip the customs line. Then I learned that "Kazakh" means "free." I thought he had an opportunity for viral marketing if he created a campaign around the e-residency card getting people to say, "I am free. I am Kazakh." Of course, once people have the card, the government can offer them services like health insurance, pension management, title insurance and any other government service that doesn't require physicality. I left Kazakhstan feeling optimistic for the country, hoping the Prime Minister promotes "Kazakh" at all costs.

Conversely, the US and China are suffering enormous backlash for making decisions to command and control its citizens. China's decision to try to prop up its currency by not allowing money to leave the country backfired. The currency went into a downward spiral and international investment is freezing up as people realize that investing in China is a "black hole" where money can come in but it cannot escape. The US's hopes to try to build a wall on the border with Mexico also backfired. It angered people on both sides of the wall for many reasons, but mostly because people believed that their freedoms were under attack. Today, a majority of the people the wall would affect want to come from Mexico into the US. Tomorrow, it may be just the opposite. Who knows which way people will want to migrate in the future?

Freedom is catching, and in my opinion, freedom is the most important feature for humanity to live prosperous, happy lives. Freedom also allows and encourages more progress than control does. Free markets allow for more liquidity and societal wealth than closed markets do. Free speech is better than muzzled speech to identify and air problems so that rather than festering, they become opportunities for progress. Free thinking allows entrepreneurs to imagine transformative businesses. Freedom is the most important thing. Free speech. Free press. Free religion. Free markets.

It may take extra thought and effort to create a platform for freedom where people are incentivized to do the right thing than it does to just create a law that blocks people from doing something, and it is far easier to just make a new law or regulation that stops aberrant behavior. But freedom is more important than regulations. And negative incentives often seem to backfire and require more negative incentives. A little more creativity and effort in planning can create a free system with proper incentives. And as a Startup Hero, you can do just that with your own company. Create a platform for freedom that generates maximum success and the behaviors you aspire to have for your team. People respond positively to freedom and trust. Likewise, they respond negatively to controls.

The first line of the pledge: "Promote freedom at all costs," is first because I believe it is the most important line.

A Startup Hero will create an environment for freedom, while still pointing the company in the right direction. The best managers are those who set an ambitious goal and allow their people to achieve it in any way they can. The worst managers are those who tell people exactly what they have to do and give them no freedom to deviate. Freedom allows the use of everyone's ingenuity and creativity. Startup Heroes who devise a platform for freedom tend to be surrounded by people who strive to make their businesses and missions successful. Those who micromanage with regulation only allow the use of their own brain to grow a business, and they find it to be lonely at the top.

QUEXERCISES ON FREEDOM

1. What does it mean to be free?

2. How do you give freedom to your employees and still get them to perform well?

3. Have you ever had a chance to create freedom, but you created rules instead?

4. The next time you think about whether there should be a rule, instead figure out an incentive to get people to get to some improved outcome without it.

5. Be the first one on the dance floor, close your eyes, and dance and sing with all your heart.

6. What can you do to free someone? Can you free your company? Your country?

FREEDOM PUZZLE

This is called the prisoner's dilemma. There are two suspects brought in for questioning. They are separated from one another. If one of them turns the other in, he gets a 1-year sentence and the other guy gets a 10-year sentence. If they both turn each other in, they each get a 5-year sentence. If neither one confesses, they both go free. You are one of the suspects. What do you do?

Does your decision change if instead of one time, you have an ongoing relationship with the other suspect that will continue after your one-time sentence?

FREEDOM LIMERICK HONORING GEORGE WASHINGTON

There once was a king of Americas
Who said, "Make it work for all here with us."
"We'll keep it on loan."
Abdicating his throne
Every four years, new king cares for us.

I WILL DO EVERYTHING IN MY POWER TO DRIVE, BUILD AND PURSUE PROGRESS AND CHANGE.

It would be naive to think that the problems plaguing mankind today can be solved with means and methods which were applied or seemed to work in the past.

MIKHAIL GORBACHEV

You must be the change you wish to see in the world.

MAHATMA GANDHI

I was taught that the way of progress was neither swift nor easy.

MARIE CURIE

How wonderful that we have met with a paradox. Now we have some hope of making progress.

NIELS BOHR

Progress is impossible without change, and those who cannot change their minds cannot change anything.

GEORGE BERNARD SHAW

If you want to succeed you should strike out on new paths, rather than travel the worn paths of accepted success.

JOHN D. ROCKEFELLER

Without a struggle, there can be no progress.

FREDERICK DOUGLASS

THE BITCOIN STORY

The first time I ran into the concept of virtual currency was when I was talking to a wealthy Korean industrialist in 2004. He said that a new massively multiplayer online role-playing game (MMOPG) was taking Seoul by storm. Something like 40% of the population was playing it. The game was called "Lineage." He went on to say that he was really into playing the game and that he hired someone to play his avatar for him while he was at work so he wouldn't lose his virtual strength while he was away from the game.

He then told me that it was his son's birthday and he asked for a $40 sword. I wondered why he was telling me that, and I politely said, "Oh? What kind of a sword?" He said, "It is really just a picture of a sword and he can use it when he plays in the video game."

I was shocked. "He wants you to pay for pixels on the screen?"

"Yes. The sword has powers and it will help him in gameplay," He replied.

Then I got excited. People would pay for virtual products!

This revelation was an epiphany for me. It got me thinking that there was an amazing business in virtual currency coming. There were many efforts. FarmVille was a fun game that allowed people to buy and trade with virtual gold. People paid real fiat currency to buy more virtual gold. There evolved a market outside of the game for virtual gold. Some people would earn lots of it in the game and others would buy it from them to advance in the game. Something potentially important was beginning. My search for universal virtual currency was afoot.

But it wasn't until 2011 when I discovered Bitcoin. Bitcoin was a new currency. One that could be used to store value and pay for anything, not just for advancement in a video game. It was a little retro in that it was set up as a marketplace where "miners" would have to "dig" for Bitcoin. They would do it by solving complex algorithms with their computers. Miners got their computers to run simulations that could help them mine Bitcoins faster. Once found, they could be stored in a "wallet" and then spent as needed. There was a decreasing number of Bitcoins made available to be mined over time (the so-called halving), so it was likely that the price of a Bitcoin would increase in value as fewer Bitcoins were mined and its usage increased. The system was set up so that only 21 million Bitcoins would ever be created, so people would not have to worry about their Bitcoin losing value due to "overprinting," a practice that many governments have engaged in that lowers their currencies' values and causes inflation. In fact, as Bitcoins spread, and its usage increased, it was likely that the currency would become more valuable.

It felt like it was funny money for a while. But people started accepting Bitcoin instead of dollars. Legend has it that one of the key Bitcoin programmers ordered a pizza and didn't have cash to pay the delivery guy. He offered him Bitcoin and within about three months, the pizza delivery guy became a millionaire. Another person sold a house for Bitcoin.

My son Adam started an accelerator called Boost VC. He decided to completely dedicate the accelerator to Bitcoin companies (and the blockchain technologies that went with it). He was the first investor in Coinbase, which would go on to dominate the retail use of Bitcoin. He also brought together about 40 companies over two sessions, or "tribes," all dedicated to working with, innovating around, mining and trading Bitcoin.

Joel Yarmon first introduced me to Bitcoin when he brought in Peter Vincennes and his company Coinlab to pitch us. Coinlab would become a Bitcoin-focused innovator and miner. It seemed a little out there, but I liked it and we made a small investment in the company.

Then I asked Peter if I could buy $250,000 worth of Bitcoin. The price was around $6 per Bitcoin. He bought some and stored them in Mt. Gox, the largest (at that time) Bitcoin exchange. He said he would take some money and buy an ASIC, a high-speed mining chip from Butterfly Labs to get us even cheaper Bitcoin. Then two things happened that made what should have been about 40,000 Bitcoins disappear.

First, the mining chip was delayed. Rather than shipping it to Peter as ordered, Butterfly Labs used the chip to mine Bitcoins for themselves. They mined Bitcoins for months before shipping the chips to Peter, and during that time, more Bitcoin miners entered the field, so it became rarer for any individual miner to find Bitcoin. By the time Peter received the ASIC chip, we had lost our window of opportunity. And if all this mining competition weren't enough, Peter stored the Bitcoin he did mine in a wallet controlled by Mt. Gox, which Mt. Gox "lost."

Ironically, my interest in Bitcoin accelerated when I heard that someone associated with Mt. Gox had absconded with about $460 million worth of Bitcoin, including some of the Bitcoin Peter had stored for me. Initially, I was furious. I believed that that kind of a theft would wipe this novel currency out completely. After all, who would want to hold a currency that people on the inside could just steal. But the price of Bitcoin only dropped about 20% on the news and the currency continued to be traded on other exchanges. I was flabbergasted.

But I was also fascinated. I realized that the demand for this new digital currency was so strong that even a huge theft would not keep Bitcoin from creating a new way for us to transact, store and move money. Society needed Bitcoin so much that it was willing to tolerate major failures and frauds as long as they could have this frictionless, global currency.

After all, since the financial crisis, people were losing their confidence in government controlled fiat currencies. They needed something to trade that was not tied to any government. This was clearly a big sea change, and as an agent for societal improvement and change, I intended to help support and drive it forward.

I became well aware of how important Bitcoin would be as a new and potentially transformative currency and asset. I backed a number of the Boost VC Bitcoin companies, and as I was discovering more and more uses, an enormous opportunity arose. There were several nefarious uses of Bitcoin. One of the most notorious of these was the Silk Road, a group that allowed people to buy and sell anything from drugs and arms to hired assassins. And while people originally believed Bitcoin use could not be traced, the opposite was true. Since every Bitcoin has a unique path associated with it, Bitcoins that are stolen or used for illegal products and services can be easily traced. So

I expect all the crypto criminals will eventually be caught. And many have already been caught.

While I was lamenting the fact that I had lost all that Bitcoin, something happened that gave me another shot at getting involved in the Bitcoin opportunity. The US Marshall's office confiscated the Bitcoins owned by the Silk Road, and more than 30,000 Bitcoins were put up for auction. I looked at this as an opportunity to rebuy the Bitcoins I lost.

There were 31 bidders that came to the table, and the auction was a silent bid for nine blocks of approximately 4000 Bitcoins each. Most of the discussions among the bidders were about how much of a discount from market prices the large blocks of Bitcoins would sell for. The market price then was $618 per Bitcoin. At the last minute, I decided to bid higher than market price. I bid $632.

I won all nine blocks! After the inevitable buyer's remorse that happens when you know you have paid a higher price than anyone else was willing to pay, I thought about how I could best drive a positive use for these Bitcoins with a tainted past. I decided that I would use them to support the proliferation of Bitcoin through emerging country marketplaces where people didn't have confidence in their own currencies. In many countries, that lack of confidence was due to the practice of governments printing extra money for themselves, spreading more corruption and decreasing the money's value. The people are often then riddled with inflation and mistrust.

To make matters worse, people who don't have much money are not "bankable." Banks lose money on people who don't have enough money to make all the paperwork worthwhile. Banking regulations set up to protect the little guy have kept the little guy from participating in the economy—almost guaranteeing that he will remain "the little guy." These people are the "unbanked," and there are 3 billion of them. Bitcoin might be the solution for these people!

Avish Bhama, a Boost entrepreneur with a company called Mirror, helped me figure out a good plan to spread the currency to emerging country markets. The idea was to allow people from developing nations the ability to invest in anything (even to go short against their own currency) by using Bitcoin as the "rails," the conduit for the trades. We held a big press conference together laying out our plans, but since then, the plan has been changed several times. In any case, our ideas gave a lift to the general attitude toward Bitcoin, and the price and confidence in Bitcoin was boosted. Bitcoin itself has been a godsend to the unbanked, providing an economic system for people who are shunned by the currently overregulated banks.

Before I did anything with the Bitcoins, I had to accept delivery of the coins from the US Marshall's office. Avish helped me make sure we could get the Bitcoin into a safe wallet, and I also brought in Leif Jurvetson, my partner's son, who was a 14-year-old Bitcoin expert. Leif is a big Bitcoin proponent, so I invited him in to discuss the security we would be using, and he was with me when I discussed the transfer with the US Marshall's office. He was quite helpful in figuring out the best way to secure the Bitcoin.

When the transfer happened, there was some hold up. We were already a half hour into what was normally a 10-minute approval cycle and we were getting a little anxious. Then we got a report of a.0007 Bitcoin coming into the wallet. We all thought we had been hacked!

Eventually, the full transfer came in and the authenticators recognized the transfer on the blockchain. All was well with the world. We said, "Thank you," to the Marshall's office team, and hung up.

I learned later that Leif had sent the.0007 Bitcoin to thank me for inviting him into the big meeting. Great kid!

Now that I had the Bitcoins, I worked with Avish on his company, called Mirror because he would set up the Bitcoin to "mirror" the trades that happened in various exchanges. Mirror later decided to change its business model, but companies I backed later—BitPesa in Africa, Bitpagos in Latin America and CoinHako in Southeast Asia—took hold of the idea and made the emerging world their marketplace.

The obvious benefits of Bitcoin are 1) it is a currency that is accepted everywhere without any government friction or interference, 2) it is a stored value solution that doesn't require a holder to keep a room full of metals and art, and 3) it is a frictionless currency that can move automatically based on a contract without the usual drag that comes from regulations that need to be interpreted by a lawyer or an accountant. There are many uses for Bitcoin. A Bitcoin wallet can be used as an escrow for a contract in transition, as a redistribution of an estate, or as a transfer agent to distribute payments, dividends or shares of stock. And we are only scratching the surface.

The technology behind Bitcoin is called the blockchain. The blockchain also has some amazing potential. It can be thought of as a giant ledger, keeping track of money, data, inventory, contracts, etc. "Smart" contracts can be designed such that they anticipate eventualities and automatically distribute appropriately.

And corporations can use the blockchain to automatically pay employees their wages and benefits, pay shareholders their dividends, and pay noteholders their interest and principal payments, all with precise accuracy and automated accounting. Furthermore, companies can use the blockchain to pay their suppliers and receive money from their customers, handling lay away payment plans and warranties without friction or human influence.

The blockchain can manage three-way transfers with ease, and eventually will handle retail transactions without the need for credit or debit cards. Insurance companies can use it to manage their claims and automate collections. Real estate escrows and titles can all be done quickly and easily between buyer and seller. Drugs and food can be authenticated by blockchain to guarantee their origins.

And the US government (and other governments) can manage social security, welfare, Medicare, worker's comp, disability and all their data verification of citizens and businesses with Bitcoin and the blockchain, since blockchain is the perfect government service employee. It is honest, incorruptible, secure, and fair.

Bitcoin and its underlying technology, the blockchain, are changes that allow us to progress. But change is difficult for those people who don't have the spark of a Startup Hero in their eyes, and many industries will have to go through fundamental changes to adapt to the advent of this new way of thinking.

People will have to learn that the bank, being the trusted third party for centuries, will soon be replaced by computers that now monitor their holdings through the blockchain. Banking will be simpler, safer and easier than relying on people to do the monotonous work in some brick and mortar facility. Over time, people may see as I see that the money they hold at Coinbase is safer than the money they hold at Wells Fargo or JP Morgan.

Still, the luddites will say that they like to know there is something behind their money like gold or the full faith and confidence of the federal government. Well, the gold standard is no more and in the financial meltdown, that full faith was seriously in jeopardy. Computers are less likely to steal people's money. What the luddites might want to consider is that their money is already flying around the Internet in the current system, and putting it on the blockchain only makes it safer. Additionally, the blockchain banker doesn't take as much as it flies by.

This new digital currency deserves to live and thrive. It has the ability to create a new market unfettered by government politics. The currency can move across borders like gold, but be more frictionless than a bank wire. The reduction in friction (and increase in liquidity) will set the platform for a more prosperous and wealthy world.

Still, Bitcoin is going through growing pains. Over the next 18 months after I won the auction, there were many other incidents of theft and illegal use that brought fear into the Bitcoin marketplace, so the value of my coins went down. The Silk Road Bitcoins I bought dropped in value to just below $200 each. Fortunately for me and for our global society as a whole, confidence has returned, and the price of the Bitcoin has recovered as the market continues to expand and stabilize and as more uses for Bitcoin are discovered.

I believe that this volatility will be looked back on as speedbumps in the road to us getting a globally distributed, liquid and fair economy. A society's wealth and prosperity are driven in part by its ability to trade freely. Bitcoin, because it is so liquid and so flexible, can create a wealthier, more prosperous world.

It is interesting to note that countries, now recognizing that they are in competition with one another, are trying to make sure they win the Bitcoin economy. The smartest of these are either allowing

Bitcoin to prosper or recognize that they need a light touch in regulating Bitcoin to attract all the creativity, money and startups that are flooding into the field.

There are many parallels between Bitcoin now and the Internet in 1994. In 1994, the Internet was just for hobbyists and hackers. I remember when I first used the Internet, the only things I could do were buy diamonds and try to break into NORAD. There were very few uses. It took many years for the Internet to become mainstream, but when it did, it transformed industries. HTTP was the first real working protocol, so people standardized on it even though there were more elegant solutions, just as people today are frustrated with the limitations of Bitcoin but have made it a standard because of all the network effects around the early winner.

The US was wise to leave the Internet unregulated and free because all the Internet entrepreneurs created startups in the US, and the economy around the Internet blossomed. Keeping its regulatory hands light should help innovators stay in the US. At this writing, the Commodities Futures Trade Board (CFTB) and the Securities and Exchange Commission (SEC) are both taking a wait-and-see attitude as they approach the burgeoning virtual market. The SEC did claim that one new crypto vehicle, the DAO, was a security, but they are open to allowing other forms to be clear of securities laws.

Some countries have been early innovators and beneficiaries of the blockchain industry. Singapore and Switzerland have set guidelines for people to create competing crypto commodities. Both individuals and companies can create commodity offerings or Initial Coin Offerings (ICOs) that can have a mission attached to them.

I believe that losing the Bitcoin economy would be akin to losing the Internet, so countries should make sure they are well positioned to compete for the Bitcoin entrepreneurs of the world. Bitcoin is here to stay, and the countries that are the most open to it will be the biggest beneficiaries. The US won big by allowing the Internet to grow unimpeded, and Silicon Valley thrived. I would hope our new leaders would recognize the potential for Bitcoin to similarly drive economic growth and prosperity.

More barriers in society create more friction, and more corruption. Fewer regulations make societies freer and wealthier with more jobs. More liquidity creates a wealthy society; less liquidity creates more poverty. When one country overregulates its banks, or drives an inflationary or failing hopeless economy, the Bitcoin economy flourishes. In some ways, Bitcoin is a check on bad governance.

Some smart and progressive governments will see the blockchain as an opportunity. Many government services can be provided virtually through the blockchain now, and smart governments may recognize that they are not constrained by geographic borders. Governments might look to compete for citizens, both domestic and foreign, in providing virtual services like health insurance, pensions, income insurance, or universal basic income. A government's physical location or land base might become a lesser part of governance, and virtual governance might be where governments compete for us, whether we live in their geographic territory or not.

The long-term vision for Bitcoin is to give the world economic emancipation. Banks will have to adapt their services as the need for trusted third parties and financial middlemen are eclipsed by a trusted crowd of blockchain monitors. The blockchain, being a perfect ledger, may change the accountant's role to one of advisor, and smart contracts may change what it means to be a corporate lawyer. People will not need to hoard gold or hard currency since Bitcoin is a far more convenient source for stored value. Governments may recognize that their fiat currencies are inferior to virtual currencies and will have to allow more financial freedom to their citizens or risk losing those citizens. Taxing authorities and welfare service providers may be replaced by blockchain tax redistribution engines and welfare insurance wallets.

The potential of Bitcoin is only limited by the imaginations of the entrepreneurs who work to drive this new virtual economy. To monitor and keep it honest, I believe that the community of users will ultimately self-regulate, possibly eclipsing or obviating the need for the various governments of the world to regulate the crypto world.

The Bitcoin revolution is coming. It is here to bank the unbanked, to democratize economic opportunity and to reevaluate governance. I expect that it will change everything from the banks and the financial system to healthcare, democracy, and even government.

DAOS AND ICOS

A new form of fundraising is happening around the blockchain architecture. People discovered that the blockchain could be used to raise funds for projects and startups. In effect, people found that they could create their own currencies using Bitcoin as a model. These would be known as decentralized autonomous organizations (DAOs). The first of these, DAO Maker, had an inauspicious beginning. The company used Ethereum (a decentralized currency built using a protocol similar to the Bitcoin blockchain) as its platform. A hacker figured out that when money was moving from one entity to another, they could siphon off the Ethereum currency, called Ether, collected from the sale of the tokens. The hacker managed to steal 3.6 million Ether (at the time valued around $72 million) and the price of Ether dropped from $20 to about $13. DAO offerings came to an abrupt end.

But then more people saw potential in these offerings. The DAO Maker offering had raised $100 million, and entrepreneurs saw potential there. After all, DAOs (and ICOs, as they became known), could raise private money for a project relatively easily without sharing equity and with little friction from any government organization. The tokens purchased could be immediately marketable, and the price would fluctuate as the value of the underlying asset grew.

Any project could be funded by a DAO offering, and any startup could raise money by simply initiating their own currency. In fact, it wouldn't be limited to startups. Anyone could set up an ICO. Imagine the societal change and the frictionless market, the wealth and the jobs that could be created if everyone could raise their own money and have their labor valued through a fresh currency.

As of this writing, Draper Associates has funded three ICOs. Bancor has the potential to transform marketplaces for projects and startups, Tezos has the potential to change how we govern ourselves globally, and Credo can be the vehicle we all use to put a value on email attention.

The Bitcoin/Blockchain/ICO technology is transformative. The changes that we will all encounter are only limited by people's imaginations. We humans have the opportunity to progress far beyond what any of us have ever imagined. By decentralizing economic power, these tokens can open the economic world up to anyone, anywhere with an idea and the willingness to put in the work to spread their idea and their token to the world.

And, as a Startup Hero, you will do everything in your power to pursue progress and change, so you can look at Bitcoin as one of the current vehicles available to you to drive progress and change, move society forward, and drive your industry now that you have an awareness of these breakthroughs.

A NOTE ON THE POTENTIAL OF BITCOIN

Bitcoin could be as important to our world as credit cards or paper money. When money velocity is increased due to reduced friction in the economy, a society becomes wealthier. Bitcoin reduces a significant amount of friction in the economy. People no longer have to pay a "trusted third party" or a bank to make a transaction occur. With all the fraud and hacking of the banks, Bitcoin may accelerate as a currency even faster than it would have without these external threats.

Almost anything you now use your bank for, you can use Bitcoin for. The immediate applications are sending money overseas, paying for products and services, making micropayments to people who need to be paid for their services (e.g., residuals for actors or cameramen), overseas employee wages, payments by the unbanked, etc.

Longer term, any contract will be better served by being fixed on the blockchain. The blockchain allows any contract that revolves around an event (like a company sale, a dividend, a royalty distribution, a death, the outcome of a game, etc.) where cash or stock or something of value needs to be distributed or paid out, can be agreed to, executed and disbursed without a lawyer or an accountant, since the trusted third party is all of society, not a series of written documents, a regulated accounting firm and a brick and mortar bank.

Bitcoin's blockchain is technology that is open and transparent, distributed, frictionless and secure. This technology may be at least as transformative as the Internet has been. While the Internet transformed music, communications, information, entertainment and transportation, Bitcoin and its blockchain may allow governments to be virtual, banks to be unnecessary, ownership to be ironclad, insurance to be frictionless, and people to know who owns what.

ICOs have the potential to open up new highways of human creativity. Imagine services that bank the unbanked, insure the uninsurable, and give liquidity to markets that until now were illiquid. ICOs may be as big a breakthrough for economic progress as interest was for lenders or stock was for investors. I can imagine societal transformations that were only dreamt of before decentralized autonomous tokens. I expect to see a renaissance of breakthroughs in everything from finance to healthcare, from data to distribution, and from infrastructure to government.

QUEXERCISES ON PROGRESS AND CHANGE

1. What will you do to drive, build and pursue progress and change?

2. What in your world seems wrong, stagnant, or in need of revamping or renovating?

3. How will you go about making the change?

4. What forces for the status quo will you be up against?

5. How will the status quo respond? What other obstacles will you face?

6. What resources will you need? What people will you need to help you?

7. How can you take advantage of an ICO? What kind of coin would you issue? What change would it promote?

8. Meet someone on the street who will listen to you and teach them how you make a living.

PROGRESS PUZZLE

When there is too much government, the workers lose incentive to work and progress slows, but if there is too little government, businesses can create problems for society and the people are less safe. If a government takes one dollar and adds some safety and insurance to your life, but only uses 8% for the progress of society, and a company takes one dollar and uses 90% for the progress of society, and you want society to progress safely, what is the right balance between safety and progress? When you think of this, think about how much of the value of your work you would want to give to the government, and what kind of safety net you would want.

There are more complications. If government spending gets past 30%, the progress goes negative. If business goes past 90%, the progress goes negative. You are never 100% safe. The highest safety is at 50% government spending. The highest productivity is at 15% government spending.

Where would you fall on this political scale? Would you want the highest safety or the highest productivity, or something in between?

Now think about how fast you would progress each year, and remember that it compounds. If an unfettered country grows at 10% and you decide to grow at 2%, then in five years the unfettered country would have progressed 60%, and your country would have progressed by a little more than 10%. Does that change your thinking?

PROGRESS AND CHANGE SHAKESPEARIAN SONNET

The immovable object and the infinite force

The Luddite fills a certain plebeian role
To uphold, defend and secure the status quo
She sets her stubborn girth into that hole
Inertia immovable. Though change does blow

The hero comes to save us with a plan
His power vision bolder than a wave
He is however just a single man
Most of those around him say, "behave."

He tries to push the Luddite with a shove
He takes her by the hand and lightly tugs

He digs around her freeing her to move
Her hiney stuck could make her meal for bugs

As time goes by she bends to see his way
With smile and heart, she joins him in the fray.

MY BRAND, MY NETWORK AND MY REPUTATION ARE PARAMOUNT.

As I grow older, I pay less attention to what men say. I just watch what they do.

ANDREW CARNEGIE

The future of communicating with customers rests in engaging with them through every possible channel: phone, e-mail, chat, Web, and social networks. Customers are discussing a company's products and brand in real time. Companies need to join the conversation.

MARC BENIOFF

A brand is a voice and a product is a souvenir.

LISA GANSKY

You have to understand your own personal DNA. Don't do things because I do them or Steve Jobs or Mark Cuban tried it. You need to know your personal brand and stay true to it.

GARY VAYNERCHUK

A brand for a company is like a reputation for a person. You earn reputation by trying to do hard things well.

JEFF BEZOS

MY BRAND

Logo. Your logo should mean something. The initial logo for Draper Associates, designed by my cousin, Phyllis Merikallio, was a blue globe in front of a black triangle. I liked this for a lot of reasons. The triangle represented "change" and the globe represented "the world," so together these images said, "Change the world." Apple's logo was a rainbow-colored apple, which was both eye catching and meant that the products were for everyone. Nike's logo was a simple black "swoosh," which implied that Nike shoes would make you active, maybe even a better athlete, and a faster runner.

But your brand is not just a simple logo. Your brand permeates your organization. My friend, the late Don Hitchens, was perhaps the best brand advisor I ever met. He told me, "Tim, your brand is everything. Your brand is what you wear, who you work with, how you treat and incentivize your employees, how you treat your suppliers, and of course how you treat your customers." Don changed my life. I took brand to heart. I even decided to always wear the same dark suits and colorful Save the Children red ties (until recently when the charity stopped selling ties). I try to be a good example in everything I do, and I constantly try to think about how I am treating the people I work with, sell to, fund, teach and raise money from.

Steve Jobs always wore a black turtleneck and jeans. It said, "I am not wearing a tie, so I am somewhat counter-cultural (because IBM was all white shirts and ties at the time), I want to be comfortable, and I want my customers to have a more comfortable, easier life, and my products will be easier to use."

Your brand extends to your customer. There is an old saying, "The customer is always right." And that is a good motto to live by. The three greatest entrepreneurs I have backed (so far) went much further than that. Niklas Zennstrom, founder of Skype (in concert with his partner, Janus Fries); Robin Li, founder of Chinese search engine Baidu; and Elon Musk, founder of PayPal, Tesla, and SpaceX, all used the same word when referring to their customers. The word is "delight." They said, "We want to delight our users." This is the mindset that helped build Skype, Baidu, Tesla and SpaceX. And it probably should be the mindset you use as you become a Startup

Hero.

I recently talked to my friend Marc Benioff, who is the founder, chairman and CEO of Salesforce. He told me that when he spoke to Mark Zuckerberg of Facebook, Mark said, "You don't have much of a technology orientation, do you?" Marc responded, "We have a customer orientation." The customer is always right, and if you delight your customer, your brand will expand in a positive way, your business will thrive, and you will move the world forward.

MY NETWORK

Build your network. Build it all the way up and down the food chain. You never know when your largest investor will need a plumber or your janitor will need a dentist. Get to know people. Connect with what they do. Help people with their challenges. Use your network to make the people around you successful.

To start with, in order to build a link to someone, you have to meet them. In many cases, that can be as simple as turning to the person sitting next to you on a plane, or standing near you at a party, or waiting in line at the DMV and saying, "Hi, what is your work?" In other cases, you will have to target people you need to meet and set up appointments with their assistants, or figure out where they are going to be and be there yourself.

Then, get contact information. Find out how the person wants to be reached, email, telephone, WeChat, text, etc. and reach them that way. Then follow up with a thank you note or a photo reminder of the meeting that can increase the strength of the bond you have established. The bond increases, and your reputation is enhanced as someone who follows up. Subliminally, you have shown your contact that you are a hard worker. Include in your follow up anything you might have discussed or promised each other in the discussion.

And then, where it makes sense, when you have established a real connection, try to make a deal with the person, no matter how simple. Ideally, the deal will have money going one way or the other, and some service going either way or both ways. This exercise will force you into a creative mindset, where together you and this person will pursue a project with some type of end goal of progress.

The deal and its contract (whether a large legal document or a handshake) creates a solid bond. The bond shows trust between you and the other party. Trust can lead to all sorts of benefits to your business life. I have made deals with people to share a cab from the airport that led me to an entrepreneur to back. I have funded entrepreneurs on a napkin, and they in turn spread the word to all their entrepreneur friends that I have the ability to move fast. And I have hired employees with a handshake, which led to long-term loyalty and trust, and an opening up of their networks to the business.

I was named the #1 Networked Venture Capitalist by AlwaysOn magazine. Apparently, they ran a computer model looking at all the connections of all the venture capitalists, and my name came up the most often. I will use my own network in describing how to build out a network, but by no means is this necessarily the best way to do it. Everyone needs to work with their own style, their own strategy, and their own people to discover how to network best.

In my business, the venture capital business, a network is paramount. We need to spread the word far and wide that we are in the business so entrepreneurs know how to find us. We need to connect our startups with other investors, customers, service providers, suppliers, employees, and potential joint venture partners. We need to know the press so we can help our entrepreneurs get the word out when they launch a new product or service. We need to know educators, so they can send us their most promising students to work for the companies in our portfolio. And we need to know influencers who promote progress, small businesses, and entrepreneurship, so we can encourage them to support our portfolio companies.

THE DRAPER VENTURE NETWORK STORY

When the Draper Venture Network (DVN) started, I was still new to the venture capital business. I listened to the advice of many of the veterans of the industry as I was getting my sea legs. The conventional wisdom suggested that: 1) Venture capital is a local business—most venture firms would not venture more than 25 miles from their office to make an investment, and 2) Venture capital does not scale. Most venture capital firms just grew by investing larger amounts in companies and eventually graduated into the private equity or buyout business.

When people say, "This is the way it is," I start looking for reasons why that might not be the case. I took this conventional wisdom on as a challenge. I wanted to see if I could invest in companies outside of my immediate neighborhood, and I wanted to see if I could scale the venture capital business geographically. I tend to believe that if everyone agrees that something is the way it is and it will never change, it may just be time to see if I can change it. My opportunity to shake up the status quo started with a boondoggle to Alaska.

It was three years into my venture capital career. I was struggling with my fund and worrying about the money I had borrowed from the SBIC. I got a form letter from the Alaskan government asking if I would come to Alaska to discuss venture capital and possibly put together a venture capital fund there. Oil had fallen to $6 per barrel and the real estate business was also in free fall. The Alaskan government was searching for a new economic cornerstone that could supplement its core industries. I am sure many other venture capitalists got the same letter, but no one else responded. After all, Alaska was not in their 25-mile radius. But I had other plans.

I flew up on Alaska Air, landing in Ketchikan (very short runway, very icy—the nose of the plane was over water when we finally came to a stop) on the way to Juneau (the plane's wing almost hit the trees as we landed). Alaskan pilots are extraordinary.

Once I arrived in Juneau, I met with a small group from AIDEA, the Alaskan Development Authority, and discussed the venture capital business and how it might help Alaskans diversify their economy. They asked me to give an impromptu speech at lunch to what seemed to be the local chamber of commerce. I met some local entrepreneurs who had some fun, local businesses and ideas, collecting business cards as I went. One card was from David Rose, who ran the Alaskan Permanent Fund, one of the largest pension funds in the US. Certainly that was a contact I could use at a future date.

The press there asked me about the opportunities that might make good venture investments in Alaska. I had heard about everything from a fish head splitting company, to a salmon skin wallets company, to "Alaska Men," a tongue-in-cheek magazine that a very motivated woman was driving. I sensed that there was a lot of creativity in the state, and I thought there would be ample opportunity that would come out of the woodwork once the entrepreneurs of Alaska learned that venture capital was available from our fund.

Oddly, that same day, I was asked to speak to the Keidanren, a high-level Japanese keiretsu consisting of the chairmen of 20 of the largest businesses in Japan who were visiting Alaska to lobby against the unitary tax they were paying. I didn't really understand the connection, but it seemed to be a good opportunity for me to meet some of the most powerful people in Japan. Perhaps the Alaskan government just needed someone to stall the Japanese while they deliberated, or maybe it was a test for me, but I prepared and made a speech. I was very nervous speaking to such a powerful group, but I didn't need to worry. The jet-lagged Japanese businessmen kept falling asleep on me. During the speech, every once in a while, I shouted and watched all their heads bob up for an instant before they dozed back off. But I got to know some of them after the speech (they were happy to have had a nap) and they were quite helpful to me when, several years later, I set up a Japanese venture fund. You never know when efforts to build a network will pay off.

Whatever the tests were that the Alaskans gave me, I guess I passed. It took two years, but eventually AIDEA awarded me a $6 million fund to invest. After receiving the award, I heard one of the executives, Burt Wagnon, say in frustration, "This money is gone." He believed that the venture capital business had no use in Alaska and I would just lose their money. Maybe he believed it, and maybe he just knew how I ticked, because nothing could have motivated me more....

I put a team together with local Anchorage real estate businessman Jim Yarmon and fellow Harvard Business School alum Jim Lynch. The three of us agreed to put half the money in Alaska, and half in Silicon Valley. We called the fund Polaris Fund to give it local appeal, and we were off to the races. We made it work, funding a bone-stretching technology company (seemed painful, but it grew people's bones), a low-Earth orbit satellite company, and the fish head splitter company as well as a few great Silicon Valley companies. It took a few years, but we ended up returning the $6 million to AIDEA and much more. Burt can now rest easy knowing that the money was well invested.

This Polaris Fund in Alaska turned out to be the first of many network partners we would set up. Because the Polaris Fund worked out so well, I started to believe that there might be a full-blown franchise opportunity in venture capital, and with it an opportunity to significantly expand our network.

I set off to try to "franchise" venture capital. And it wasn't difficult. After Polaris, people started coming to me. I got a call from Todd Stevens, a classmate of mine from Harvard Business School, and together with Zions Bank money, we set up the Wasatch Fund in Utah. The bank was looking to participate in this new form of finance, and we were the perfect ticket. We put a team together and started investing in and around Utah. In Washington D.C., I teamed up with Stanford fraternity brother John Backus to raise a fund we called Draper Atlantic. In Los Angeles, another Stanford fraternity brother, David Cremin, had decided to leave the music business just as the Los Angeles Community Development Bank asked me to put together a fund for me to run, which we called Zone Ventures. And there were many others that followed (Timberline in Seattle, DFJ Gotham in New York City, DFJ Portage in Chicago, DFJ Mercury in Texas, Access Ventures in Colorado, and DFJ New England in Boston). We even decided to go international in 1999 and set up DFJ ePlanet as a joint venture with Roderick Thompson and Asad Jamal, two very bright but somewhat mysterious people who had hunted us down to use our newly minted but effective brand to build a global franchise.

This group of venture funds became the DFJ Network. Our network became unique in the world of venture capital. As a group, we became the #1 most prolific venture investor with our network boasting over 50 general partners who were investing in more than 100 companies per year. Investors from all over the world were discovering that they could help each other with deciding on investments, making introductions to new companies to invest in, making connections to potential customers for portfolio investments, and sharing investments and syndication. Because of our model, and the system we built, many new venture capitalists were created and trained, and hundreds of portfolio companies have been funded around the world. The network became a major asset for us. Arguably, we would never have backed Skype and Baidu if we hadn't created the network.

In 2008 though, the markets collapsed, and the network was beginning to unravel. Many of my DFJ partners who had not been around for the creation of the network (and missed out on Skype and Baidu) wondered why DFJ would tarnish the brand with groups that had spotty results. I argued that some of the funds had done quite well, and that all venture funds went through a dry spell during this period because of a lack of liquidity, and because confidence in the global markets was low. The network limped along for several years until we hired Gabe Turner, who steadily and systematically brought the network back to life, rebranding it as the Draper Venture Network (DVN) because of branding confusion issues we ran into, and building on its strong global reputation.

Today, the DVN spans 14 relationship firms, with 8 alumni firms, covering over 50 cities around the world and managing several billion dollars in nearly 1000 companies. And the power of the network is unprecedented for deal flow, due diligence, best practices, and the connections the teams make for their portfolio companies around the world. Companies in the network include Right-Click Capital in Australia, Dalus Capital in Mexico, Wavemaker in Singapore and South East Asia, Blume Ventures in India, as well as the various Draper branded funds: Draper Dragon in China, Draper Athena in Korea, Draper Nexus in Japan, Draper Esprit in the UK, Draper Triangle in the Midwestern US, Draper Aurora in Russia, and Draper Associates in Silicon Valley as well as three smaller firms in our DVN beta program, and we are adding more partners every year.

A network provides network effects. More nodes on a network increase the power of the network as the square of the number of nodes on the network increases. This concept is known as Metcalfe's Law, after entrepreneur, venture capitalist, educator and pundit Bob Metcalfe. The DVN allows me to evaluate and potentially fund any company from anywhere in the world. My deal flow has also expanded and improved. My judgment can only have been improved by seeing more companies from more regions, and Draper Associates' returns should continue to improve because we see so many more companies for each one I invest in. Additionally, my entrepreneurs can easily grow their businesses internationally because our network has such great reach. I would never have envisioned the awesome potential of Bitcoin to bank the unbanked if I hadn't spent so much time evaluating and working with startups from other countries around the world.

The DVN network boasts nearly 1000 companies, so we are able to get quantity discounts on travel, insurance and the like. The network also becomes a large marketplace itself. The companies can sell to each other, or band together to pitch a large customer with multiple needs. Because of the size of the network, we are able to attract large companies to come to an event we have called the DVN CEO Summit, where business development teams from Fortune 500 companies gather to connect with our startups and see which ones they can work with on partnerships, joint ventures, or as customers. Some of the attendees are also looking to acquire our companies.

THE BEYOND NEWS HAT STORY

Beyond the formal network created by DVN, we have a network of entrepreneurs whose companies we funded. We backed Scott Walchek and his company called Beyond News. Scott was a confident, good-looking man with a swagger. He negotiated a very tough deal with us, but we liked him, and we liked Beyond News's business plan. We invested in the company partly because it had a very sweet deal with Lexis Nexis, the legal data firm. But, two weeks after our investment cleared, the Lexis Nexis deal fell apart. We were very circumspect thinking we had bet on a deal that the company may have known was going to fall apart and the company may have waited to tell us until the check cleared, but Scott said, "Look, it happened. We are just as surprised as you are. We are telling you this right away." Then he told us, "This is a blessing. We have another plan to take this company forward, and it is a better model." John was confident that Scott was on the up and up, and Scott appreciated that, but I was still a little suspicious.

Instead of Beyond News, I started to call the company "Beyond Belief," because I was not 100% certain of what we had invested in. I even told the Scott that I would eat my hat if we ever got our money back on our investment in Beyond News. Scott shrugged, and without missing a beat, laid out his new plan for the business. He would do online comparison shopping. His enthusiasm was catching.

The business did start working. Scott and his team were building some strong momentum, and he got a call from a potential partner. Scott described the event to John Fisher, who represented us on the board of Beyond News.

Scott said, "We were talking with David Peterschmidt of Inktomi, and he said he wanted to buy the company. When we asked how much he hoped to pay for it, he started writing on the chalkboard. First, he put a '1' down, and we were about to walk out of the room thinking we were worth way more than one million dollars. Then he put a '3' down, and we thought, 'Wow! Thirteen million dollars is awesome!' But we kept our mouths shut and he kept writing, and he added a '0.' After he wrote the word million, we smiled and quickly shook his hand to seal the deal." We sold Beyond News for $130 million in Inktomi stock!

The San Francisco Giants hat I brought for the closing dinner tasted like ink and cardboard.

The Inktomi stock shot up from there almost tenfold. Scott made so much money he became a venture angel. Since we stood by him when he was down, he brought John a great lead.

I came to John saying we need to fund the search engine for China. He said, "What a coincidence. Scott just sent me a lead on a startup called Baidu that does just that and he is already a seed investor." Baidu grew to be worth over $60 billion and eventually became one of our greatest investments ever, but it wouldn't have happened without the network.

Build and support your network!

Think about what your network is made up of today. How can you potentially expand it? How might it be helpful to you in the future?

MY REPUTATION

A reputation can be built over 40 years, but it can be ruined in a day. The infamous blue dress put a damper on all the good things Bill Clinton had done for America and the global economy when he was in office. Watergate hangs heavy over Richard Nixon's legacy even though he did some extraordinary work, including opening up the US's relationship with China. Enron and WorldCorp were great companies before they overplayed their hands and got into accounting messes.

In a crisis, the best way to avoid ruining your reputation is to pause, accept what the fates have in mind for you and just work through it. Do not overplay your hand! Sometimes in a crisis people resort to trying to correct the problem with a shortcut or a lie. Or they try to overcompensate and hide the problem and then they get in deeper. I don't know for sure, but my best guess is that the notorious schemers, Ponzi, Madoff and Sanford, all started out their businesses with honest intent, and then made some bad choices to try to prop up their results, ruining what might have otherwise been stellar careers.

Handling a crisis is best done by coming out with all the bad news right away. When Gavin Newsom was mayor of San Francisco, he was caught having an affair. Almost immediately, he came out to greet the press saying, "Everything you have heard about me…is true." That honesty nipped the story in the bud and ended the news cycle. Gavin went on to become lieutenant governor (and at this writing, he is the frontrunner for governor of California).

Tylenol was one of the most successful over-the-counter products of all time when some nefarious person laced some of the bottles with cyanide. Seven people died from these contaminated pills. Johnson & Johnson was Tylenol's parent company, and its chairman, James Burke, had to protect the people and save the product. The company immediately told customers not to use Tylenol, and they took it off the shelves at great cost to the company. Ultimately, they were able to resume shipping the product with better security on the bottles. The Tylenol consumers so appreciated the company for keeping them safe that sales shot up after the repair of the scare. Rather than trying to cover it up, the company came straight out and told consumers the truth. The company was then seen as the victim of tampering, not the killer of seven (or more) people, and the customers soon came back with even more confidence in the brand.

Don't try to cover it up. You will save your reputation if you open up and tell the whole story. Your reputation is paramount.

QUEXERCIZES ON BRAND

1. Does the brand make the product or does the product make the brand? Charles Schwab built his brand and then created products around it. Hotmail and Skype built the product and allowed it to spread from person to person with very little friction.

2. Think about the brands you trust. Why do you trust them?

3. Design your personal brand with an edge. Who are you and what do you stand for? Then take an action toward building that brand. Then tweet it out to your network and respond to the reaction you get from your friends.

NEURON CONNECTORS PUZZLE

1. How many connections are made in a network of one? How many in a network of 21?

2. There are two physical volumes of an old encyclopedia sitting on a shelf in a college library. One volume is labeled A-M and the other N-W. Is the third volume X-Z missing?

3. What is the highest score you can get in Scrabble on the first move?

BRAND, NETWORK AND REPUTATION PETRARCHAN SONNET

Winning your community

Community is like a pack of wolves
Responding to a lead dog purely loyal
His reputation--acts that made him royal
Their memory imprinted with symbols

Connecting with a pack requires proof
To prove your worth through deeds is a hard toil.

Competitors bring your startup blood to boil
A steady build will surely raise the roof

We trust the brands we know like Skype and Tesla
But some like Bell have somehow lost their lusta
It's Metcalfe's Law that defines how great our network
Those people in your tribe are how you'll get work.
A network build requires dedication
Be thoughtful as you build your reputation

I WILL SET POSITIVE EXAMPLES FOR OTHERS TO EMULATE.

I actually think that the most efficacious way of making a difference is to lead by example, and doing random acts of kindness is setting a very good example of how to behave in the world.

MISHA COLLINS

A return to first principles in a republic is sometimes caused by the simple virtues of one man. His good example has such an influence that the good men strive to imitate him, and the wicked are ashamed to lead a life so contrary to his example.

NICCOLO MACHIAVELLI

I think the only kind of acceptable evangelization is the evangelization of good example.

ANDREW GREELEY

Whether we like it or not, we are high-profile athletes. We're role models. Kids come up to me all the time to talk and it makes me remember when I was a kid and I got to meet Jerry Rice and how much that meant to me. And how we've got to set a good example.

JONATHAN VILMA

If there is such a thing as good leadership, it is to give a good example. I have to do so for all the Ikea employees.

INGVAR KAMPRAD

Innovation distinguishes between a leader and a follower.

STEVE JOBS

Leadership is a skill, and it requires commitment.

Great leaders are fair, just and honorable. Great leaders allow their team to shine. Great leaders lead by example. Great leaders know when to be there for their team, and when to let the team drive the task.

When an entrepreneur starts a company, he or she rarely has any idea that in 10 years the company they started may be employing thousands of people. And even fewer entrepreneurs understand that those employees will pick up their memes (a meme is like a gene, but it is a learned character trait rather than a born one. The word meme is now used to describe a short video or GIF that spreads quickly). We have seen very positive memes spread throughout the best of companies.

There are many ways to lead an organization. Vivek Ranadive, founder and former CEO of Tibco, led by sending a message to his team of continued improvement in serving the customers. He said, "We just work to keep improving. We improve everything. We improve ourselves. We improve our products. We improve our services. Our customers seem to love it."

Elon Musk of SpaceX put out an imaginative challenge. He said, "We are going to Mars!" When he said it, he clearly didn't mind that the vast majority of people who heard him would think he was crazy, because by saying it, he also attracted the best and brightest engineers to work at his company, since great engineers want to work on something exciting and ambitious.

Marc Benioff of Salesforce gives his 25,000 employees a very clear direction and goal, and then monitors their progress toward that goal regularly. He does not tell them how to do their job. He trusts them to figure it out. In his book, "Behind the Cloud," he describes it like this:

"V2MOM, an acronym that stands for vision, values, methods, obstacles, and measures. This tool (pronounced "V2 mom") has helped me achieve my goals in my past work and helps make salesforce.com a success. V2MOM enabled me to clarify what I was doing and communicate it to the entire company as well. The vision helped us define what we wanted to do. The values established what was most important about that vision; it set the principles and beliefs that guided it (in priority). The methods il-

lustrated how we would get the job done by outlining the actions and the steps that everyone needed to take. The obstacles identified the challenges, problems, and issues we would have to overcome to achieve our vision. Finally, the measures specified the actual result we aimed to achieve; often this was defined as a numerical outcome. Combined, V2MOM gave us a detailed map of where we were going as well as a compass to direct us there. Essentially, V2MOM is an exercise in awareness in which the result is total alignment. In addition, having a clarified direction and focusing collective energy on the desired outcome eliminate the anxiety that is often present in times of change."

In all three of these cases, the leader set a direction for people. The employees in each case knew what they were doing the work for. The best leaders make sure their employees know how they contribute to the company's success.

There is no single Startup Hero leader. They can come in all forms and shapes, and the approach can vary widely, but in all successful cases, the leader puts a clear direction into people's minds so that they have a purpose to their work.

You will have to decide what kind of leader you want to be. What do you want tens of thousands of people to be like? How will you manage them? What should they stand for? How should they conduct themselves in society?

I remember the brainwashing I got when I worked at Hewlett Packard (HP). We learned about the HP Way, and how we were expected to conduct ourselves. Our clear mission was to care for all the stakeholders around us: our shareholders, customers, suppliers, employees, and our community. All employees abided by a dress code of button down shirt and slacks, and we all spoke in three letter acronyms to shorten our conversations. I remember watching my boss to see how I was expected to act if I was to succeed in this caring culture, so I know the brainwashing worked on me.

I noticed my friends at Sun Microsystems take on not just the aggressive thinking of their leader, Scott McNealy, but also his mannerisms and wording. "Awesome" was Scott's trademark word, and he regularly said, "the networked computer is inevitable." His employees started chanting the same mantras and they even took on his fashion sense, wearing the same t-shirts and jeans that he did. He encouraged a very casual tone among his employees so that they knew that he just wanted them to get the job done (not to wait on protocol) and they responded accordingly.

Steve Jobs created the meme of calling his employees "evangelists" so Apple employees would take on his religious fervor for the company. Many even wore jeans and black turtlenecks to emulate the great man. Bill Gates prided himself on his high IQ, so everyone at Microsoft was focused on being smart. Some employees even wore glasses that looked like the ones Bill wore whether they had a vision problem or not.

Being a great leader forces you to think about how you live your life, because you will see others trying to emulate you. It is often painful for an entrepreneur to do this because often, for them, the mission is all that matters. Damn the torpedoes, full speed ahead. But leaders need to understand what it is they are spreading. If a leader smokes, his or her employees will smoke. If a leader drinks heavily or takes drugs, so will his or her employees. If a leader leaves garbage around, that leader will soon find that his or her offices are unlivable. If a leader overeats, the company might have healthcare issues down the line. If a leader is short-tempered, the employees may fight.

But, as a Startup Hero, if you are kind to people, they will be too, and the company will be known as a nice place to work. If you are enthusiastic about the mission, that optimistic force will lift the company to new heights. If you live clean, the company will keep their vices at home. If you are honest, the company will run on trust, which is so much more efficient than one run on suspicion. If you love what you do and show it, your company will be a family of people who help each other lead happier, more successful lives. And don't forget to have a little fun at work and celebrate the small successes. People need a release from whatever it is you have them doing day after day.

Lead by example, and put your beliefs and values up on the wall for all to see. It is important for a Startup Hero to know what he or she wants to accomplish. Sometimes a mission can change or become muddled. It is important for you to keep a clear mission for your team, communicate that mission, and guide your team to work toward that mission. A constant reminder of why you are all here is good for employee morale. It keeps the team excited about your mission, and it helps everyone focus to a goal.

Set positive examples for others to emulate.

QUEXERCISES ON POSITIVE EXAMPLES

1. Have you ever done something that you might not have done if you had a child with you?

2. Have you ever done something that you would not have done if a reporter had seen you?

3. Have you ever led a team in any aspect of your life? What did you do right? What would you have done differently?

4. Have you ever been surprised because someone was watching you to emulate you?

5. Help an old person across the street, or help a short person to get their carry-ons from the overhead compartment, or watch someone try to do something and see if you can help. And then bend down and pick up some garbage and throw it into a garbage can.

BRAINTORNADO ON POSITIVE EXAMPLES

If you have 15 magnets linked together from left to right, and the first magnet is positive on the right side, what is the polarity on the right side of the sixth magnet from the left?

POSITIVE EXAMPLE HAIKU

If I walk, you walk
Follow me through the gauntlet
If I soar, you soar

I WILL INSTILL GOOD HABITS IN MYSELF. I WILL TAKE CARE OF MYSELF.

Good habits formed at youth make all the difference.

ARISTOTLE

You've got to get good habits of working hard so that when that play comes up during the regular season that you're able to complete it and do it the right way.

AL KALINE

I'm taking better care of myself by eating healthy, exercising and doing my best to keep my stress level down as well as role modeling good habits for my kids.

MONICA POTTER

You, yourself, as much as anybody in the entire universe, deserve your love and affection.

GAUTAMA BUDDHA

Take care of yourself. You need to be healthy and happy to be an effective Startup Hero. Your health is tied to your life and vice versa. Dr. Dean Ornish, a regular Draper University speaker who wrote the book *Reversing Heart Disease*, states that you can change your habits and your body will reform. Your heart, your brain, your demeanor can all be changed by a change in lifestyle. He found that just by eating well, exercising regularly, and loving friends, that people could physically change and a bad heart could become a good heart, both figuratively and literally.

THE WHOLE 30 STORY

My wife saw that I was getting a little overweight even though I exercised for about an hour almost every day. She noticed that I had become a chocoholic and would eat anything I could get my hands on at night. I stored dried fruit in my desk and I would eat ice cream by the pint when I got in front of the TV. My sisters both hinted at my weight gain, but otherwise, people were too polite or too scared to tell me to lose weight. Only my best friend, Cree Edwards, was cruel and kind enough to tell me I had gotten fat.

I noticed that my knees, my back and my hips were giving me trouble more often, and I had chronic plantar fasciitis for more than six years. I chalked it all up to just getting old. I could lose a pound or two when I starved myself, but I would always come back to the trough with a vengeance, and go back to my old weight, or heavier. As an optimist, I could always see the good angles as I admired myself in the mirror, and I am tall, so I can hide a lot of extra weight.

Being overweight was affecting my moods and my business. I was one of the top well-known venture capitalists in the world, but still it was a struggle to get my first independent venture capital fund raised. Subconsciously, I believe that people might have thought I would eat up their profits, or that maybe I had gotten lazy. But as it turned out, I was just eating the wrong things.

One day, my wife looked at me critically and said, "**WE** should try this." It was a program called The Whole 30, where for 30 days I could eat as much as I wanted, only it couldn't include sugar, bread, dairy, or grains. I could eat any meat, vegetables, fruits, potatoes, and selected nuts. And although my wife always looked good and probably didn't need to lose weight, she did it with me. It worked out well. She kept me on the straight and narrow. We made it fun and collaborative. It turns out that there is added sugar in almost everything--most bacon, canned goods, cereals, and of course ice cream and chocolate.

Similarly, bread seems to be one of our staples. You can find bread in meatloaf, every sandwich, pizza, pancakes, tortillas, and even the "meat" in some fast food burgers. Dairy is in milk, butter, ice cream, yogurt, cheese, pizza...even on most salads and in salad dressings (which also have sugar). Grains include rice, wheat, and corn, all difficult to avoid in our current culture.

After the initial shock of not eating any of my staples, I pursued this new lifestyle. Rather than looking at it as a sacrifice, I decided that this "diet" was just a "food adventure." This was my startup diet. I needed to transform an industry dominated by a fat monopoly (my metabolism), and do it by creating a new startup (my new eating habits). As the great Startup Heroes do, I had to go all in, and my wife and I made up the founding team.

We both enjoyed the new challenge. She did most of the cooking, but both of us started to be conscious of every single thing that went into the pan. It turns out, some garlic salt has sugar in it, for instance. Day three was a panic for me, when my body started to freak out seeing that it was not getting what it used to get. I had diarrhea and was peeing more than ever. This was a typical startup process consisting of tremendous life changes, a singular focus, a vision, and a hope for a better life at the end of a dark tunnel. But weirdly, I was never hungry. Having a diet where you can eat as much as you want feels like you are not really sacrificing the way you believe you should be when on a diet. Maybe this could be not just than a diet but a lifestyle.

I shed 15 pounds during those 30 days, and at this reading, I am one year into this lifestyle change and 40 pounds lighter. It is like magic. The pains in my knees, back and hips are almost totally gone. I have no more plantar fasciitis. My energy level is up. I am thinking clearer, and my work is more effective. My wife similarly lost weight and still looks awesome. I had to get some new clothes, because my pants were falling off. Now, I can go back deep into my closet to find those clothes that I bought for a younger, lighter me. I also had to retrain myself in basketball, since I was an "in the paint" defender, but without the extra weight, I was less effective there, so I am trying to learn how to shoot. And now I have noticed that the subconscious societal biases against the overweight are not affecting my work and more of the things I want done are getting done.

Smoking has some similar qualities to obesity. Smokers really irritate nonsmokers. Some of the same subconscious thoughts keep nonsmokers from wanting to do business with smokers. I never smoked, so my advice here should be taken with a grain of salt, but I have gotten four students at Draper University to quit smoking through this method. As I see it, to a smoker, smoking is an enjoyable experience, and except for the high likelihood of dying of lung cancer, smokers don't seem to see any downside to their smoking habit.

To counter this misconception, I created a little exercise at my university. When students at Draper University smoke, we create friction, so they don't feel that the experience is so enjoyable. Every time they smoke a cigarette, they are asked to go pick up 10 cigarette butts from the alley and throw them out, and then go up and change their clothes and brush their teeth. This request does a few things:

First, it makes them think before they light up. These chores give them friction to smoking. Picking up the cigarette butts makes them appreciate the littering they have done and makes them think of what they are leaving behind in this life. And second, being forced to change their clothes and brush their teeth every time they smoke reminds them of how their breath, clothes and carelessness are affecting other people.

But to use this Draper University startup method to quit smoking, you need to understand how cigarettes are marketed. A cigarette pack is the perfect size to fit nicely in your hand. It is the same size as a pack of cards and an iPhone, two other addictive consumer products. Packs are in attractive boxes and each cigarette is like a new gift. A cigarette is nicely rolled and can be thought of as a substitute for a baby pacifier for those of us who still love to suck on things. Cigarette companies have mastered the marketing art. Cigarettes themselves are addictive, but so is the whole process of consuming them. Cigarette companies have found an ideal way to create a habit in people. And if you smoke, you are their stooge, their mark, their putz.

If you are going to be a Startup Hero, use something else in place of cigarettes. Gum and Tic Tacs are better habits, although they may clash with the Whole 30 diet above. Almond butter is now packaged in nice beautiful containers, so you can just carry those with you whenever you feel like lighting up. There are plenty of things that can be substitutes if you look around. And if you don't find any, just go start a company around a product that is packaged to fit in the palm of your hand, comes out in sticks, allows you to light something on fire and you get to suck on—but doesn't give you (and the people around you) lung cancer.

You must stay healthy. You must stay healthy to make the changes you envision and see them through to completion. I once read that 33% of the Forbes billionaires were teetotalers. By contrast, approximately 2% of the US adult population doesn't drink alcohol, and most of them are Mormons or in Alcoholics Anonymous (AA). Very few successful CEOs are overweight. Most of them eat well and have very rigid exercise routines. Instill good habits in yourself. Take care of yourself.

QUEXERCISES ON HABITS

1. What are your best habits?

2. What are your worst habits?

3. How can you make modifications to your lifestyle to get to your goal?

4. How can you remain emotionally steady when you go through difficult times?

5. When can your business tolerate you taking a vacation?

6. Are you taking care of yourself?

7. Exercise every morning before you eat breakfast for 30 days. Eat nothing with processed sugar, grain or milk in it.

HABIT PUZZLE

How many times do you have to do something to make it a habit?

Three nuns live together. They are all in roughly the same shape. Every Sunday, they pick up their habits, light their candles and go to their church. Two of the nuns won't walk together, but both of the others get along with the third nun, who we will call Susie. None of them will walk alone unless they are walking back toward their home. When Susie is fresh, she can go at 4 mph for a mile in a fun nun run. Her second mile is more of a jog at 2 mph. She needs a 15-minute rest to fully recuperate. She can go forever at their 1 mph walking pace. The candles can't burn out before they get to church, and the candles usually last about four hours. The church is three miles away. What is the least distance their combined steps will walk on any given Sunday? And can they keep all the candles burning until they are in the church?

THIS BODY, MY TEMPLE

(To the tune of "In-a-gadda-da-vida," by Iron Butterfly)

In this body, my temple, baby
(From the garden I'm eatin')
From the fruits of my labor, honey
Don't you know that I'm reaping rewards

Oh, won't you stretch with me
Just take my hand
Oh, won't you run with me
Explore this land
Do it by hand

In this great mind, my temple, honey
Don't you know that I process the news?
In this clear mind, my temple, baby
Don't you know that my words will be true

Oh, won't you work with me
Give me a hand

Oh, won't you dream with me
And mold this land
Give me a hand

In this body, my temple, honey
Don't do drugs and no smoking too
In this body, my temple, baby
Don't you know that it's not good for you

Oh, won't you sing with me
Strike up the band
Oh, won't you spar with me
Go hand to hand
Please play your hand

In this body, my temple, baby
(No desserts and no feed-in)
In this belly of muscle, honey
Don't you know that I don't overdo

Oh, won't you dance with me
Give me your hand
Come celebrate with me
We've built this brand
Please take my hand

I WILL FAIL AND FAIL AGAIN UNTIL I SUCCEED.

Success is not final, failure is not fatal: it is the courage to continue that counts.

WINSTON CHURCHILL

Think like a queen. A queen is not afraid to fail. Failure is another steppingstone to greatness.

OPRAH WINFREY

Failure is simply the opportunity to begin again, this time more intelligently.

HENRY FORD

Sometimes by losing a battle you find a new way to win the war.

DONALD TRUMP

Competition is always a good thing. It forces us to do our best. A monopoly renders people complacent and satisfied with mediocrity.

NANCY PEARCEY

I've been up against tough competition my whole life. I wouldn't know how to get along without it.

WALT DISNEY

Strength does not come from winning. Your struggles develop your strengths. When you go through hardships and decide not to surrender, that is strength.

ARNOLD SCHWARZENEGGER

Sometimes when you innovate, you make mistakes. It is best to admit them quickly, and get on with improving your other innovations.

STEVE JOBS

An optimist can be called naive or childish, but it is the optimists of the world who change it. An optimist may not always be right, but a pessimist never accomplishes anything.

TIM DRAPER

OPTIMISM

An optimist can be called naive or childish, but it is the optimists of the world who change it. An optimist may not always be right, but a pessimist never accomplishes anything. Ted Leonsis, the founder of Redgate, is a charismatic leader who sold his company to AOL, and became one of the group presidents there, and later bought the Washington Wizards and the Washington Capitals. Ted once said to me, "Some people would rather be right. I would rather just win."

Frank Herbert said in his classic science fiction epic, Dune, "Fear is the mind killer." Pessimists are fearful. Fear has destroyed many businesses. An interesting exercise is to watch the local news and count how many stories evoke fear. For some reason, the news and other media programming have tapped into the "fear" path of our survival instincts, giving us a negative endorphin rush that keeps us coming back. What it does to society is keep people from living full lives. People feel so much empathy for the victims portrayed on TV that they don't realize how distant they really are from the danger they are seeing. I know one woman who was so wrapped up in the fear she saw on TV that she was too afraid to leave her house!

This fear is often transferred into the work world. Many people are so afraid of losing their jobs or changing their situations that they don't want to try anything new. But it is the new and the change that drives progress. It is the new and the change that makes great breakthroughs. It is the new and the change that makes humanity come alive! Ironically, you are probably more likely to keep your job if you take a few risks along the way. Fear not!! Go forth and try stuff.

Here is a riddle:

Question: What do electricity, Velcro, penicillin, Reese's Peanut Butter Cups and America all have in common?

Answer: They were all mistakes. People were out doing things. They were flying kites, sailing for the West Indies, feeding dying orphans moldy bread, or (if you believe the old commercial) tripping into each other while holding a snack.

They were exploring, experiencing life, and having adventures. They were just out there having fun or hard at work trying things that helped them make some of the most important discoveries in history. And it is not just the great inventions that were mistakes. All of my best investments started out as something else that for one reason or another failed or were abandoned.

The Hotmail founders first came to us pitching a lookup table for people's personal and contact information on the Internet. It was only when they were walking out the door that Steve Jurvetson asked if they had any other ideas. It turned out that their riskier, less safe idea was free, web-based email. The Skype founders initially pitched me on using peer-to-peer technology to generate shared Wi-Fi, then changed course and took on the long-distance carriers with Skype. Google, Baidu, and Yahoo were only search tools that were growing but hemorrhaging money before they all got wind of what GoTo was doing with paid search. When they copied the GoTo model, they were able to build profitable business models. JustinTV was a network of people creating their own real-time video channels when the team discovered that 40% of the business was about people watching other people play video games, and that led them to rebrand and focus only on the e-sports world, which led to Twitch.TV.

All of these people were out trying things. Opportunity came up in a variety of forms. Not only was it important that these people were out there trying something, they were also able to recognize when they had made a discovery that was not the original intent and then adjust and pivot to the other, bigger and better direction.

So...try stuff. Be fearless. It is OK to plan and discuss possible outcomes, but it is the trying that creates the failures that ultimately lead to extraordinary success. Action is everything. Action separates those who just dream from those who make something happen. Those who feel they need to wait until the stars align rarely close the deal, achieve their dreams or make possible the impossible. The spoils go to those who act. If you don't ask that potential soulmate to the prom, he or she won't go with you. Your soulmate will go with the person who asked him or her. Similarly, in business, those who stick their necks out, create, and try are those who win. And even if they don't win, they learn so that they can be better and potentially win the next time.

Have a willingness to fail. When we were building out the DVN, we had a long discussion about how if we each sent out emails to the whole network, we would all be inundated with emails. Our concerns were that we would each be promoting our businesses too much and we would be overwhelmed with connections. Instead of banning "reply all" emails, we just decided to take the action approach. Our motto became, "Just hit send." It turned out that no one overused the network and all of us benefitted from the freedom to take action when we needed to "Just hit send" became a way of thinking throughout the network, so rather than waiting until the stars aligned, the DVN was building a bias for action.

THE YAHOO STORY

Here is a story about my own failure to act. My father introduced me to Jerry Yang and David Filo. They were leaving their PhD programs at Stanford University to start a little business that would organize the World Wide Web, a newly opened up DARPA/academia project that was now available for everyone. I followed up by biking over to Stanford to meet Jerry and David in their trailer. They showed me a chart showing how fast people were trying out the service. It was extraordinary. People were using their index for searching for all sorts of information and the charts were impressive. They joked that they might call their company Yahoo! because when people explored the Internet it was called surfing, and when people caught a wave in the ocean, they screamed "YAHOO!" I told them they had to use that name, and I wanted to invest in them. They were interested in getting funding, but they were more interested in finding a CEO to help them run the company. I sent them a number of CEO candidates because I was so excited about what they were doing. One candidate met with them and asked me cynically, "What do you think will happen with this company they are calling Yahoo!?" Being a believer, I told him that if he joined the company now, he could make as much as $10 million. (If he had accepted the offer, he could have made 100 times that much.) In any case, I was having trouble finding a suitable candidate to run their company.

While I was searching for a CEO for Yahoo!, Jerry and David had ample time to meet with other venture capitalists. I knew that I should have just written them a check and suggested that it go into the next round, but not knowing what that round would look like or who the ultimate CEO would be held up my decision. Since I was not absolutely positive about all the possible outcomes of an investment in the company, I was slow to commit, and I lost the deal.

By the time I made them an offer, it was a pittance compared to their other offers, and Jerry and David went silent on me. Eventually, Sequoia Capital did the financing and got Tim Koogle to come be the CEO. I tried to pile on with the Sequoia financing, but I was just too late. Both my candidate and I missed out on all the success that would have come from being a part of Yahoo! We weren't willing to make the leap without more information, and we both lost big.

THE NAPSTER STORY

One instance of fear killing off a great company was in the case of Napster. I was familiar with the case since one of our network partners, Draper Atlantic, had made the first convertible loan to Napster.

Napster was started by Sean Parker and Shawn Fanning. They created a new file sharing technology that allowed people to share files frictionlessly and for free. The technology had many potential uses for digital product distribution. Several other companies had used the technology for other purposes, but Napster created a product that was easy to use and only focused on music files, called MP3s. It was extraordinary technology in that people could now easily download music in the form of MP3 files to their computer and store it there for future use. Teenagers and music lovers everywhere glommed on to this new service and realized that they could get all the music they wanted from each other for free. They felt that it was OK since music was often shared at dances, parties and concerts, and this was just another form of sharing as long as someone originally bought the music. At its peak, Napster had over 80 million accounts.

Most of that music was copyrighted, but there was no clear case for the difference between playing a CD for others to share in a dorm room and sharing a file through the Internet. These MP3s spread so quickly and freely that they started to have a detrimental effect on CD sales in the music industry.

The music industry was an oligopoly. Sony, Disney, Universal and BMI pretty much controlled the entire spectrum of music. They decided which musicians would become famous and which would become obscure. They drove the marketing of music through the radio. They determined which music would be sold through the record stores. They had music and its industry completely wired. But then Napster's free service came into being and it threw the music industry into a tailspin. The established music companies felt they were under attack. They were riddled in fear of losing their oligopoly, so they lashed out.

The music industry brought lawsuits against Napster, but they went much further than that. They sued everyone they could think of. They even sued the teenagers that were sharing the music. They cleverly called the file sharing "piracy," and rallied the help of the top musicians to make it clear to the public that file sharing was "theft of services." They lobbied the government to force a shutdown of Napster and hoped to put the management of Napster in jail.

And Napster responded with fear. The Napster team feared the repercussions of a lawsuit, or going to jail, so they hired a music industry veteran lawyer as CEO to help them manage through their concerns. It is hard to imagine whether this was the right choice, but in retrospect, it didn't work. Lawyers are generally trained to anticipate all the things that can go wrong in a business. They inadvertently might spread fear in a company leading people to be careful rather than bold. I would argue that being bold might have had a very different outcome. A bold move might have been to go after the music business head on arguing that they have operated an oligopoly for years and Napster was finally there to democratize the music industry, allowing musicians from all over to participate and spread their music without having to run through the friction of the music labels. They could have argued that sharing music through digital files was no different than sharing music with friends in a dorm room. They could have argued that Napster was allowing artists to spread their music far and wide to places that could never have heard it before. But they were fearful, and they didn't.

Instead of boldly challenging the music industry by arguing that they were not breaking any laws because no law regarding music sharing existed, or by calmly going to work negotiating a contract with the industry, Napster went into fear mode, worried that the music industry was going to ruin them.

And the music industry played on that fear. They sued Napster for gazillions of dollars, asking Napster to pay the equivalent of the retail price of every song shared by every teenager everywhere. One executive at Napster said that a music industry lawyer showed him a picture of his own house stating, "See this? Your house is going to be mine." They event sued the teenagers!

The Napster team was paralyzed. Fear spread, and they handed over the keys to the business, a business that was probably worth billions of dollars had it been able to rationally come to terms with the music industry, or even more if they had boldly run their business with no eye toward what the music industry would do.

Fear is indeed the mind killer and in the case of Napster, it was the business killer too. The music industry's fear hurt the music industry too. Instead of embracing a new technology and figuring out how to charge users, they panicked and lost out on what would become one of the most valuable technologies created and exploited over the next decade.

Steve Jobs ended up winning this market by coming in with a "white knight" idea. He would create a file sharing application called iTunes, sell each song for 99 cents, and cut the music industry in on the success of the product. He negotiated with the music industry leaders and made iTunes one of the most profitable parts of Apple's business. However, the music industry got a worse deal than they would have had with Napster, and Napster had to shut down its service.

Incidentally, this failure didn't deter the founders from trying again. Both have become enormously successful with their post-Napster efforts. Sean Parker went on to help Mark Zuckerberg in the founding of Facebook, and Shawn Fanning started a flurry of companies around derivations of the file sharing theme. Fail and fail again until you succeed.

Make a list of all your failures. Your failures should make you proud. Keep failing. Keep living. Keep trying.

As much as I recommend trying and failing, I also believe a Start-up Hero should be wise and learn from their mistakes. Entrepreneurs should not desperately hold on to bankrupt ideas or defunct deals. A good entrepreneur recognizes failure, then realigns and acts again without hesitation. Sometimes you will need to pivot, to give up, to accept defeat and move on. There will always be other mountains to climb. And you need to recognize when an idea might not be worth the effort. It could be because of competition, or the team you signed up with, or a failure to communicate your vision, or just running out of money, but failure happens, and you need to learn the lesson, move on, and let it go when it does.

Failure hurts, but failing is a part of the free market. It is a part of economic renewal. The nature of my business, and venture capital in itself, requires me to accept failure. By my estimates, I have failed about 600 times to date. A willingness to fail allows me to take bigger risks with my investments, which on the whole, has generated more extraordinary returns than if I had not been willing to fail. Nevertheless, I have experienced a few enormous failures that were hard to walk away from and equally hard to learn from. Here is one.

THE DRAPER FISHER JURVETSON MEVC STORY

One such failure was when we invested in and helped raise Draper Fisher Jurvetson MeVC, a company set up to bring venture capital to the individual investor. Only large institutions, accredited investors (millionaires) or so called "sophisticated investors" are allowed to invest in venture capital today. This is yet another example of the government protecting you from yourself, which ends up being to your detriment. [Note: see my next book, "The Startup Government," for some potential remedies.]

Everything was going smoothly. The company built the platform out, and then we easily raised $300 million through a brokerage firm from small investors who wanted to participate in the returns venture capital could provide them. Our pitch was simple. DFJ had an extraordinary track record, and we had a great global network of funds that could all generate deal flow for the fund. We pitched that we would manage the fund, and that was an even bigger attraction. Our thinking was that we would be able to invest alongside our existing funds with the same terms we got for our private investors, and the public would finally be able to invest in venture capital. All of this was cleared and recleared with attorneys and government officials.

We went public on the New York Stock Exchange to great fanfare. But then, after we raised the money with the terms presented, the SEC changed course and our attorneys told us that the partners at DFJ could not manage the money because we would also be investing our private fund money, and there could be conflicts of interest. It was quite embarrassing. We had sold the fund on the premise of investing the money for the public investors, and now that we had it, the SEC made it clear that we couldn't do it. Of course, the SEC reports to no one and its word is final, so we demurred.

We decided to hire a top team to take our place and handed over management to John Grillos, a proven investor and successful entrepreneur. John was excited because his team would be able to manage the money and take advantage of the deal flow from the entire DFJ Network, representing a cornucopia of opportunities.

But then, we got more bad news from our attorneys. The SEC said that investing in companies in the DFJ Network would be disallowed as well because the network could also conceivably be conflicted. Our fund was now isolated from all of us--the promoters and presumed fiduciaries of the fund--and we could not use the intelligence and portfolio companies of the DFJ Network. So rather than having a strong fund managed by the team that pitched it taking advantage of the enormous network we had built, DFJ MeVC was now being managed by a new team that was hamstrung--not able to invest in certain companies, and isolated from its promoters. To all the public investors in the fund, I am truly sorry I was regulated out of doing what I had hoped to do for you.

I now wonder, "If the SEC was going to disallow any of our activity from being involved in creating a new public fund, why did they let us raise the money in the first place?" It would have been far easier for all of us if they had just stated flatly that we could not raise a publicly raised fund while we also managed a privately managed fund. Or ideally, to have just let the market decide.

Since we could not manage the fund, or use our network to help the fund, we decided that we should not take fees from the fund. But to ensure the vision of allowing the individual investor to invest in venture capital, I would at least help out at the board level pro bono. But even with this philanthropic effort, we hit a tumult.

The Internet bubble burst in March of 2001, and the stock of DFJ MeVC fell to half of its IPO price, valuing the company at below the cash that the fund had in the bank! It was so cheap that some clever hedge fund managers bought it up and repositioned it. By trying to protect the investor, the SEC ended up seriously harming the investor while destroying the entire premise of the investment. The investors wanted a venture capital fund managed by DFJ that could take advantage of the deal flow provided by the DFJ Network, and they ended up with a hedge fund managed by people they didn't even know. Unintended consequences of regulations can be worse than if the regulations didn't exist in the first place.

I have always prided myself on my ability to change the world for the betterment of society, but when this hope for the individual investor was finally gobbled up by hedge fund managers, I decided to take the learnings and just let it go.

One embarrassing day came when Associate Justice of the Supreme Court, Sandra Day O'Connor, told me she had invested in DFJ MeVC when it went public. I apologized profusely, but in retrospect, I should have discussed with her exactly what the SEC had done to the company, because she may have been in a position to do something about it!

THE XPERT FINANCIAL STORY

The failure in MeVC helped me understand more about finance and regulations, but it didn't deter me from trying, and failing, again. I started a company with my friend Thomas Foley and my son Adam to try to create a system where private companies could be tradeable. We called it "Xchange." I invested in the company to get some good software engineers to make it easy to research, evaluate and trade private companies. We had a few competitors in Second Market and SharesPost, but we were determined to create the best user experience for people who wanted to be able to buy and sell stock in private companies, since the regulations, known as Sarbanes Oxley, were deterring companies from going public and deterring people from investing in the public markets.

The press wrote some nice articles about us using our name, "Xchange," and they were picked up by people at the SEC. The SEC sent us a message that we would have to change our name or face the wrath of being regulated as an exchange. Again! Argh. In its noble effort to protect the individual investor, the SEC was keeping individual investors from being able to share in the growth of private companies, and in doing so they stifled the growth in jobs and the economy that could come from the startup investments.

In response to the SEC, we changed the company name to Xpert Financial and we learned to use the words private market platform rather than private exchange. Rather than being regulated by the SEC, we were now regulated by the Financial Industry Regulatory Authority (FINRA), and we would have to apply to be a broker/dealer.

Since I was a large shareholder and board member, I was forced to study so I could pass a test to earn my Series 62 credential. We would not be allowed to pursue the business unless I passed. We hired an expensive tutor, and I got accelerated training to make sure that I wasn't the bottleneck to getting the platform built. Fortunately, I just squeaked by with a 76 (70 was required to pass). But then we needed to hire an expensive compliance officer and expensive lawyers both in Silicon Valley and Washington, DC to work to comply to make it so we could trade private companies. For a startup, we were spending a lot of money just to get into business!

Our engineers put together a platform for the masses, so that anyone could participate. Then we got word from our attorneys that our platform could only be used for high net worth clients and qualified institutions. We had to rewrite the software to clear customers in advance to make sure they were considered high net worth. This was in addition to all the regulations built around KYC (know your customer), fraud checking and AML (anti-money laundering). It was a lot of red tape that stood in the way of our progress.

In the meantime, we were testing the market for our product. I knew instinctively that investors would love to have more liquidity in their private shares, since the illiquid markets were making it difficult for investors to get any money out of their holdings in private companies, and that entrepreneurs would like to sell some of their shares too to pay for a house or send their children to college or whatever.

It turned out that investors did want more liquidity and that the entrepreneurs were enthusiastic about having the ability to sell shares in the private market, both to grow their businesses and to personally raise cash to buy that house or pay for college. But when they all got together to discuss the Xpert option among their boards, they all found that as fiduciaries, they were much more conservative about our new platform. While they all liked the idea in principal, none of them wanted to risk a business for the improved liquidity, so we were having a very difficult time finding any company willing to go first. Without a willing customer, we decided to close up shop.

We ended up selling Xpert Financial to another financial firm for the value of a broker dealer license, and Thomas went on to build the product with the new company. We investors took an almost complete loss, and still, private companies were illiquid. My vision where everyone, rich or poor, can be a venture capitalist, and everyone, rich or poor, can have tradeable, liquid private shares in companies still looked like a pipe dream.

At this writing, the tide may have finally turned. The JOBS Act passed into law, allowing the small investor to participate in private company investing. And although years have gone by and the rules and regulations are still not clear, it seems that there is an opening there. Some new platforms are being built for private companies to be traded. At Draper Associates, we have backed Equidate and EquityZen, two promising platforms for high net worth investors to trade private stocks, and AngelList, Crowdfunder, and others may be working toward allowing investors in private companies to become more liquid. Electronic share companies like eShares and Capshare may be able to easily manage the logistics of trading private shares.

And ICOs, since they are currencies rather than securities, may also pave a new path to funding and liquidity for creative entrepreneurs for their endeavors.

And now, even if the US SEC continues to keep the small investor from investing in the private markets, the British government is allowing both a MeVC and an Xchange to occur. In fact, recently, Draper Esprit, the London-based Draper Venture Network partner, just listed on the London Exchange without all the problems that we faced at MeVC. And crowdfunding company Crowdcube (that Draper Associates recently backed) allows any individual investor to buy private company stock. Soon, we expect to see a full private market evolve, albeit in London. I hope to soon see Silicon Valley follow suit with the SEC's blessing.

Fail and fail again until you succeed. In my heart, I know that allowing the individual investor to be able to participate in funding private companies is good for society, and I hope to continue to drive toward a solution, creating failures and maybe some success along the way. I do understand that if people have not been trained to invest, they may inadvertently lose money, and that the government is just trying to protect them, but by keeping them from failing, the government is keeping them from learning about investing. Maybe the government will think "educate" rather than "regulate."

Even though these failures were tragic in my mind, the failures that really hurt are the failures to act. In the venture capital business, when I have made an investment in a company that failed, it was never that big a loss since we make so many investments. But when I missed investing in Google, Yahoo!, Facebook, Airbnb, Uber and others, those were my true failures. Here are some other failures I have experienced in my career.

THE ACTIVISION STORY AND THE NETFLIX STORY

I tend to jump to the answer. I take great leaps and make assumptions about the future that may or may not come true, but once I am convinced, I assume that everyone else will easily jump to the same conclusion. This failing has not just kept me from getting my visions accomplished, it has given me extraordinary frustration over the years. What I needed to be able to do was to understand how to bring people along to my way of thinking. Former Secretary of State George Schultz was a true visionary, but he was also a master of communicating those visions. He would start many of his speeches by saying, "Let me take you through my line of thinking." It helped people come to his realizations through the path that he took to get there. But I had never learned how to do that.

Just out of business school, I went to the board members of Activision, my dad's old partners at Sutter Hill Ventures, and asked to become the CEO. Activision had just gone public at a very high multiple and I thought I could use the high-priced stock to buy up the whole software industry, since all of the other companies were private and valued lower. I told them that as Activision's CEO, I would use the public stock to buy up Microsoft and Lotus and a bunch of other software companies that were all private and valued low. In retrospect, they should have done it, but they looked at me with cocked heads and politely showed me the door. It has taken me many years to understand that while I had the right idea, people have to be brought along my path before they will come to my conclusion. I failed to convince them, and though I suffered frustration, the experience made me work on my abilities to persuade people to come to my way of thinking. Now, I strive to keep what I call "the George Schultz method" close at hand when I promote my ideas.

Another Failure:

Reed Hastings, founder and CEO of Netflix and former founder of Pure Software, is a master of understanding how to bring people along to participate in his visions. We had tried to invest in Reed at Pure, but he turned us down. After selling Pure for a big win, he came back to me with Netflix. The idea was that he would create a website where people would list their favorite movies and Netflix would deliver them through the US Mail to their door. My immediate reaction was, "That is ridiculous, Reed. People are already streaming movies directly to their computers. Why would you want to waste all that money building out a delivery service when high speed Internet is right around the corner." Reed said, "They aren't ready for streaming yet. We will capture the customer and stream to them later." I disagreed and passed on seed investing in Netflix.

OUCH!

Weirdly, Reed also knew that people would respond better to supporting charter schools than they would for my passion, voucher schools, so his California education initiative passed while mine failed. My next book, "The Startup Government," will cover that topic in more depth. Reed Hastings has incredible vision. What is next for you, Reed?

I still jump to conclusions easily, but I have learned to try to understand the path I tread on to come to those conclusions, so that I can take people along my same path. My failures have taught me well, but I still have a long way to go.

Many potential Startup Heroes see the endpoint and often fail to get there because they haven't charted the proper course. I recommend charting a course that shows people how you get to and share your conclusion. But also, be willing to try a course and fail and try another course and fail before you find your course to success.

There is a corollary to fail and fail again until you succeed, and it is:

Ask stupid questions until you are smart.

THE STUPID QUESTION

At an inauguration party, I got a chance to meet the famous and brilliant interviewer Barbara Walters. I asked her what advice she would give to my daughter Jesse, who was starting her own web talk show called "The Valley Girl." Barbara said, "It is all about the second question." It was the kind of answer that makes you think. I believe her thinking was that the first question is the fundamental one and is used as a set up. It can sound stupid and fundamental, but it paves the way for the second question, which can be the zinger!

I find that it is the stupid, but fundamental, question that is the most enlightening, whether I am interviewing entrepreneurs or asking a question of a speaker or professor in front of a large audience. I find that as stupid as the question sounds, it is often the question that is on everyone else's mind too.

At Draper University, the students meet in a room we call "The

Egg Room." The students sit on bean bag chairs and blow up chairs that look like eggs. The whole room has the look of a giant chicken incubator. On their first day, I tell them about the book "Stranger in a Strange Land," by Robert Heinlein, in which a Martian comes down to Earth and seems lost and remains totally silent for a long time. Then, one day, in perfect English, he blurts out, "I am only an egg." He means that he is still too new to Earth to know anything, but he has already learned the language, so he shows brilliance in his first words. I tell these heroes in training that they are only eggs, and to break out of their shells, they need to crack them open by raising their hands and asking the stupid questions. It seems to work well. Draper University graduates seem to be willing to ask the stupid question, and then become ambitious, aggressive and inquisitive. (See if you can find the other reference I make that comes from Stranger in a Strange Land in this book.)

I remember a meeting I once had that showed the brilliance of the stupid question. An entrepreneur came in to pitch me on his business. He kept using the terminology "Web 2.0." We all thought we might have some inkling about what he was talking about, but it wasn't until I asked the stupid question, "What is Web 2.0?" that we really learned anything. We learned that he was a pretender. The question stumped him. He had been throwing the term around in a bunch of meetings, and no one had ever asked him what it meant. My simple question cleared the whole situation up for us. We realized that this was not someone who would set a trend, but someone who was "trendy." This one stupid question saved us hours of uncertainty and deliberation, and maybe even some money. It turns out that Web 2.0 had thousands of definitions (computing in the cloud, the wireless net, social networking, etc.), so maybe he was just stumped by not knowing which of the thousands of answers he could give, but the company never went anywhere, and we were better off not investing. The stupid question was smart.

Ask the stupid questions. Get smart.

Have a willingness to fail, to look stupid, to ask the stupid question to set up the next one. It is far better to do something embarrassing and win than to run the risk of pretending to be smart and ending up losing big. And just by trying, you will learn more and have more success in the long run than the person who doesn't try.

QUEXERCISES ON FAILURE

1. When have you failed? What did you learn?

2. What did you try to accomplish when you failed? What did you accomplish instead?

3. Are you ready to try again? What would you do differently this time? Did you just need to stick it out a little longer or was it strategically wrong?

4. What good can come out of your failure? Have you ever wanted to ask a question and thought it might be stupid, so you didn't?

5. If you have, here is an exercise for you: Go find that person you wanted to ask the stupid question to and ask the question. Now, wouldn't that have been easier if you had just been willing to look a little stupid and just asked the question the first time when the person was right in front of you?

6. Is there something in your spirit that is so important to you that you are willing to fail and fail again for it? If there is, you may be ready to be a Startup Hero.

7. Play the game "Really Bad Chess" against the computer until you reach a rank of 80. Or, make your own bow and arrows and shoot at a target 100 feet away until you hit a bullseye that has a -inch diameter. Fail and fail again until you succeed.

FAILURE PUZZLE

What is the relationship between the square of the sum and the sum of the cubes?

FAILURE IN SEUSSIAN: TRIAL AND FAILURE

In the boring old town of Carefulosippi
Lived an awkward young girl whose ideas were quite trippy.

Her name was Catina Cecurity Cafety,

for all of the names in her brood rhymed with safety.

The people all lived in the safety of bubbles,
that kept them from horrors of Kaptos and Ubbles.

For Kaptos were mistakes and Ubbles were failures,
and neither would sit well with the leaders and Pharaohs.

But Catina was different, she got into trouble,
and sometimes she would even take off her bubble.

In her mind she explored the wonders of Thudd,
An island she dreamed up on the planet of Drudd

She invented a robot called Carramasoo
That taught you some Martian while tying your shoe.

And a head-mounted wirey slipmaroday
That filled in the words when your brain went away

She envisioned a country without any maxxes,
no limits, no boundaries, no prisons, no taxes.

She called it Flandora and filled it with benchens
so she could create and construct all her inventions

Her parents were embarrassed every time she would speak
of the fractile of life that lived alongside bird's beaks

And her friends called her "nutball" and "quirkly " and "ignorama-
mace,"
when she tried to invent a time-portable suitcase.

The town was of course so safe and secure,
because bubbles were an integral part of life pure

For they feared all the accidents that could appear,
if they took off their bubble that they held so dear.

The bubbles of course could protect them from rain,
and comets and bee stings and the Blue Valley strain.

The bubbles could save them from near certain death
that might come if they encountered the old black dog's breath.

But then one day the mayor received a dark note.
A bubble malfunction caused the bubbles to float.

The citizens started floating in air,
and all they could do was to wonder and stare.

It became a big deal when Rebecca Aim Certain
got trapped on her roof with a tangled-up curtain.

The town rose through the air higher and higher,
for none of them was willing to fail, be a trier.

Till Catina said, "Let's try doubles."
"Hold hands with a partner and unclamp a few bubbles."

Her friends all ignored her or shouted their insults,
while townspeople floated just measuring results.

Till Tommy Bartonkey
the ne'er do well monkey
said, "Let's give it a chance,
I just peed in my pants."

So Tommy and Catina unleashed just one belt
and floated to Earth like a bundled-up pelt.

The town cried, "We can't, it's not in our bylaws."
For centuries we've gotten by without "try" laws.

But two by two they broke with old norms
without even filling the requisite forms.

Catina saved them all in Carefulosippi,
and the bubbles were thrown out with the Crippy.

"We owe Catina our lives and salvation,"
said the mayor through people's cheers and ovations.

And now they all know that a failure is progress
And the new town motto is "Try it, say yes!"

I WILL EXPLORE THE WORLD WITH GUSTO AND ENTHUSIASM.

Success consists of going from failure to failure without loss of enthusiasm.

WINSTON CHURCHILL

We have to straighten out our country; we have to make our country great again, and we need energy and enthusiasm.

DONALD TRUMP

Apathy can be overcome by enthusiasm, and enthusiasm can only be aroused by two things: first, an ideal, which takes the imagination by storm, and second, a definite intelligible plan for carrying that ideal into practice.

ARNOLD J. TOYNBEE

Flaming enthusiasm, backed up by horse sense and persistence, is the quality that most frequently makes for success.

DALE CARNEGIE

Willie Mays could throw better, and Hank Aaron could hit more home runs. But I've got enthusiasm. I've got desire. I've got hustle. Those are God-given talents, too.

PETE ROSE

Nothing great was ever achieved without enthusiasm.

RALPH WALDO EMERSON

THE BUCKET LIST STORY

When I was 32 years old, before anyone knew the term "bucket list," Ted Leonsis and I were leaving a Preview Travel board meeting on a plane heading from Lanai to Honolulu. It was a very turbulent flight and we were starting to think that this might be our last one. Ted turned to me and said, "Make a list of the 100 things you want to do before you die." Ted told me about the list he had made and how he was knocking things off his list one by one.

Being in a plane that looked like it might go down kicked me into action. I immediately started making my list: Run a marathon, build a house, plant a tree…. Being an overachiever, I included 101 things to do on my list and the list has been a great diversion for me throughout my life. Some of the items on the list have been huge challenges for me, but as I try to complete each item I have forced myself to try new things, to step away from the treadmill for a while, and to find new ways to create and live my life.

A bucket list allows you to follow through on your dreams. It also allows you to create stories for yourself and maybe for your grandchildren. Starting a company is rewarding, but knowing that you are accomplishing life goals builds follow-through, helps you overcome barriers you have in your mind and encourages you live a life with gusto and enthusiasm.

If you want to be a Startup Hero, you will want to create your own list. Entries on your list should include anything you have dreamed of doing. And as you accomplish the items on the list, you will find that each of them makes you a more worldly, fuller, interesting and creative person. I believe that your list will actually help you become the Startup Hero you want to be, and even though it may distract you from your business vision, it will help you achieve it in a bigger, faster and more economic way than you ever imagined you could.

In any case, writing seemed like a good distraction from the scary bumpy plane ride, so I got my pen out while we were getting bounced up and down and I wrote my list in very sloppy handwriting. I have since reordered and organized the list by "F" words—so that I remember that a big part of being a Startup Hero is failing. It is also fun. Each of these items that I have accomplished (and some that I have tried and failed at) have a story attached to them, some of which I have written about below. The accomplishments and the stories attached to them have led me to more success and more happiness. So thank you Ted!

Before reading my list below, write your own list. Then come back to read my list and see if you want to adjust yours.

Now, feel free to take a look. The check marks highlight the ones I have completed as of this writing.

FAME

1	✓	Get on a TV show (Startup U, The Naked Brothers Band)
2	✓	Get in a movie (Heartless)
3	✓	Get a speaking part in a movie (Naked Brothers Band)
4		Write a novel
5		Write a non-fiction book (I guess this is it, but some would argue that this is my novel)
6	✓	Get on the cover of Upside or The Red Herring magazine
7	✓	Throw a party for 1000 guests (2001: A Cyberspace Odessay)
8	✓	Be a guest on a talk show (Stephen Colbert)

FORTUNE

9	✓	Buy an island (Lupita Island)
10		Make an investment in Mongolia
11	✓	Buy some serious land on the water (DreamFarm Ranch)
12	✓	Seed five public companies (PTC, TSLA, DIGI, Overture, BIDU, many more)

13	✓	Collect Amazing Fantasy #15 and Willie Mays rookie baseball card (Bought both)
14		Get a patent (decided to give the ideas away so far)
15		Buy art by Vincent Van Gogh

FAMILY

16	✓	Have four children (Jesse, Adam, Billy, Eleanor)
17	✓	Get married (Melissa)
18		Go backpacking with my kids
19		Start a business with my kids
20	✓	See a baby being born (saw all four)
21	✓	Buy a sailboat (Flying Scot)
22	✓	Buy a motorboat (The 100 Feet)
23	✓	See all kids Graduate from College (UCLA x3 and USC)

FAN

24		Visit all 50 states - spend a night (46/50)
25		Visit 100 Countries - spend a night (68/100)
26	✓	Go to a World Series (Go Giants!!!)
27	✓	Go to a World Cup (at Stanford)
28	✓	Go to a Super Bowl (Ravens over Giants)
29	✓	Play chess in Washington Square (lost 3 games)
30		Play tennis at Wimbledon
31		Drive across the country
32	✓	Go to DisneyWorld (fun!)
33		Go on a safari in Botswana

34	✓	Go to the Consumer Electronics Show in Las Vegas (many times)
35	✓	Visit the New York Stock Exchange (BizWorld and MeVC)
36	✓	See the opening of a Broadway show (Crazy She Calls Me)
37	✓	See Steve Miller Band in concert (with the Doobie Brothers at Shoreline - met him later)
38	✓	Visit the pyramids (and Ramses II)
39	✓	Go to the Olympics games (Summer in Atlanta, Winter in Utah)

FRIENDS

40		Play touch football with Joe Montana
41		Meet each U.S. President since Richard Nixon (so far, so good)
42	✓	Meet Barry Bonds (he helped coach my kids' T-ball team)
43		Meet Charles Barkeley
44	✓	Meet Michael Milken (spoke at the Milken Institute)
45		Meet Michael Jackson (I had backstage passes to his concert in London, but he died before the concert was scheduled to begin)
46	✓	Meet Phil Collins (at the Oscars)

FREAKS

| 47 | ✓ | Attend a funeral (this has happened too many times) |
| 48 | ✓ | Be in a hurricane (swam during Hurricane Bob) |

49	✓	Be in an earthquake (dove under my desk at work)
50	✓	Be in a flood (our dog had to swim through the house)
51	✓	See an active volcano (in Pucon, Chile, and Mount St. Helens, both from the sky)
52	✓	Visit a prison (Sonora State Prison with Defy Ventures)

FULFILLMENT

53	✓	Create a board game (Stanford: The Game, Voter's Choice)
54	✓	Create a game for a class (BizWorld)
55	✓	Paint 10 good paintings ("good" is in the eyes of the painter)
56		Plant a tree that lives
57	✓	Build a treehouse with my kids (at my parents' house before they tore it down)
58	✓	Produce a movie (The Tic Code, The Naked Brothers Band, Stella's Last Weekend)
59		Produce a CD-ROM title (I think technology has moved past me here)
60	✓	Get 10 articles published (most are about supporting entrepreneurship and driving technology)
61		Write a very long poem
62	✓	Make a success of a dropout (there have been many)
63	✓	Get jobs for 10 friends (very satisfying)
64	✓	Grow a vegetable garden (it attracted crows)
65		Free a prisoner

| 66 | ✓ | Get a law changed or eliminated (made school vouchers legal) |
| 67 | ✓ | Teach a class at Stanford Business School (with Bill Sahlman) |

FASCINATION

68		Learn more Japanese
69		Learn to play 3 songs on the piano well
70		Read 1000 books (I am at 350)
71		Learn to make one spectacular dessert
72	✓	Read the Bible (Old and New)
73	✓	Read the Koran (brilliant legal document)
74	✓	Read the book of Mao (he was awesome, then he was awful)
75		Read The Book of Mormon
76		Shoot below 85 in golf (best score 86; typical score 110)

FOOLISHNESS

77	✓	Bareback ride an unknown horse (with my brother-in-law in Hawaii)
78	✓	Hang glide (crashed and cracked the mast)
79	✓	Pilot an airplane (bush plane in Alaska)
80	✓	Parasailing (in Mexico)
81	✓	Drink snake blood in Snake Alley (in Taiwan)
82	✓	Swim in the Crystal Springs Reservoir (so muddy!)
83		Fly a bicycle plane
84	✓	Streak (check!)

85	✓	Fly in the Concorde (with Melissa on her 40th birthday)
86		Walk on the moon
87	✓	Ride an elephant (in India and on Sand Hill Road)
88	✓	Ride a jet ski (crazy fun)
89	✓	Scuba dive again (ran out of air in Africa the first time)
90		Skinny dip in every ocean (all but the Arctic, brrrr!)
91	✓	Swim in a water tower (Point O' Woods in Michigan)

FEATS

92	✓	Run a marathon (I hit the wall)
93	✓	Escape from Alcatraz (made sure I started from Alcatraz, brrrr!)
94	✓	Barefoot waterski (in Sacramento Delta)
95	✓	Climb a mountain (might go for a higher peak here)
96		Cliff dive at Hyatt Regency Kauai
97	✓	Catch a marlin (caught a baby one in Mexico)
98	✓	Catch a salmon in Alaska (caught an Alaskan Grand Slam!)
99	✓	Bike to the ocean from home (hit the wall at 63 miles)
100		Walk to the top of the Empire State Building
101		Make another list

Now review your bucket list and see if you want to make any changes. Your list will guide you off the track and help you to experience life, to better understand the world, and become a better person.

Having a list will inspire you to actually do what you wrote down, and it will help you fulfill your ambitions. It is likely that if you want to be able to check items off your list, you will need to explore the world with gusto and enthusiasm. And to be a true Startup Hero, you will not just want to check them off, you will want to over-achieve each one, hitting it out of the park.

The list has created more than 70 stories I can tell my grandchildren, but I will share some personal stories about my experiences with the adventures that I took because of my list. The list has helped me drive forward in life, have some fun and do some stupid stuff along the way.

LUCKY NO. 13: COLLECT AMAZING FANTASY NO. 15 AND WILLIE MAYS ROOKIE BASEBALL CARD

Number thirteen on my list of 101 things to do before I die led me to meeting my heroes, Willie Mays and Stan Lee.

Willie Mays, Hero.

I used to love baseball. I guess I still do, but not with the reverence I did when I was nine years old. I collected baseball cards, studying the people, the positions and the statistics of every player. I listened to games on the radio, scoring every pitch as I listened. I read the green sports page in the newspaper, studying the leaders, the standings, and the stats. I learned more math looking at the statistics on the backs of baseball cards and reading the sports section of the newspaper than I did in school. I was a pretty good baseball player too, at least until high school when pitchers learned to throw curve balls and discovered that I couldn't hit them.

I remember camping in sleeping bags in our backyard with Cree Edwards, staying up until midnight listening to a game on the radio when Bobby Bonds hit a grand slam in his first major league at bat. I remember when my dad brought us to a San Francisco Giants game and we saw Gaylord Perry pitch a no hitter. The star of the team was Willie Mays. He was the one who could hit the big home runs. He was my hero and I always wanted to meet him.

At 42, I invested in David Kaval, who started a new minor league called the Golden Baseball League. He was even a bigger baseball nut than I was. As a challenge, he and a friend saw a game in every major league stadium in 30 days. The idea behind his startup was that major league baseball had gotten to be a monopoly and he was going to challenge the monopoly. The company was well thought out, and David was a real go getter, but it failed after about four seasons. I got to play in one game for one of the teams called the Chico Outlaws. I played three and one-half innings in right field and struck out swinging in my one at bat. All curve balls. David Kaval eventually became the general manager of the Oakland A's and offered to have me come out and throw out the first pitch at a game—something that I should have included on my list.

Back to Willie Mays. His rookie baseball card was made by Bowman in 1951. It was remarkably hard to find, and it would be expensive if in near perfect condition. I didn't want to spend money on what many would think was a silly thing, but I had it in the back of my mind that I needed to get it because it was on my list.

Back then, before eBay changed the whole marketplace, there was a very imperfect market for baseball cards. A Willie Mays rookie card might have been $2000 in San Francisco or New York where he played for the Giants, but in other cities, he was just the guy who used to beat their team, so his cards were not worth as much there.

One day, I was in Boston on a business trip. I had visited a company along Route 128 called Polygen that might change all of chemistry by simulating molecules on the computer. I had also just visited the team at Parametric Technology, and I was feeling good about that investment. I had a few hours to kill, so I went for a walk. I walked by a hole-in-the-wall sports collector store. I decided to go in. I wandered around trying to remember the old players I saw depicted on the cards. Then I saw it. The Willie Mays rookie card. Bowman. 1951. The card was in excellent condition and on sale for $640.

Of course! It made perfect sense. No one in Boston would want that card. Collectors would pay a lot more for a Carl Yastrzemski card, because he had played for their local team. The crazy Red Sox fans probably hated Willie Mays. I negotiated with the storekeeper and got the price down to $600 before walking away holding the card like it was the President's nuclear codes. I negotiated my first geographical arbitrage, not recognizing at the time that the Draper Venture Network would also someday take advantage of the same strategy.

I got a chance to meet Willie Mays when he came out to help coach Barry Bonds' son, who was on my son's T-ball team. Meeting him was a great moment for me. I told him he was my hero, then I shook his hand. It was the biggest hand I had ever shaken.

Stan Lee, Hero.

I had a big party for my 21st birthday and on the invitation I asked my friends for "unique and expensive" gifts. Doctor Dave Mohler gave me the core of a nuclear power plant. My Stanford roommate, Doug Carter, gave me moldy bread that he declared was an early form of penicillin. But my childhood buddy, Bobby Jacobs, gave me Amazing Spiderman comic book #162. Great fun. But when I read it I realized that this comic book was the middle of a story, so I had to go buy #161 and #163 to figure out what happened.

Years later, I became a major comic book collector and felt that to understand everything about Spiderman, I had to buy and read the entire series, including Amazing Fantasy #15, the first appearance of Spiderman, even though a good copy of the comic sells for more than $10,000. So naturally, I needed to add it to my bucket list.

Apparently, my love for superheroes and the passion I found for comic books is genetic. My son Adam also has a love for comic books, and naturally, I supported the idea that my children would learn new technologies, exercise good values, and possibly become heroes themselves by reading comic books.

Adam and I went together to Comic-Con, the big comic book conference. We had a great time watching the people come dressed as their favorite comic book characters, meeting with the writers and artists behind various comics and picking up fun art and comics as we explored. We found an old guy dressed like a Swiss watch repairman at a booth that had a bunch of different old comics in it. We talked to him for a while and I mentioned that I was potentially in the market for my bucket list item, a copy of Amazing Fantasy #15.

He called across the aisle and a copy of the comic I was looking for magically appeared. Adam and I looked it over to make sure it was legitimate, and I asked if he was willing to sell it and for what price. After some haggling, we got the price down to $6400, and I bought it. We walked out of Comic-Con on cloud 9.

The creator of Spiderman, as well as Ironman, the Fantastic Four, and many other imaginative superheroes is a man named Stan Lee. Stan is a legend in the comic book world and gets big money for every autograph and photo he gives out at Comic-Con. I had always wanted to meet him, but our paths never crossed.

Then one day, Adam asked if I would like to join him for lunch with Stan Lee. Apparently, through his Boost accelerator, Adam had met a friend of Stan's and told him of his love for superheroes. In fact, Boost VC's stated mission is to help entrepreneurs to build an Ironman suit.

I jumped at the chance to meet this creator of superhero worlds. After all, my entire career has been in supporting, funding, and educating heroes. Stan has had a major influence on my work life.

We met Stan in a nice restaurant in Los Angeles. There were six of us at the table, but Adam gave me the honor of sitting next to Stan. He was 91, but I would have guessed 70. He was delightful. He was quick-witted, funny, and very sharp and dynamic. We got along famously. He told me all about how he came up with the concepts of "true believers" and "with great power comes great responsibility." He was talking about his next projects as if he were 31 years old rather than 91. I think Stan will continue to live a long life, because he still has so much left to accomplish, and his imagination is still very much intact.

I was well prepared for the lunch. I brought along my copy of Amazing Fantasy #15, maybe to have him sign it or just to show it to him. I didn't know which, but the opportunity was so extraordinary, I felt like I couldn't pass it up. If he signed the comic book, it would lower its resale value, but the emotional value would be astronomic. When he saw the comic, he lit up. He went into a great story about how it almost got him fired. The editors didn't like the idea of Spider-man, but he caught them at a weak moment. They were at the end of the line with the Amazing Fantasy series, and they didn't seem to care what would go into the comic, so Stan put in his Spiderman idea. At first, they were very upset with him, but then the comic book flew off the shelves and people were asking for copies long after they had run out. Realizing that they had a big winner, the publishers asked Stan to start a whole new series around Spiderman.

We had been sitting with Stan for over two hours, but our time with him went by like a flash, and I no longer felt like I had to have anything from him. Instead, I felt like I owed him a great amount of gratitude. I showed him pictures of Draper University and Hero City with their superhero themes, where pictures of superheroes are paint-ed on the walls. I told him about how I got Adam and his brother, Billy, to swim laps for their swim team by bribing them with Marvel Masterpiece cards. Then I asked him if he owned a copy of Amazing Fantasy #15, and to my surprise, he said, "No, those things are too expensive."

After a slight hesitation, I was compelled. I gave Stan Lee my copy of Amazing Fantasy #15. He had had such a profound impact on me, my life, and my business that I felt it was my duty to somehow reward him. Stan was so flattered and so thankful, that I knew I had done the right thing. A Twitter follower of mine said it best when he told me, "So generous of you. The universe is back in balance now."

I got a chance to do something for a hero of mine. It was won-derful and almost cathartic. I never really knew what I was going to do with that comic book anyway. By the way, if Willie Mays doesn't have his own rookie card, I would be happy to take him to lunch.

NO. 81 DRINK SNAKE BLOOD IN SNAKE ALLEY, TAIPEI, TAIWAN

I was in Taipei with David Lee and the board of his company. Many years earlier, David founded a company he called Qume, where he invented the daisy wheel printer, a printer that looked like a tiny plastic bicycle wheel. He started this new company that man-ufactured peripherals in Taiwan, which he also called Qume, and we were there to look over the manufacturing facility. We had a wonderful trip.

We experienced a lot of firsts there. We ate shark's fin soup, donkey, and chicken feet since they were among the local delicacies. I had my first karaoke experience. Bob Dilworth, CEO of Zenith Data Systems, and I stood on stage in front of 150 non-English-speaking Taiwanese and sang *"Put your head on my shoulder."* At the end of the song, I put my head on Bob's shoulder. It was a big hit, but since they didn't speak English, no one but Bob and David knew why I put my head on his shoulder.

But the defining moment of the trip was when we got to Taipei's famous "Snake Alley." David jokingly asked, "Who wants to drink snake blood?" Since the shark fin soup was so tasty, I said, "I am game for anything at this point." So we went to a very dingy alley where we met a man who opened a basket and showed us the cobra he had caught. David negotiated some sort of arrangement with him in Chinese, and the man asked me to stand on a box. A crowd of people gathered around, and I started wondering if this was as typical as it seemed when David first suggested it. The man spoke some Chinese and David translated, "He says it is very good for vision." I took this to mean figurative vision or future vision, but it is possible he just meant "eyesight."

Then the man picked up the cobra by the tail, whacked its head against the box and skinned it like he was peeling a very long banana. He then hung it upside down for the blood to run into a small glass jigger, and finally, he took something that looked like a bloody bean (the cobra's gall bladder), crushed it with his fingers and plopped it into the jigger. Then he poured some clear liquid into the cup, which was apparently rice wine. I don't drink alcohol, but in this case, I made an exception. I downed the contents of the jigger in one gulp to great fanfare and cheers from the crowd.

My face went from glee to horror. The stuff was awful. It tasted like blood. Duh! I should have known. I felt awful the rest of the night, like all the blood had left my face and was raising havoc in my stomach. The next day, I was fully recovered. I believe that I got this "vision." I am not going to say that I can see the future, but I am not going to say I can't. In any case, it is undeniable that my eyesight is no better, but I have been pretty lucky since then.

NO. 9 BUY AN ISLAND

Chased by a Cape Buffalo.

Tom Lithgow, a good friend of mine, grew up in Tanzania. Tom runs an African tourist company called Firelight Safaris. He and his then wife, Belinda, took my family on safari. He explained that the cape buffalo, which are notoriously dangerous animals, weigh about one ton, are about seven feet tall and can take down a pride of lions. Two days later, we all witnessed a cape buffalo fending off about 14 lions. They are spectacular creatures.

The next day, we spotted a cape buffalo that was lying down. Tom and I decided to quietly take a picture of me alongside the buffalo. I then went into the hut and told my kids to come out and get a picture of themselves by the cape buffalo. My daughter Jesse passed on the invitation saying she needed a nap and heading into her room. My son Billy said, "Dad, I am already living on the edge here. I don't want to get anywhere near these animals." I said, "Come on, Billy, live a little." After some cajoling, he, my son Adam, my daughter Eleanor and I all went out to greet the cape buffalo. Adam and Eleanor ran right up to the 2000-pound creature, which was now standing up! This was a very different scene than when I got my picture taken, and it seemed significantly more dangerous. I knew we should probably make it a fast photo shoot and get out of there.

Billy started to advance toward the buffalo so he could get in the picture, when from the other side of the cape buffalo, a Maasai warrior (who was there to protect us) spotted us and saw what we were doing. He waved his hands, whistled and shouted, "Get away from the cape buffalo." The buffalo now felt surrounded by people. It got spooked and decided to charge us. Billy turned around and started running, then Eleanor took off after him, and Adam after her. I stayed back to lure the buffalo away from the kids, so then it came for me, a large, easy target. I furtively looked around to see what I could do, and saw a small tree about 20 yards away. It was only about 3" wide at the base of the trunk, but it would have to do. I ran to the tree and scurried behind it.

The cape buffalo came right up to the tree and stopped. I realized that he could easily just lunge through it and gore me. But he stopped, looked down at me with one eye and one horn on each side of the tree and then ran around it to my left to see if he could gore me on my left side. I moved to the right to dodge him, and juked him the way I used to juke my sisters when they chased me around the kitchen table. He veered back to my right and I moved left. We did this several times. Eventually, and luckily, the cape buffalo gave up, and with his head turned back to watch me, he ran away down the hill.

Once I was safely out of range, I ran up to give my kids a hug for reassurance. Billy shrugged me off and said shrilly, "Dad, get inside."

The next day, an enormous bird of prey, a black-shouldered kite, flew down, hit me in the head and stole a sandwich out of my hands. My guard was heightened for the rest of the trip, and I have a cape buffalo head on my office wall to remind me to always be alert and aware, and that life can end at any minute.

These experiences brought me closer to Tom and Belinda Lithgow who eventually led me to buy Lupita Island, which allowed me to check off #9 on my list.

Lupita Island.

I was always enamored with the idea of owning an island. The freedom to start a new utopia, the feeling of being open to the air, and having fresh water surround me. I also like the idea of being able to reinvent a world. Islands have also meant adventure and relaxation to me. My grandfather once gathered my extended family on an island called Palm Island. The discoverer of the island had written a book about his adventure. He had survived alone on the island for years before being discovered by travelers. Rather than returning to civilization, he made the island into a rustic retreat for people to enjoy. I think owning an island is a life adventure. It is part Robinson Crusoe, part James Bond villain, and part Hawaiian vacationer.

After our family safari in Tanzania, I decided to look for land there, believing that the world would eventually discover such a beautiful place. The Lithgows identified an island we could inhabit on Lake Tanganyika, and we decided to buy it and build our island paradise. Tom and Belinda were our partners on the venture, and we moved forward on the construction of Lupita Island. Tom would oversee the construction and Belinda, who had a strong penchant for design, would handle the interiors.

When the island was offered to us, it was bare rock and foliage with no permanent habitation--a blank slate. Construction began in 2004 and was completed in 2008. If you are going to build habitation on an island, you have to be prepared because things can go wrong. A worker we hired to design our airplane runway was killed in a boating accident. They had to saw the cruise boat we got for the island in two to get it under a bridge, and then weld it back together once it got to the island. Some of our workers incinerated garbage too close to the clubhouse and burned the entire clubhouse down. We did rebuild it better than before, but it was a real setback and doubled the cost of construction. Wherever possible we utilized locally sourced thatching, wood products and bricks, and employed tradesmen from the local region. We had to employ security guards so that the island didn't get looted, but that didn't stop the chimpanzee who lived alone there from regularly stealing food from our storage facility. My friends Doc Mohler and Alfred Mandel went on an early excursion to the island where Alfred laid the Wi-Fi and David did some medical work on the locals, but they had to fend the island off from pirates. The villas that Belinda designed and Tom built are possibly the most beautiful pieces of property on the earth today, but a lot of blood (literally), sweat and tears went into building them. We consider the island "rustic luxury," and it has attracted some of the most famous and wealthiest people in the world to come stay there. There is no title insurance, and we don't have the paperwork that says it is ours from the Tanzanian government. All we really had was the OK from the nearby town. If push comes to shove, we may just declare it a new freedom country and see what happens.

Our island is marketed quietly because we want it to stay special. We have mostly focused on wealthy families who want to have large gatherings. Occasionally, we host exclusive conferences there. Of course, celebrity couples celebrating their honeymoons are particularly thrilled because they can totally get away from paparazzi and crazed fans.

When I travel to Lupita Island, I typically go with 20-30 friends or family members and take over the island. These trips are ideal. Everyone gets to know each other so well, and the things we see or do are things we couldn't do anywhere else. We helicoptered to the second highest waterfall in the world in nearby Zambia. We even dropped like James Bond out of the helicopter into the lake from about 40 feet up. We went scuba diving with rare freshwater fish. We saw the chimps that Jane Goodall studied. One day, I swam with my friends Larsh Johnson and Will Edwards to a neighboring island where we met islanders who live purely off what they catch in the lake.

All of our experiences have been extraordinary, but one thing I will never forget is waterskiing on the lake where I was behind the only boat for miles in every direction. The locals all stared and waved thinking that somehow I was walking on water.

The island investment at its surface seems to be a total failure. The island operation loses money every year, and we can't sell it because our title is tied up in a slow and seemingly arbitrary bureaucracy, but to me, Lupita Island is an escape hatch, a possibly free trade zone, a dream of a simple life and an ongoing option on what I expect to be a coming boom in African tourism.

NO. 54 CREATE A GAME FOR A CLASS

Creating a game for a school class is #54 on my bucket list. The opportunity to check it off came when my then eight-year-old daughter, Jesse, asked me, "What do you do?" Rather than tell her what I do, I decided to show her. I set about creating a game about business for her third-grade classroom. It was fun to design. The curriculum would be taught over four days: Design Day, Manufacturing Day, Marketing Day, and Finance Day. Each day would have the students go through the motions of building a business. My daughter loved friendship bracelets, so I decided that I would turn her classroom into an industry of friendship bracelet manufacturing companies.

I begged her teacher for months to let me have four mornings with the class. Her teacher kept putting me off until one day in May she finally said, "What the heck, they are finished with testing, go ahead and see what you can do. But I suspect that your idea will only take about 15 minutes of class time and I will have to take them back from you." I told her that would be fine if it happened that way, and started teaching. I broke the class into six groups of six students, and made each of the groups a company in the friendship bracelet industry.

On Design Day, the groups incorporated, raised money from a banker or venture capitalist, used the money to buy crayons and paper to do theoretical design, and then chose which of the six designs the whole team would manufacture the next day. There were a lot of fights about whose design was more beautiful and whose would be the easiest to make.

On Manufacturing Day, the students purchased string, tape and bags—most teams would start out as a job shop where each student worked independently on his or her own bracelet, but some of the cleverer teams would discover that, in general, the girls could make bracelets better than the boys could, so they would form some sort of an assembly line.

On Marketing Day, the teams were asked to make a slogan, a logo, a sales pitch, and a commercial. We then asked the fourth-grade class to be discriminating shoppers, to go around the classroom to the various "companies" and make purchases based on the attractiveness of the marketing and the quality of the bracelets. It was a remarkable success. The classroom looked like a Turkish Bazaar. Kids were up on tables shouting, "Get your bracelets here." Teams were trained to keep track of their money, and then on Finance Day, we got them to create their own balance sheet and income statement. Based on the value of each company, we picked a winner.

What happened after that was phenomenal. By the third day, the teacher had given me full control of the classroom, and brought in the school principal to see the action. At the end of day four, she said, "You have to come back next year." The principal said, "You have to teach my fourth, fifth, sixth, seventh and eighth grade classes." I thanked them both, told them that I had another job and could not spare the time, but I knew I was on to something.

Two years later, I taught the class to my son Adam. I videotaped it and created a program so that anyone could teach it. I made it easy for teachers and parent volunteers to lead the program in any classroom anywhere. Around the new content, I founded BizWorld, the non-profit organization that teaches children how business works. BizWorld celebrated its 20th year in 2017, and has been taught in all 50 states and in more than 100 countries. More than 600,000 children have taken a BizWorld course.

As a non-profit, BizWorld needs to raise money to create the packages that train the teachers and volunteers and spread the word. Every year we hold the BizWorld luncheon, an event where we invite people to come, donate, and interact with students who sell them bracelets. We also have a fireside chat where I interview top luminaries and successful entrepreneurs. The first interview was with Eric Schmidt of Google. I asked him whether he learned anything about business when he was in grade school. He said, "No." He had to learn on the fly. During another interview with Ronnie Lott, famous 49er cornerback with Super Bowl rings on all his fingers (except the one), gamely asked the kids business questions, which they were able to answer adroitly because of their experience with BizWorld. The event has since been named "BizWorld's Riskmaster Award Lunch," and has attracted some real luminaries.

Elon Musk of Tesla and SpaceX, Marc Benioff of Salesforce, Richard Rosenblatt of Myspace, Chad Hurley of YouTube, Tom Seibel of Seibel Systems, Jenny Johnson of Franklin Fund, Aaron Levie of Box, Eric Migicovsky of Pebble, Brian Armstrong of Coinbase, and Peter Gotcher of Digidesign and Dolby have all come to do fireside chats at the BizWorld luncheon. Ironically, none of them seemed to have had any business training in grade school. BizWorld also raises money from an annual dinner in which Joe Saunders of Visa, Paul Jacobs of Qualcomm, and Meg Whitman of eBay were honored in the past. Pursuing #54 on my bucket list has led me to build relationships with some of the most powerful people in technology.

BizWorld also led me to the California initiative for school choice (school vouchers). When I first taught BizWorld, I noticed how stark the classrooms were in my daughter's school. I started asking questions, and I realized there were structural issues that made it difficult to teach and manage schools now. I decided to see how I could help change the system. My activism led me to being appointed to the California State Board of Education, and my tenure there drove my efforts to become author and supporter of a statewide initiative for California to allow parents the right to choose the school their child attends. It was called the school voucher initiative, proposition 38 Yes.

Here is what I learned. Schools and teachers were not accountable. Bad teachers couldn't be fired, and good teachers couldn't get raises. The principal of a school had no influence over who could teach in his or her school, nor did he or she have influence over the teachers' salaries and bonuses. The teachers' union (California Teachers Association) had developed such a hegemony of power over education in the state that they controlled everything from teachers' salaries to their work hours to the process under which they could be replaced. They influenced laws to make sure that there was ample taxpayer money to support teachers, and to make sure there were more and more teachers hired. After all, teachers pay dues to the union, so more teachers equals more income to the union bosses. And parents were stuck with the school that was in their district with no recourse and no way to get their children out of a bad school. Schools needed choice. They needed accountability. They needed a market system.

School vouchers are a market system that allows parents the right to choose the school that is right for their child, where taxpayer money follows a child into the school their parent chooses. I decided to see if I could drive our state to create this market system, this choice for parents.

I started with a website. It was the first political website anyone had ever made. It was called LocalChoice2000.com. On the site, I asked for suggestions for how best to build this initiative. I got 10,000 suggestions, and settled on one that seemed ambitious but simple and fair. I hired a team to conduct a poll and it showed that 80 percent of the people were in favor of giving parents a choice and allowing the money to go to a school the parent chooses. I thought this would be an easy win, so I threw my heart and soul (and a lot of money) into a campaign for school vouchers.

To my surprise, after a valiant effort, the campaign lost big in November 2000. The CTA and the NEA (the teachers' unions) proved too much to overcome. They got their teachers out en masse to campaign, spent $100 million against it, and to make matters worse, I got my tires slashed twice, my office was broken into and my campaign files were stolen.

Barry Hutchison worked for the campaign in PR, and he likened the campaign to a circus fun house. He said, "You never know which way to turn and you never know if what you are seeing is really what is there."

Still, it was a great experience to try to drive change, and even though we lost the initiative, I was able to check off #66 on my list--change a law. Despite the loss, through my efforts, the Supreme Court of the United States met and agreed to allow school vouchers as a viable option for states in May of 2002.

The school voucher battle also allowed me to meet and inform John McCain about the benefits of school vouchers at a Ted Forstmann event in Aspen. Senator McCain subsequently promoted school vouchers in his presidential debate with Barack Obama. I have had multiple meetings with both Presidents Bush, Former Governor of California Pete Wilson, Former Governor of California Arnold Schwarzenegger and many other powerful politicians on the topic of school vouchers since, and eventually, I believe school vouchers will come to pass. Even though my efforts were an enormous failure, ultimately the campaign may influence people to restructure education so that parents have a choice and schools and teachers have to perform to succeed.

NO. 25 VISIT 100 COUNTRIES

Visiting 100 countries is a goal I have had since my father ran the UNDP and counted 110 countries that he had visited. My imagination about all those different lands and cultures gave me an itchy foot. I needed to see more countries. At this writing, I am only at about 70 countries, but the experiences I have had by opening up to this enormous and varied world have given me so much! Here are some stories about a few of the countries I have visited and what each visit led to.

China.

My father was the Administrator of UNDP, and he took me to Beijing, China and Ulan Bator, Mongolia, where he would attempt to raise money from China so that UNDP could use it to save Mongolians from starving in the coming winter. The Berlin Wall had fallen, and the former USSR was disbanded so support that had previously gone to Mongolia was no longer available, and people were going to starve if UNDP didn't come through with some aid money.

Mongolia was fascinating. We saw people living as nomads moving their yurts by yak from place to place as they hunted and gathered food for winter. The city of Ulan Bator reeked of death, as it was built around a slaughterhouse. The government buildings were all Soviet grey and drab. We learned that as an artifact of Soviet rule, the government allowed trade only on Sunday mornings from 10-12. I vividly remember one elderly woman standing behind a table with three sewing buttons on it, making a case for someone to come buy her buttons. We met the president of Mongolia, and I remember Dad telling him that he should open the markets up all week, and the country would get better for his people. As we were leaving, the president told me in a spiritual, almost desperate voice, "You will come back here to help my country." I still haven't been back, but I plan to one day.

Our trip to China was even more eye opening. Since Dad was a VIP, we got very special treatment. We arrived at the Peking (Beijing) airport and were led out by an entourage of soldiers. We got into a car, the only car we saw on the whole trip. We were driven on the only paved road I saw anywhere in Beijing. And we stayed in what was the only international hotel in Beijing, a place called "Friendship Hotel." We watched as people rode bikes and traded vegetables out of baskets that looked like woven straw—so called "Chinese hats."

By contrast, present day Beijing has rings of highways as far as the eye can see, traffic everywhere and thousands of very high-end international hotels. Very few bicycles still operate on the streets and there are beautiful and delicious grocery stores and restaurants everywhere.

I went back to China 15 years later on a fact-finding mission, and had the opportunity to speak with the then Minister of Finance in Beijing. He told me, "You must invest in our country." I said that I had heard a story about a chocolate company an American started in China. The company had grown to generate $90 million in sales annually, but the Chinese government took it from him and nationalized it. Then I asked, "Why would I want to invest here, if your government will just take it from me later?" He then asked me what I would suggest he do to attract foreign investment.

I told him that if he wanted people to invest in his country, he should make sure that the first people who invested in Chinese companies made money and had an easy time repatriating that money, so that the investors would go back and tell all their friends about it. Hearing of the early investors' success would attract many investors. I told him that if he did this, he would have more investment than he ever imagined.

I forgot about our conversation and didn't return to China until we had set up the DFJ ePlanet fund in 1999. DFJ ePlanet had raised money from the Singapore government and one of the early hires was Finian Tan. Finian thought there was something interesting about investing in China, so I made another trip to see what progress the country had made.

At that time, everything we heard about China was depressing. The American media led us to believe that there was no infrastructure, the people were untrustworthy, the government took over any business that got to be worth anything, and Chinese businesses just stole everything that was developed in the US.

With the US press biases as my backdrop, I went back to China. Finian took me to Shanghai this time, and I saw something there that inspired me to overcome what I had heard in the media, and consider taking a chance by making a few investments in China. Here is what I saw that changed my thinking.

Finian and I were taking a long drive from Shanghai to Hangzhou. We had been in the car for about two hours and we still had another hour or two to go, and it was getting pretty boring. I was looking out the window and noticed something unusual. I saw rows and rows of open-to-the-air concrete tilt ups with dirt driveways that went on for miles and miles. Then I noticed one house with blue windows, a golden spire on the roof and a paved driveway. I thought nothing of it until I saw another one, and another and another. I projected that China was modernizing, and that the culture would change from one of pure communists, where everyone is the same and lives in squalor, to a free market where everyone wanted to be like their wealthy neighbor. It would be like "keeping up with the Joneses" in the US in the 1950's, only in this case it might be keeping up with the Hwangs or the Lis and it would be with more than one billion people. I thought, "The blue window salesman is going to make a fortune," and surmised that eventually they would all buy blue windows and spires for their roofs, and then they would also buy refrigerators, computers, cell phones, and software. I decided to take the plunge into the unknown water and start investing money in China.

When we got to Hangzhou, I met some government officials who were very anxious to build a "free market economy with Chinese characteristics" there. I saw a technology center with lots of well-educated engineers and scientists.

The first investments our team made in China were in companies where people said they had good government connections. It turned out that this strategy might have been effective investing in the private equity business, but it was a contra indicator for venture capital. We pretty much lost all the money we invested in those "government connections" businesses.

But we also took another approach. We invested in some dynamic young entrepreneurs who were setting out to change the world, as we did in Silicon Valley. They seemed to be in the weakest of positions in China--all heart and with no connections, no money, and very little hope of success. To us, these entrepreneurs represented hope for the country and excitement for an enormous new market. And we liked being first. When you are first, you are the only game in town, so everyone wants to play with you. We met all the leading minds in technology in Beijing and Shanghai. And we funded some of them.

They included Robin Li, Nick Yang, Jason Jiang, and Bin Tang.

These were the entrepreneurs that started Baidu, Kong Zhong, Focus Media, and YeePay, and there were many others that would help make the Draper name synonymous with venture capital in China for years to come. I did meet Jack Ma, the founder of Alibaba, and while he seemed like a very passionate entrepreneur, our discussion was somewhat lost in translation, and I passed on funding him (adding to my long list of failures to act).

In China, we could see successful companies created in Silicon Valley and then fund similar companies in China. I worked with Robin Li on his business plan for Baidu while he was getting started, and I was able to get him to include paid search and real names in the Baidu platform—both fundamental to the business's success. I had learned about Clear Channel when I met with Founder Lowry Mays, so when I met with the copycat Focus Media team, I knew that we should invest. And PayPal's success in the US was a harbinger for Bin Tang, who would be building a payment system called YeePay in China.

Robin Li was the toughest negotiator. We thought that by investing $9 million for 28% of Baidu, we were paying too much for too little, but that was the deal I came home with after a heated discussion in a taxi cab ride with Robin and Finian. It turned out that 28% of Baidu today is worth well over $20 billion, so maybe we paid too little.

China grew because it was so open and unregulated to start with, but government officials often get schadenfreude, and they forget where their country's success came from. I think this is the case in China today where the Chinese government seems to be trying to control business in the country and the government of China is tightening down with regulations, fines, fees and taxes.

For example, the government shut down YeePay for several months based on new regulations they had adopted that forced the company to pay a large fine. Then a government S.O.E. (State Owned Enterprise) came in and compelled the company to sell to them at a deeply discounted price. At this moment, the government is not even letting money leave the country, so the opportunity to invest in Chinese companies may be waning. In response, we have put our Chinese efforts on hold because if money can't leave the country, there is no reason to invest any money over there. But, I am still a great lover of all things Chinese, and I hope the government comes around and reintroduces a free market. Being the first Silicon Valley venture capital investor to invest in China allowed me to back some of the great Chinese companies, and to set standards for venture capital investment there.

Germany.

In the fall of 1997, I was in Berlin to attend the European Round-table for Technology (ETRE) for the first time. ETRE was led by emcee extraordinaire Alex Vieux. The panel I would be on was enti-tled: "Venture Capital. Is this the end of the Macarena?" My obvious answer to the question presented was, "No way. Venture capital has many great years ahead." But, this would be my first real foray into Europe, and I wanted to do something memorable. I got a CD of "The Macarena" and bought a very cheap German CD player.

My plan was to answer the question by getting the audience to dance the Macarena. I needed to start with my co-panelists. I went to John Schock of Asset Management first, who I knew the best and thought would be the most receptive to the idea. His response was, "Tim, your antics will fall flat on this conservative audience. Do not do this under any circumstances."

Undeterred, I went to my friend from Sequoia, Pierre Lamond, who I thought would be the toughest nut to crack. He said, "Oh, the Macarena?" and he showed me a few Macarena dance moves. The others on the panel were European and kind of looked at me funny, but shrugged their shoulders. When I mentioned the idea to Alex, he was conflicted between panic and excitement.

When I faced the audience of dark suits and dull frowns, I knew I was doing the right thing. This group needed a lift, and I needed to make sure they knew that venture capital from Silicon Valley was different than what they experienced in Europe. It was a 1:30 pm panel and people were just back from lunch. After a brief introduc-tion from Alex, who is not known for brief introductions, I took the stage and suggested that everyone get up and stretch after such a big lunch. To my glee, the entire audience of 250 suits kind of looked at each other and reluctantly got up. Then I said, "OK, now put your left hand out." Everyone put their left hand out. When I turned on the CD player, we all started dancing. When the song came to an end, I concluded, "Alex, it is clearly not the end of the Macarena, and venture capital is just beginning, particularly here in Europe!"

Since then, the ETRE audience has been one of my favorites to keynote. They have grown to expect the unexpected. I wrote two songs that I sang to them, "The Riskmaster" and "Take My Money." After the attack on the World Trade Center, when people were still in shock, I asked the ETRE attendees to all hold hands and say something nice to the person sitting next to you. When ETRE was in Stockholm, after the mortgage collapse, I defended free markets against an onslaught of calls to regulate.* All in all, I have enjoyed a long relationship with the ETRE audience, and the organization has helped me explore the European continent with gusto and enthusiasm!

*Incidentally, even today, very few people realize that the US government is responsible for the financial collapse. The government told banks to loan to high risk borrowers so everyone could be a homeowner, and they said that they would guarantee the loans. The banks made risky loans as instructed—after all they were to be government guaranteed. In retrospect, it seems so obvious to predict what would happen next. When the loans inevitably turned bad, the government was called on to make good on their guarantees. Somehow the story became that it was the banks' fault, and the government had to "bail out the banks," but it was the government's contracted obligation to do so.

Singapore.

I have always had a strong bond with Singapore. The country might be a 17-hour flight away from Silicon Valley, but it is very aligned with the Startup Hero on how to drive progress. My experience started when Finian Tan, then working for the Singapore government, called to say that he would like to invest $100 million from the Singapore sovereign wealth fund, GIC, into Draper Fisher Jurvetson ePlanet Ventures. We were so impressed with Finian, that several months later we hired him to run our Asian office. We set up an office in Singapore, and worked hard to make the GIC. a great return during what turned out to be a challenging venture capital environment.

Through that ongoing relationship, we met then Deputy Prime Minister (now President) Tony Tan. Tony and his son Peter got involved with my efforts with BizWorld, bringing BizWorld to many of the country's junior high schools. Tony later asked me to serve on Singapore's Economic Development Board's International Leadership Council, where I served for 18 months advising Singapore on their economic development. I got to meet Prime Minister Lee Kwan Yew, the founder and leader of the Singapore miracle. He led the country through 40 years of prosperity and free markets. Although he was well into his 80s, the Minister Mentor still had extraordinary energy and wisdom.

The Singapore government is very pro-business, and they pursue it with vigor. During one dinner, I was seated next to Tony and I suggested that Singapore set up a stock market that operated as one big corporation. People's share of ownership in the corporation could be tied directly to how their individual portfolio investments performed, share for dollar. If done right, foreign investors would only pay taxes when they repatriated their money to their home country. He must have liked the idea, because he went right to action. He arranged a breakfast for me the next day where I sat between the head of the Singapore SEC and the president of the Singapore Stock Exchange.*

*Imagine how great the US would be if that kind of efficiency of action happened in our government.

Singapore runs much like a company, improving constantly, and competing with the other countries for capital and positive impact citizens. Singapore has the best education system in the world and the best healthcare. My breakfast meeting seems to have had an impact. As I write this, the big corporation idea is still buried, but the Singapore Stock Exchange is working to make private companies tradeable.

Nigeria.

One of my students who showed great promise was Toro Orero from Nigeria. Toro wanted to create a Draper-like ecosystem in Nigeria. He was excitable and dynamic. There was something exciting about his mission and he seemed to have the gusto and enthusiasm I knew it would take to make something happen in Africa. I decided to back him in his mission by investing in his venture capital fund. After about nine months, Toro invited me to come to Accra, Ghana and Lagos, Nigeria, for two conferences that he arranged. All the people around me advised me not to go. They feared the dangerous environment that the US media tended to promote whenever they reported a story on Nigeria. Seeing my determination, my loyal assistant Karen called ahead to get me security detail. When I got to Lagos, I was met by a two-car caravan of black suburbans with four guys hanging out the windows holding machine guns. They were very good at their jobs, but in my estimation, totally unnecessary. If anything, the guards brought attention to me as a possible target.

Toro called the conferences Speedup Africa, and both conferences were terrific. In Accra, I visited with more than 50 credible entrepreneurs, where Toro led the group in some shenanigans, bringing a spirit of change and dynamism to Africa that had never been there before.

Several years ago, I made an investment in Pagatech, a payment system for the unbanked in Nigeria. I took the opportunity to visit Tayo Oviosu, the CEO and founder of Pagatech, to see how it was working. Tayo took me around to some of the poorest parts of Lagos and showed me a system of finance that I was having trouble fathoming, where Pagatech agents take cash from the unbanked and pay their bills for them. The alternative for the unbanked is to wait in line for as long as 24 hours to pay their electricity, water or Internet bills so that their utilities are not shut off.

This African trip led me to what I hope to be a very important investment in BitPesa, a Bitcoin pan-African payment system. Africa, like China was back in the 1990s, is unchartered territory for venture capital. The rules and regulations have not been set and opportunities for entrepreneurship are everywhere. As a startup, Africa has the benefit of having little infrastructure or regulations limiting its innovations. Similar to how China was able to skip over land lines and go straight to smartphones, Africa will be able to skip over banks and go right to cryptocurrency.

There are many other countries and experiences I have had that might be enlightening, but suffice is to say, world travel has been good for me, and as you become a Startup Hero and as your business expands, I believe it will be good for you too.

NO. 70 READ 1000 BOOKS

For me, reading a lot of books is an aspirational goal. The number could have been 100 or one million. But 1000 is about 20 books per year for 50 years. I have not kept pace, but I am at over 300, and while I am nowhere near the scholar I would like to be, I have read enough good books to make the following recommendations to you as you drive toward becoming a Startup Hero.

Here is my Startup Hero reading list:

Dune by Frank Herbert

The Startup Game by William Draper

Bionomics by Michael Rothschild

Foundation by Isaac Asimov

How to Win Friends and Influence People by Dale Carnegie

Man and Superman by George Bernard Shaw

Zero to One by Peter Thiel

Harry Potter and the Philosopher's Stone by JK Rowling

Physics of the Future by Michio Kaku

Moneyball by Michael Lewis

The Botany of Desire by Michael Pollan

The Epiphany by Cree Edwards

...and this book you are reading right now! Read *How to be The Startup Hero* by Tim Draper.

Notice there are not a lot of business books listed. A Startup Hero must be well rounded and must understand people, philosophies and cultures. Your reading should not only be focused on your own business, but also be time you spend to understand the human mind and what it is capable of. Take the time to read. Startup Heroes read.

NO. 22 BUY A MOTORBOAT

Bruises in the Boardroom.

I bought a motorboat. It has created countless adventures, and taught me the hard way about the caution you need to have to be a good ship captain. This story is from when I was still a sloppy ship captain.

It was about 10pm. My sister missed the ferry from Long Island to Fire Island where we were spending our family vacation. I took my son and my father in my boat to go get her. I had had several summers of experience as captain of the boat, but everything looked a little different driving the boat at night. I needed to cross the Great South Bay and then, when I reached the big red buoy, cut up toward the ferry dock. It was a beautiful night. Calm, clear, black. The air was fresh. The boat was cutting through the water like a knife. I kept looking for the buoy. I was sure it was nearby.

I saw what looked like a long stretch of seaweed, and for fun, I gunned the engine to have the boat cut through it. But it wasn't seaweed. I was too late to see what it was. "LAND!" I shouted, and the boat flew 100 feet over a beach and through some high reeds to come to a startling halt. My son casually mentioned his toe hurt, and then stuttered, "Pops is d-d-dead." Sure enough my father had gone head first through the anchor door and wasn't moving. I shook him back alive, saying, "No way!" He is not going now. Finally, his foot started to move, then his arm, and then he started to slur a few words that didn't make sense. Relieved, I said, "See Adam, he is fine."

We used the radio and were eventually saved by SeaTow, a boat towing service, but they broke a cable trying to get our boat back on to the water from the land. We had to leave the boat, but they took us back to Fire Island. When we got back, Dad took a bath and invited everyone, including the nanny (to her horror) in to see this enormous bruise he had gotten on his butt. Dad still seemed a little delirious from the concussion he suffered, but we were all used to his unusually open personality, so we guessed that he would be fine. And fortunately, he was back on the tennis court and telling everyone about the accident the next morning.

Two weeks later, back in Silicon Valley, Dad was telling the story to West Shell, the CEO of Netcentives. The way my dad describes it, he was in West's office, which was surrounded by glass and on the second floor overlooking the whole company. Dad felt obligated to show West his butt to put an exclamation point on the story. He took down his pants in the glass office situated in the middle of the company and said, "See." Then he went home and told my mother about seeing West and taking down his pants. Mom started laughing and said, "But Bill, the bruise is gone." For years after, former Netcentives employees that I have met have mentioned that time when my father flashed their CEO.

Gusto and enthusiasm can bring on trouble, but as my father says, "When things get bad, just think of what a great story it will be later."

NO. 1 GET ON A TV SHOW

Originally, running a marathon was at the top of my list, #1 changed when I organized the list by "Fs."

Startup U.

My exposure to Hollywood had been only through my sister, Polly Draper, who was, among many other leading roles, a star in a TV hit series called "Thirty Something." She later created a movie called "The Tic Code" and after that the Nickelodeon hit "The Naked Brothers Band," built around her sons, Nat and Alex Wolff, with cameos from me, my sons and my daughters. My daughter Jesse had a large role as the boys' nanny. I was the character "Principal Schmoke," a wacky school principal.

I learned some of the ins and outs of Hollywood through helping Polly with the business side of these shows. What I generally learned was that money goes into Hollywood but it doesn't come out (like a black hole, the Roach Motel or Hotel California).

I learned firsthand how strange a monopoly provider operates as a business when we decided to do a reality show called "Startup U." I suspected that something big was coming in creating shows around entrepreneurship. I thought it would be fun to be a part of one. I even made several trips to various studios and met with several producers for about 10 years making suggestions for shows, from comedies to competitions to game shows built around our industry. But it wasn't until I got a call from Mike and Tim Duffy of the Ugly Brother Studios that I got an entrepreneurial show going.

Mike and Tim were terrific. We bonded immediately when I heard that they were professional producers that were spinning out from the big studios to do something entrepreneurial themselves. We decided to work together to design a reality show around Draper University. They could visualize all the amazing things they could do with a show built around our unusual and exciting school. I loved that we could make the school famous and show the world that a school could be created to drive to the needs of students who would mold the 21st century.

We sold the show to ABC Family, a network that I thought could provide some reach and then potentially bring the show to a much larger audience with their parent company, ABC. There was some turmoil there, people coming and going, being fired and leaving, but eventually, we got the "green light" to produce the show.

Making the show was great fun. There were 10 students hand-picked to be the main characters. To keep it manageable, we kept class size to a total of 30 so the 10 students could easily be focused on. The students included a wide mix of exceptional talent including former Miss USA Erin Brady and her then husband Tony Capasso, Instagram star Ana Marte, social entrepreneur Sharon Winter, and medical marijuana delivery king David Kram. Lectures were given by the founders of Lyft, SolarCity, Airbnb, and several other household names. Among the speakers were Michelle Kwan, Jane Buckingham, and the Valley Girl herself, Jesse Draper.

The students came up with a wide range of interesting companies to pitch. I agreed to invest in the top three in hopes that the show would help them get off the ground. The team did an outstanding job and the show was terrific. When the show aired, we had great expectations because we knew we had created something special. The students participated in a variety of activities and there was even some drama and comedy from the group. We estimated that ABC Family spent $7 million to make the show. But all the money went into production. I thought it was weird that after spending so much money to produce the show that their entire marketing budget seemed to be less than $50,000. Maybe ABC Family knew something we didn't. Not long after we launched, they scrapped all their reality TV shows and changed the name of their network.

The show totally bombed. The audience for the network was mostly young teenagers. They were not the best audience for this kind of show, since they were still a long way from thinking about their careers and were nowhere near ready to become entrepreneurs. ABC Family did stick it out for the full 10 episodes, but didn't advertise them and decided not to renew the show. I think the show will be a hit once it finds its audience, and there are some indications that it will. The network sold the rights to Startup U to the History Channel in Latin America recently, and when I went to Monterrey, Mexico, everyone I met seemed to want a selfie with me. They kept saying, "Startup U," "Startup U!!" I was thrilled that the show had aired there. After each selfie, I would say something like, "Nice to meet you." And everyone seemed to have the same reaction. It seemed that they didn't like my voice since they thought I would sound like I did on the show, which had been dubbed in Spanish!

Win or lose, I am so glad we tried the show. I often think fondly about my co-stars, who are all amazing people and doing great things, and I think the show, even with the tiny audience, helped us market Draper University.

NO. 29 PLAY CHESS IN WASHINGTON SQUARE

I was in New York City one beautiful day and I discovered that I had a two-hour block of time to kill. Rather than go back to my hotel room to catch up on my email, I decided to pull myself off the work treadmill and get one of the 101 accomplished. I walked from midtown about 60 blocks to Washington Square, and found a wonderful older man with a curly graying beard and worn sandals who wanted to play chess with me. He brought out the clock he would use for the game. "Five minutes each," he said, and I realized that this would be tougher than I thought. I am a pretty good chess player when I have unlimited time, but on a clock I was sure to be challenged. When we started, he kept having to push my clock for me because I didn't remember it was there. He moved as quickly as my grandfather did when he was doing his magic tricks for me. He made mincemeat of me in about 20 moves. Then he looked at me and said, "One more game...." Each game was $5 to the winner and while I wanted to play again, I realized that this could be an expensive afternoon. So we played another game. I thought I had him this time. It was his turn and he was down a pawn. He nonchalantly got up, wandered over to a tree, and peed on the tree. It threw me completely. He checkmated me in about four more moves. Then he pleaded, "One more game...." "How," you might ask "is this story ever going to help me become a Startup Hero?" My answer is simple. If you find yourself in a bind, try something unexpected.

NEXT STOP: TOP OF THE EMPIRE STATE BUILDING

This one will be a challenge for me, because since 9/11, people aren't allowed to walk up to the top of the Empire State Building unless it is the Annual Empire State Building Run-Up, the one day a year that marathoners run up it. I might have to run another marathon to get to check this one off. However I do it, I hope to do it with gusto and enthusiasm.

HAVE ADVENTURES

Explore the world with gusto and enthusiasm. And although I highly recommend a bucket list, I don't recommend that you obsess over it. Some of the greatest moments of my life happened when I just went on adventures or took on challenges.

We have some very good family friends that all vacation together on Fire Island: the Chandlers, the Kiernans and the Shumways. We all have similarly aged children and we have watched them all grow up. The activities we share include board games, tennis, body surfing, boating and fishing, as well as social activities and challenges.

These families are up for anything and they do it all with gusto and enthusiasm. When my right hand was injured before a big tennis match we call "The Trash Talkers Invitational," Dave Chandler got us all to play with our opposite hand, and it was so much fun that we continued to play lefty long after my hand was healed. I once challenged John Kiernan to a four-mile swimming race from Fire Island to Long Island, and John Shumway agreed to follow us in the boat, bringing along his then teenage daughter and her friend. Everything went swimmingly until, in the last half mile, we were hit by an unexpected hurricane. We swam on, but the waves sent us in circles. It was disconcerting to swim 20 strokes and look up to discover that 10 of them had been in the wrong direction, but neither of us was willing to stop until we finished the race. But the boat was in trouble and starting to sink. John was starting to panic, and his daughter and her friend were screaming and crying, so he got us to abandon our quest not more than 400 yards from our destination. Undeterred, we tried it again the following year with John Kiernan's daughter, who literally swam circles around us—but we made it.

Gusto and enthusiasm can be a challenge. Make sure you get some enthusiastic and adventurous friends to explore the world with you.

QUEXERCISES ON GUSTO AND ENTHUSIASM

1. Who is the most enthusiastic person you know?

2. What holds you back from being the most enthusiastic person you know?

3. What is your greatest adventure to date?

4. What adventure would you like to go on to make your life fuller?

5. Go to a baseball game and cheer relentlessly for the visiting team.

GUSTO AND ENTHUSIASM PUZZLE

What is the highest score you can get in Scrabble on your first move?

COUPLET FOR GUSTO

A pessimist is always spreading fear.
An optimist builds all that we hold dear.

I WILL TREAT PEOPLE WELL.

We learned about gratitude and humility - that so many people had a hand in our success, from the teachers who inspired us to the janitors who kept our school clean...and we were taught to value everyone's contribution and treat everyone with respect.

MICHELLE OBAMA

The real act of marriage takes place in the heart, not in the ballroom or church or synagogue. It's a choice you make - not just on your wedding day, but over and over again - and that choice is reflected in the way you treat your husband or wife.

BARBARA DE ANGELIS

Beginning today, treat everyone you meet as if they were going to be dead by midnight. Extend to them all the care, kindness and understanding you can muster, and do it with no thought of any reward. Your life will never be the same again.

OG MANDINO

Do right. Do your best. Treat others as you want to be treated.

LOU HOLTZ

The magic formula that successful businesses have discovered is to treat customers like guests and employees like people.

TOM PETERS

Kindness is a mark of faith, and whoever has not kindness has not faith.

MOHAMMED

And know that I am with you always; yes, to the end of time.

JESUS CHRIST

Small things matter. They define you. Give gifts on special days. Write thank you notes. Help people with introductions and challenges. George H.W. Bush always wrote thank you notes for everything anyone did for him, and he became President of the United States. His notes were short, funny and to the point, but he got them done. Set aside one day each week to write notes to people who helped you in some way or threw a party or gave you a gift. Make it quick, but get them out. It doesn't matter if they are handwritten or texts. It only matters that you send them. This is all a part of the Startup Hero mentality. Treating people well isn't just about doing things for people and not expecting anything in return; it is also about recognizing people for the good that they are doing for you, or for anyone around you.

GINA

Gina Kloes, a Tony Robbins acolyte, has become one of the most sought-after team building leaders in the world. She inspires everyone she meets to be better. She has taught groups from Africa to Fiji, and she is a regular at Draper University. My wife, Melissa, and I have gotten to know Gina well over the years. Once she took Melissa and me out to try Cryo Wave, where we were put in a freezing chamber for three minutes each in Manhattan Beach, California, to make sure we were keeping fresh. She got us boogie boards and volleyballs to welcome us to the neighborhood there. She makes us themed baskets for our birthdays.

Gina has a knack with people; she inspires the people around her to be better, and she encourages them to try new things. She makes them overcome their fears and their hangups. She helps them see a better person in themselves.

At Draper University, she works tirelessly, sometimes from 8 am to as late as 3 am. She takes students through a process that starts with dancing just as they wake up, gets them to bare their souls to help them understand where they might have mental blocks, and then encourages them to break boards with their hands and to eat fire from a torch to get them to overcome their fears and to open their eyes to see how much they are really capable of. She gives it her all. She stays up working through student problems and challenges.

She is filled with ideas for improving Draper University and she gives me suggestions without judgement.

Incidentally, Gina has written a book called "Magical Moments," which encourages people to think about and make the best of their lives. Check it out. Be like Gina. Gina knows how to treat people well. And she writes "thank you" notes. Maybe she should be President.

CO-WORKER GIFTS

When I was getting started, I so appreciated all the work my team did for me. Since we were only a small team, it was easy to do the small thoughtful things for these people who did all that work. But the business grew, and I developed a problem. How do you scale a personal touch? When I started Draper Associates, I had very personal connections with each of my co-workers. For birthdays and the holidays, I gave each of them individual gifts that were particular to them, generally with a story behind them. Steve Jurvetson loved his various curiosities and toys, so I got him a giant toy box that I labelled Steve's Toys. I gave Jennifer Fonstad a golden axe in a particularly difficult year when she had to fire the CEOs of three of her four startups. I made a work of art with money from various countries for our finance team. I gave our PR manager a megaphone. But the team kept growing and growing and I found I couldn't keep up. I wanted to keep it personal, but I didn't have the creative time to do it.

I have a trunk that I bought in Africa. It is beautiful, but my wife thought it was ugly and didn't want it in our house. I also have many people who work with me, and as we grew, I realized that I wouldn't be able to remember to get gifts for each person on every birthday. I also have hundreds of active portfolio investments and service suppliers who send me gifts on occasion, which are not really just for me, but for our firm, the institution. I put these three factors together to create the "birthday trunk." Whenever I get a gift from a portfolio company or a service company, I put it in the trunk, and when it is someone's birthday, they get to take one item out of the trunk as their gift. It works well. Sometimes people get a very expensive bottle of wine or an iPhone and sometimes they get a beanie or a t-shirt. But, through this trunk, I have a way of making them feel appreciated even though this process is universal and the gifts in the trunk are all regifts. It is nice to add a little fun to their birthday that seems like a personal touch but doesn't require a lot of extra effort on my part.

Since we moved into Hero City, we have another birthday prize. On their birthdays, people can get up on the perch at the top of the stairs, bang Captain America's shield with Thor's hammer and say, "It's my birthday," and declare something that people (including themselves) will have to do on that day. People have made rules like you have to sing to each other, or you need to smile at everyone you talk to.

I also try to deliver candies or teddy bears to employees on Valentine's Day or a fun surprise for the holidays. I find that the process allows me to better connect with my team. I have arranged outings and trips for the team, given out gifts for holidays, and written poems or songs that include all the people in the company and the contribution they have made over the year. I love doing it and I think they appreciate the effort.

Treating people well isn't all about giving. Being a Startup Hero takes forethought. For example, as you hire people into your startup, you will need to set up your company to promote fairness. You will need to make sure people are not treated differently for similar jobs. You will need to explain a rationale for one employee getting more money or stock than another. Are there job levels? Is there seniority? How is performance measured? All of these questions are best solved in advance, so that when someone is hired, they understand the entire picture and will feel as though they were treated fairly.

Additional forethought should be used to handle issues like how your business will handle travel and expense requests, how you will compensate people for personal days or sick days, how you will handle medical insurance and medical issues, how you will handle exits when people leave. The government gives guidelines (and laws) that you will have to follow, but make sure you are not just doing what the government tells you with respect to how you treat your employees. They are much more important than that. Figure out how to humanize the work and treat people well.

QUEXERCISES ON TREATING PEOPLE WELL

1. How will you set up your startup?

2. How will people be compensated?

3. How will they be fired?

4. What will they get if they leave voluntarily?

5. Will you give them more money or stock when they do great work?

6. Will you set up any exceptions?

7. What will you do to make them feel special?

8. Call your mother.

9. You and your partner start a company and decide to split the company 5050. After six months, you discover that your partner has decided to take a job somewhere else. Name six ways you can rearrange your company to part amicably.

BRAINTORNADO ON UNDERSTANDING OTHER CULTURES

50+50=140

There is a planet where this is true. How many fingers do the aliens of that planet have on each hand?

FREEFORM FOR TREATING PEOPLE WELL

Attila the Hun shared the spoils of war
Genghis Khan lived up to his own laws
Napoleon planted trees for soldier shade
Winston Churchill gave people hope and grit
Steve Jobs drove his team to strive to perfection
Elon Musk inspired his people to shoot for Mars
Deng Xiao Peng said, "Some of us will get rich first"
Lee Kwan Yew remodeled his troubled country with honesty

What will you do for your people?

I WILL MAKE SHORT-TERM SACRIFICES FOR LONG-TERM SUCCESS.

Success is no accident. It is hard work, perseverance, learning, studying, sacrifice and most of all, love of what you are doing or learning to do.

PELE

Let us sacrifice our today so that our children can have a better tomorrow.

A. P. J. ABDUL KALAM

Great achievement is usually born of great sacrifice, and is never the result of selfishness.

NAPOLEON HILL

Football is like life - it requires perseverance, self-denial, hard work, sacrifice, dedication and respect for authority.

VINCE LOMBARDI

In order to become prosperous, a person must initially work very hard, so he or she has to sacrifice a lot of leisure time.

DALAI LAMA

We all naturally want to become successful...we also want to take shortcuts. And it's easy to do so, but you can never take away the effort of hard work and discipline and sacrifice.

APOLO OHNO

One life is all we have and we live it as we believe in living it. But to sacrifice what you are and to live without belief, that is a fate more terrible than dying.

JOAN OF ARC

The great secret of true success, of true happiness, is this: the man or woman who asks for no return, the perfectly unselfish person, is the most successful.

SWAMI VIVEKANANDA

Know when to hold 'em. Know when to fold 'em. Know when to walk away. Know when to run. There'll be time enough for countin' when the dealin's done.

KENNY ROGERS

SACRIFICE

If you are going to be a successful entrepreneur, your mission has to be number one. You are not going to be able to do a lot of things. If a big customer needs you during your daughter's championship soccer game, you will have to take care of the customer. But this line of the pledge is not really intended to be about your sacrifices at home, but a guide to the decisions you make at work.

Startups often have to make difficult decisions as they grow. Should I take $5 million from a reputable venture capital firm or should I take $15 million from a corporate who has a reputation for taking trade secrets. Should I hire my loyal friend who is an adequate coder, or should I risk that relationship to hire an outstanding coder who has a tendency to need adulation? Do I take this order from this customer now in hopes that we can make what they need delivered in time, or do I lose the order to a competitor and hold off on shipping until it is absolutely ready for market?

The best entrepreneurs raise the money clear of restrictions, hire the best people they can, and ship on their own timeframe, but none of the answers are as clear cut as they would like.

THE APOLLO COMPUTER/SUN MICROSYSTEMS STORY

Here is an example of when an entrepreneur made a short-term sacrifice for long-term gain, but broke all the other rules of engagement to make sure he won the game. In the summer of 1983, I was working at Apollo Computer as the assistant to Charlie Specter, the company president. Charlie had just landed an enormous order with Computervision. This order would be the company's largest one to date and would represent 25% of Apollo's business going forward. At that time, Apollo was the leading workstation company, but they had one competitor in Sun Microsystems. Sun was run by some young aggressive people out of Stanford. It had a less powerful, less expensive product, and Sun sold one quarter as much volume as Apollo sold. But the industry was growing fast, so both companies were on a roll.

For Apollo, this Computervision order was a very large opportunity. For Sun, it was everything! The Sun team looked at this sale as mission critical to avoid getting marginalized by Apollo, and the order had already been given to Apollo. But even though the ship had sailed, Sun didn't give up. Sun did something unprecedented. It offered to supply Computervision the computers at cost, and offered 5% of their company to Computervision if they would scrap the Apollo order and go with Sun. It was a big sacrifice to give up some of the company and the profits that would come with that many sales, but Sun felt that it had to win this business or Apollo might run away with this enormous market. Computervision went back to Apollo and asked Apollo if it too wanted to give up 5% of the company and sell the computers at cost, but Apollo said no, feeling that it already had the order in hand and that Computervision would not renege. They also assumed that Computervision would choose Apollo's superior technology. And giving away a piece of the company to a customer was unprecedented!

Computervision dropped Apollo and went with Sun. The decision doubled Sun's business, making the company's sales almost equivalent to those of Apollo. This sale also gave Sun incredible momentum. The order was so large that Sun was able to lower its manufacturing costs, which allowed the company to start selling equivalent products cheaper than Apollo's. Its high volume with Computervision made its open operating system, UNIX, the standard in the industry. That order ended up making Sun's success. Apollo continued to grow and ultimately became a successful public company, but its business now had a serious challenger.

Texas Instruments (TI) did something similar with pricing. TI had run through many product cycles in the semiconductor industry. Common practice in the industry was to focus on short-term profits. When costs were high, companies priced their products accordingly, and as volumes increased and costs came down, then companies would offer their customers lower prices. This practice allowed the semiconductor companies to "skim" the early adopters of their products and later allow the prices to fall as volumes increased and costs went down.

Chips are made in batches. The process involves etching a pattern on a semiconductor wafer that is then cut into multiple chips. The "yield" is a measure of how many good chips they get out of each wafer. In practice, the yields would increase over time and the costs would decrease as volumes increased. Because the process of making a new semiconductor required so much equipment, and the product yields were low, companies would try to recoup those costs as quickly as possible from early customers.

But TI had seen this pattern happen many times, and it had the capital to run at a loss for a while, so it decided to price its chips to the future costs rather than the current costs. The company knew that over time its yields would increase, and it could make chips for less, so it priced them "forward." TI decided that it would get more design wins by giving customers the lower pricing and once its customer's products started to scale up, it would have better yields and its costs could be low enough to make a profit. This strategy was a great success. Customers enjoyed TI's forward pricing and signed up for its chips.

TI and Sun both made short-term sacrifices for long-term success and in each case, it paid off.

SIZE MATTERS, START SMALL – SAVE TIME, TIME IS MONEY

As a Startup Hero, you will need to prioritize your time. It can get tricky, but you should always try to qualify your leads to make sure you are spending your time wisely. A Startup Hero can waste a lot of time on unqualified leads. Always do your homework on the people you deal with. Before you go too far with a potential customer, ask questions. Can the customer pay? How big will the order be? How long will it take to make a decision? How long before the product will be in use?

Approach small customers first. Small customers typically decide faster and give you practice before approaching large, more complicated customers.

Similarly, when you are raising money from a venture capitalist, ask qualifying questions. How long have you been investing the current fund? How much dry powder is left in the current fund? How do decisions get made? How long does it take? What is your typical investment size? Of your investments, how many did you lead?

In hot times, venture capitalists have a lot of money to invest and put to work in startups. Don't let the pressure they feel affect the way you run your business. When times get lean, they are nowhere to be found and you will have to make do with whatever you have.

My advice: Raise their money, but don't spend it. When they say, "Scale the business," your response should be, "Not until we have the product/market fit nailed down."

Money is also often wasted in startups. The best startups raise as much money as they can and spend it only when they have to. This frugality is particularly important while the product is being developed. Many companies overhire and overspend during the development phase, and all those extra employees often become a time suck and a money drain on the company. Once the Startup Hero's company finds a few customers and he or she is satisfied with the product and the product/market fit is a lock, he or she should then and only then start spending on marketing. When the product/market fit is locked in, then time is of the essence and the entrepreneur needs to push hard so the competition doesn't have time to catch up. Of course, your company should always be frugal, but when customers are excited about the product, the company should pour it on and win the land grab.

HIRE SLOWLY, FIRE FAST

Perhaps the most important short-term sacrifice you can make is to fire someone who is not a good fit.

You always want to take your time before bringing a new person into your startup. Getting just the right fit is something that doesn't always come easily. It took me 75 interviews before I met Karen Mostes-Withrow, who would become my assistant for the next 30 years...and counting. Karen was by far the best hire I ever made. She has become almost linked to me at the brain. She handles all the work I need done but can't get to, she anticipates what the business needs and acts accordingly, and she has supported me through some very tough professional (and personal) challenges. I remember saying things like, "Do you remember that guy who...?" and before I said another word, she would respond with, "Yes, John Smith from Acron Systems." And she would be spot on.

But I have made some mistakes in hiring (and firing) and funding too.

Over my years as a venture capitalist, I have had to fire quite a few CEOs, founders, employees, and several partners in the DVN. In most cases, I believe that it is important to do it immediately, so that the person who is fired has as much time as possible to find his or her next job, and so that rumors do not circle. It should also be done with sensitivity and tact, and with finality. The rule of thumb is to guide the person to his or her strengths before explaining why there is not a fit with the company. And there should be no wiggle room. A firee should not be thinking about how they can get their job back, but about where they can go from here.

Here is a typical scenario where a founder gets fired. A founder is CEO (by default). The board decides (whether right or wrong) that the company needs to hire a new CEO. Sometimes the new person is expected to work alongside the founder, and sometimes the new person is there to replace the founder. Interestingly, the latter case may be cleaner, but when a company loses its founder, it often loses the heart and soul of the company.

I tend to favor keeping the founder of a company on as CEO as long as possible. Often the worst decision a founder makes is when he or she hires an outside CEO. Sometimes it is a mismatch culturally, sometimes it is someone who has done it before and the newness has worn off, and sometimes it is someone who has done it before and doesn't really understand that the marketplace and the technology have changed since they did it.

As much as I love it when the founder of a company is able to drive the company through all its growing pains, sometimes companies really do need new CEOs to guide them. When a new CEO comes in, there is always a reshuffling of the company. They can be useful in getting rid of "sacred cows," the people or customs that have outlived their usefulness to the company. They can also be leaders who understand better how the people in the organization should be managed.

THE CLOWN FIRING STORY

I followed my own rule and it backfired. There are always exceptions. I was chairman of a small company with a very young charismatic founder. He co-founded a company with a technical lead who he was related to. He was always in sales mode. The company was constantly overselling and underdelivering to its customers. We had a small board, and we decided that the company needed more of a leader to come in and manage customer expectations as well as the team. We brought in an experienced CEO who came in and enthusiastically invested his career and some of his money into the business.

The results were abysmal. The company sales slowed, and the new CEO created too much overhead for us to support. The company ran out of money, and we had to make a decision. We decided we had to fire the CEO and then we could make a small investment to see if the company could recover with the original team. It was Halloween, and I was dressed in a clown suit, but I had to tell the CEO immediately. I took him aside and told him that we were going to let him go. It was surreal.

After he left, I walked into the bathroom and looked in the mirror at a scary clown face. I remember thinking, "This was bad. I should have waited until tomorrow when I wasn't in a clown suit." About five years later, the man I had fired committed suicide. He had other issues, but I couldn't help thinking that I could have contributed to his downfall.

THE SOCIALTEXT STORY

By contrast, my best experience was with a more stable and mature founder, who was initially resistant to the idea of hiring someone else as CEO, but then turned around and (like a good politician) got in front of the parade. Ross Mayfield is a brilliant visionary and blogger who created SocialText, a company that uses wikis to manage a social enterprise. After we made our investment, there were a few things that didn't seem right. We scheduled a board meeting, but Ross missed it because he was in Europe hiring programmers and didn't bother to tell us that the meeting was off. I remember arriving to an almost empty office and there was no explanation for his absence. Since his product was for people to be able to communicate virtually within their company, it was ironic that they were having a hard time communicating with one another. His team was losing confidence in the company's ability to succeed. The board decided that the company needed a new CEO.

I told Ross that this decision was made, and while at first he felt that maybe we should have given him another chance, he then did something extraordinary. He got out in front of the decision. He had an enormous following in the blogosphere, and he capitalized on it. He wrote to his blog audience that he was looking for a new CEO to take his company to the next level. He then helped in the hiring of the new CEO, who ended up being Eugene Lee. Eugene brought the team together with a kumbaya management style and eventually created a successful exit for the company.

THE HARVARD BUSINESS SCHOOL REUNION STORY

In the spirit of making short-term sacrifices for long-term success, I use my class at Harvard Business School as an example. I have kept in touch with a few of my classmates, but mostly I see them every five years at our class reunions.

When I graduated from Harvard Business School in 1984, the people who seemed to know exactly where they were going were the ones who took the "safe" route. They joined investment banks or consulting firms with big salaries or joined large organizations like Sperry Univac and Ford Motor Company. At the five-year reunion, those people who took those relatively safe routes were puffing their chests out with pride at their success. Meanwhile, my classmate Jerry Shafir decided to start a healthy organic soup company, and at the five-year reunion, he was broke. Another friend, Ron Johnson, took a job in retail, where no self-respecting MBA would tread, and at the five-year mark, he was scraping gum off the floors of Target stores. A third classmate, Steve Wiggins, was struggling to start one of the first health maintenance organizations (HMOs). He also was broke. I started the venture capital company and at the five-year reunion, I was $6 million in debt to the US SBIC program, and the people there were calling my loan.

By the ten-year reunion, Jerry, Ron, Steve and I each still had our problems, but the safe bets weren't looking quite so safe. Sperry Univac was disappearing fast and Ford Motor Company was seeing Japan cut into its market share. Consultants and investment bankers were finding their careers flattening out and were wondering if this was all there was to life.

By the fifteen-year reunion, Jerry was selling a lot of soup. Ron was a leading figure in retail and would go on to create the first Apple Store and run retail for Apple Computer. Steve's company, Oxford Medical, was worth hundreds of millions of dollars, and my venture capital business was hitting the knee in the curve of what became the technology boom. At the twenty-year reunion, many of the people who took the safe routes were asking the four of us for jobs.

I think it is one of life's ironies that the people who played it safe ran into trouble, and the people who took big, seemingly reckless chances wound up "safe." The world changes rapidly. I highly recommend taking the risks of guessing what the future may look like and then pursuing a business that looks like that future. At first, you will look silly, but you will not be at anyone else's mercy, and over time you might just be considered the wise one.

Make short-term sacrifices for long-term success. Your life will likely be long, so you should anticipate and drive to that long life.

QUEXERCISES ON SACRIFICES AND SUCCESS

1. What decisions have you had to make that were short-term/long-term based?

2. What did you do?

3. Did they pay off?

4. What decisions do you anticipate having to make?

5. Will the long-term benefits outweigh the short-term sacrifices you will have to make? They usually do.

6. Have you had to fire anyone?

7. How will you approach it when you do?

8.   Plant a seed.

SHORT-TERM/LONG-TERM PUZZLES

Your company and your competitors are trying to drive each other out of business. Each year, each of you has one target to go after and you each always go after the strongest target (the company with the highest probability of driving its rival out of business). Your first competitor, Astro Space Systems, has a 50% chance of driving one of you out of business each year they are in business. Your second competitor, Base Space Labs, has a one in three chance of driving either you or Astro out of business as long as they are in business. Since your business, Creative Space, is a startup, you have just a one in four chance of driving your target out of business in any given year. Each year is discrete, in that in any given year, each of you has to pick a target to drive out of business for that year and can only switch when the dust settles. Which company is the most likely survivor? What is the probability of each surviving?

You have 300 individual physical Bitcoin tokens. You wish to transport as many as you can to a place 100 lightyears away in a Spaceuber; however, the captain only takes cash, and your spouse will only allow you to carry a maximum of 100 Bitcoins at a time, and the captain takes one Bitcoin for every lightyear he travels with you in advance. You can load and unload as many Bitcoins as you want anywhere safely. What is the most Bitcoin you can bring all the way to your destination?

SHORT RHYME FOR THE LONG GAME

The long game
Play the long game
Don't live for short fame
Threw a party and nobody came
No one wants to go when the plan is lame
It is well worth the time to make your customers tame
Build them up and make them proud when they say your name
Think it through, design it well and make it beautiful and no one's to blame

I WILL PURSUE FAIRNESS, OPENNESS, HEALTH AND FUN WITH ALL THAT I ENCOUNTER... MOSTLY FUN (FOLLOWED BY A DANCE)

It is not fair to ask of others what you are not willing to do yourself.

ELEANOR ROOSEVELT

It's just better to promote love and fairness and equality than it is to promote something you think is based on your religious beliefs.

JANE WIEDLIN

Fairness is not an attitude. It's a professional skill that must be developed and exercised.

BRIT HUME

The grass is always greener on the other side. We are busy applying fairness creams while people in the West go bare-bodied on the beach to get a tan. Indian girls have ruled the roost when it comes to beauty pageants. I flaunt my complexion, and I am proud to be noticed as an Indian wherever I go.

SHILPA SHETTY

Ensuring fairness in the American workplace should be a cornerstone of our economic policy.

TIM SCOTT

Fairness is what justice really is.

POTTER STEWART

Let go of certainty. The opposite isn't uncertainty. It's openness, curiosity and a willingness to embrace paradox, rather than choose up sides. The ultimate challenge is to accept ourselves exactly as we are, but never stop trying to learn and grow.

TONY SCHWARTZ

Remember that breath walking - as with any meditation technique - should not be pursued with a grim determination to 'get it right.' The point is to cultivate openness, relaxation and awareness, which can include awareness of your undisciplined, wandering mind.

ANDREW WEIL

Tolerance, openness to argument, openness to self-doubt, willingness to see other people's points of view - these are very liberal and enlightened values that people are right to hold, but we can't allow them to delude us to the point where we can't recognize people who are needlessly perpetrating human misery.

SAM HARRIS

One of the main characteristics that differentiates Dubai from other commercial centres is its openness to innovation and the freedoms it grants people and institutions to operate.

ABDUL AZIZ AL GHURAIR

The best weapon of a dictatorship is secrecy, but the best weapon of a democracy should be the weapon of openness.

NIELS BOHR

One of America's strengths has always been its openness to the new: both new ideas and new people.

CESAR PELLI

Days 16-27 Goodbye cravings, hello Tiger Blood!

MELISSA HARTWIG

To enjoy good health, to bring true happiness to one's family, to bring peace to all, one must first discipline and control one's own mind. If a man can control his mind he can find the way to Enlightenment, and all wisdom and virtue will naturally come to him.

BUDDHA

A healthy attitude is contagious but don't wait to catch it from others. Be a carrier.

TOM STOPPARD

To enjoy the glow of good health, you must exercise.

GENE TUNNEY

The foundation of success in life is good health: that is the substratum fortune; it is also the basis of happiness. A person cannot accumulate a fortune very well when he is sick.

P. T. BARNUM

If you obey all the rules you miss all the fun.

KATHARINE HEPBURN

Just play. Have fun. Enjoy the game.

MICHAEL JORDAN

Never, ever underestimate the importance of having fun.

RANDY PAUSCH

Just keep taking chances and having fun.

GARTH BROOKS

When you have confidence, you can have a lot of fun. And when you have fun, you can do amazing things.

JOE NAMATH

Dance like nobody's watchin'.

WILLIAM W. PURKAY

FAIRNESS

Fairness. Entrepreneurs need to pursue fairness. The best companies are fair all the way through. Fair with society, customers, shareholders, suppliers and employees. How people are paid and incentivized should be understood by each employee and they should know what they need to do to get paid more. With employees, this can be more difficult than it seems. Some people think fairness means everyone gets the same pay, but it becomes clear that this doesn't work when someone stops showing up for work or someone works extremely hard to bring in the big sale. Some people think fairness is only a meritocracy, where the stars get all the money, and the rest of the rank and file get nothing. That situation can generate just as much dissatisfaction since employee results can vary broadly over time. One month's star can be next month's black hole and vice versa. Some people think everyone should just get ownership like stock or options. This setup can be fine for long-term motivation, but stock is generally illiquid, and people have mouths to feed.

There are many issues that come into play when you are trying to compensate people fairly. How much credit do you give to the early employees who have built the business? How much to the current team who will drive the business forward? How much do you pay for experience? How much for institutional memory? How much of the decision should be based on industry comparisons? How much should be tied to people's needs (mortgages, private schools, etc.)?

I can think of four vehicles for creating fairness in employee pay. They are salary (or wages, in the case of hourly workers), commission, bonus and stock. Salary is best used to keep everyone fed, pay mortgages or rent, and should be enough to make sure the employee is not looking over his or her shoulder to see if the tax man or the credit card company is on his or her back, and also enough to be sure they feel treated well. I have known people who did crazy things to try to make ends meet. One friend took a second job cage fighting; another tried to sue people who she thought might pay her off to go away; yet another sold his car and computers so he couldn't get anywhere or do any work at home. All three of them would have been better off just telling their employer about their problem. No matter what the situation, most good employers will figure out how to make it work for their employee in order to keep him or her happy and healthy. A Startup Hero keeps salaries high enough to make sure the team's fundamental needs are met.

Commission is best used to motivate sales people, but it can also be a good vehicle for team building when the company needs all hands on deck focused on getting customers in. Toyota, for example, had overbuilt one year and they had built up an enormous inventory of cars that were not moving into customers' hands. The president changed everyone's job to sales. The mechanics, the support staff, and the assemblers all became salespeople until they moved out the inventory. And it worked. Not only did they sell all the cars, but the workers all had a better understanding of the customer and came up with better ways to make and design cars. The best commission plans are those that make sense to the workers. I remember that as a startup, Apollo Computer had an accelerating commission plan where people would get something like 5% up to their quota, 10% until twice their quota and 15% above that. But as a more established company, HP would offer 2% up to their quota, and 1.5 % of anything above it. Both made sense. Apollo wanted to grow fast and anything they could do to make that happen was mission critical. HP wanted people to feel secure in their jobs, not encouraging anything that would engender jealousy in the employees.

A bonus can create fairness when an employee has done outstanding work. Bonuses are the hardest for everyone to understand, so the best CEOs are very deliberate about how bonuses are determined. Some extraordinary CEOs lay out about five things they want each employee to focus on for the next year, each equally weighted (one should always be the "extraordinary" or "other" category). Then the following year, they go over the five things and see how well the employee has accomplished them. The goals should guide the employee towards the goals that the company needs that employee to accomplish to become successful. For example, for someone in the finance department, the goals can be 1) Focus on reporting. Make sure the executive team gets appropriate reports. 2) Focus on technology. Make sure the team is using the best technology to provide the reports required. 3) Focus on frugality. Make sure the team doesn't go over budget or hire too many consultants to do the jobs the employees can do. 4) Focus on teamwork. Make sure the team is enjoying working with the employee and there is mutual respect there. And 5) Focus on other. The "other" category allows people to veer off track if they see something unexpected that might change.

Someone in the marketing department might have five other goals. 1) Focus on users. Make sure the audience for the product is growing. 2) Focus on sales support. Make sure the sales team has everything they need. 3) Focus on beauty. Make sure the product is beautiful. 4) Focus on customers. Make sure the major customers are fully engaged and the product becomes mission critical for them. 5) Focus on other. Make sure the company is not missing out on any opportunity that comes in.

I have funded companies based on milestones, and the milestones we set in place were irrelevant when they came due. It didn't matter that the company had made its milestones, because it did it at the expense of the business. Make sure the employee is thinking for themselves and making decisions that are good for the company, not just hitting the numbers.

Stock is perhaps the best and fairest motivator for a team. Stock represents ownership in the business. An owner thinks very differently from an employee. The difference is analogous to the owner of a property vs. the renter of a property. For example, I will contrast the actions of Tom Ford, real estate owner, with that of the Kappa Alpha House at Stanford University when I lived there.

THE TOM FORD VS. KAPPA ALPHA STORY

I remember walking around with Tom Ford when he owned 3000 Sand Hill Road, which at the time was the most famous address for venture capitalists (now it might be Rosewood or Hero City in San Mateo, California).

Recognizing that his venture capitalist friends were beginning to get wealthy and that they tended to work together, but had few employees, Tom built out four office buildings with many small offices where many small teams could reside in each building. He made the offices luxurious and tailored, but he made the buildings open and communal so people could both have their own space but still feel like they were part of a community.

Tom initially went around recruiting venture capitalists to move into his space. At first, people balked since the buildings were out on a hill in the middle of nowhere. Most people, my father included, wanted to stay in Palo Alto, where they would have more of a "status" address. No one had heard of Menlo Park, but Palo Alto was considered one of the big cities of the peninsula. But Tom kept at it and finally recruited some top venture capitalists to come work at the Sand Hill Road location.

It became known as the place for venture capitalists. The press wrote it up regularly as the venture capitalist's equivalent of Wall Street. Tom was a big success. The property is probably worth nearly $1 billion today. Walking around 3000 Sand Hill Road with Tom Ford was enlightening. He showed me around the property with great pride. Four times he bent down to pick up cigarette butts. He made mental notes of a drain that had been bent and some paint that had unwittingly covered a square centimeter of a window. He noticed a car he recognized from a tenant that was parked in a "visitor" spot. He asked what else he could do to make the property more attractive to the young venture capitalists. He was an owner. And a good one. Owners think like owners. They think long term. They work to delight their customers, and no detail is too small to take care of on the spot, right there and then.

By contrast, my fraternity, the Kappa Alpha House on the Stanford campus, was a rental. Forty college boys (including myself) each paid about $300 per month to stay in a building that was built in a similar style to the buildings at 3000 Sand Hill Road. But we were renters. We knew that not only did we not have any vested interest in long-term livability in the house but also that we would only be living in our rooms for about three months at a time, and then we would switch rooms. Walking around with the frat president the conversation would go something like this:

"This is where we hit golf balls off the roof and into the lake--that window is broken because we are not all good golfers. This hole in the wall is where one of our actives shoved a ski through it to wake up the pledge sleeping in the adjacent room. Here is where people arrange all the pillows at parties so that we can dive off that loft. Here is where we created a hot tub out of logs and cement, but that was a few years ago, hence the mold growth that has developed there and there. And these rug tracks are here because one of our actives likes to ride his motorcycle up the stairs so he can park it in the bathroom."

You get the picture. As renters, we had no ownership of the building. We didn't think to repair or replace anything. We had few thoughts of the people who would come to stay later.

In a startup, ownership has the same effect. An owner is thinking about what he or she can do to make the company work better, to operate leaner, to delight the customer more, to innovate harder, to market more cleverly. A renter is someone (like a consultant) who is just in it to put in the hours and collect a paycheck.

A note here about hiring consultants. Consultants (using out-sourced engineers, managers, marketers, etc.) can provide a very valuable and positive contribution to a business. They can get a product out quickly if they have the expertise in house and have experience doing it before. They can help with a product marketing launch where the business can take advantage of the expertise of someone who has provided similar services to other companies.

However, in my experience, consultants have often been trouble for startups. Startups need "owners" whose goal is to make the company better and stronger, to deliver the product sooner, to make the customer delighted with the quality and the price they pay. They need to be flexible and make repairs and redesigns quickly and effectively.

A consultant is more interested in his or her own business, and that business is better served if the consultant is able to bill more hours and keep a given project going. When changes need to occur, while an owner would just make the changes as quickly and competently as possible, a consultant might think twice. A consultant might first calculate how many hours he can bill for the change order, then decide how long they want the job to last, and then determine how to handle the change order.

Make sure the business has institutional history in house. You don't want to have a consultant design and create technology for you and then suddenly stop because they get a bigger customer somewhere else. You want your team to be able to keep the product evolving without losing momentum. A Startup Hero might hire a consultant to get a working prototype into the hands of customers quickly, but also build an in-house team to build the long-term product so that they can make the changes when needed. A Startup Hero might hire a PR consultant to help launch the business with the media, relying on deep contacts from the consultant, but then hire an internal PR person to follow up and drive the long-term relationships.

OPENNESS

Be open to people and ideas and keep an open mind. Maybe you aren't right the first time. The founders of Hotmail originally came to us as an index for websites. The Skype founders' first plan was to do shared Wi-Fi. Elon Musk started with a Lotus car body before designing from scratch with the incomparable S-car. Ideas can come from anywhere and anyone. If you are closed to people and their ideas, opportunity will never come your way. If you keep an open mind, and let those ideas in to percolate, you will be surprised at how exciting your business can become.

Being open is so important. Woody Allen said, "90% of success is just showing up." But it is more than that. Being open to new people, new ideas and new opportunities is what makes a success. My father is the most open man I know. He is extraordinarily successful. He has succeeded in the private sector as he pioneered the venture capital business, with the public sector with the US Export-Import Bank, in politics with the UNDP, and in the non-profit sector with Draper Richards Kaplan Foundation. He says that his secret to success is saying, "Yes!" In fact, his office mates made a poster of him looking like James Bond, and they entitled it, "Dr. Yes."

If you watch my father at a social event or business conference, you will see him talking intently with complete focus with whoever he is with, whether that be the host, the caterer, the president of a country or the plumber. He learns as much from taxi drivers as from corporation presidents, and each of them becomes a part of his network and adds to his overall success. When the president of a country needs a plumber or caterer, Dad is there with a solution. But there is more to it. Wherever he goes, he spreads openness and goodwill. He identifies opportunities, and he connects people. And if there is indeed a karma scale, his is overflowing. He has done so many favors for so many people that if he needs something, there are people ready to help. So, he succeeds. Just say, "Yes!"

Dad once saw a man with a huge smile and a front tooth missing, and he asked, "Why don't you get a replacement tooth." The man said, "That will cost me $300." Dad believed that the tooth was keeping that man from the success he was capable of, so he sent the man to his own dentist where he got the tooth replaced. The man was eternally grateful, and the dentist didn't even charge my dad.

HEALTH

So many people rely on their doctor to take care of themselves. But with the exception of Kaiser and a few other unusual medical systems, doctors, while bound to the Hippocratic Oath, do not have a financial incentive to keep you well. Of course, most doctors comply with the motto, "First, do no harm," but it is ironic that the third greatest danger to your body behind heart attack and cancer is to be in a hospital. Doctors want to heal. But there have been so many lawsuits against doctors for malpractice that every doctor has a little voice in the back of their mind saying, "I better do something that won't get me sued," instead of just thinking, "What can I do for this patient?" Malpractice insurance is 25% of all the expenses a doctor endures. Patients are effectively paying an additional 33% for their healthcare because we as a society punish doctors when they make mistakes. Trust is free. Lack of trust is expensive.

The weird thing about medicine in the US today is that there is little discipline on government spending. Medicine, for the most part, is almost free for the patient. There may be a copay, but it is usually minimal. People are welcome to go to the hospital with any ailment they have. Their visits are paid by the insurance companies. Insurance companies get their money from either taxpayers (in the case of Medicare) or corporations who are forced by the government to provide healthcare coverage for their employees. There is very little disincentive for a patient to go to a hospital. And there is often an incentive for the doctors to give their patients the most expensive treatments available, because insurance pays based on the type of treatment, not the outcome. This situation can lead to doctors having a perverse motivation to misdiagnose a patient so that they or their hospitals can generate more revenue.

THE THERANOS STORY

One day, my daughter Jesse's best friend, Elizabeth Holmes, came into my office and said, "I am going to change healthcare as we know it." At 19 years old, she understood that all the current incentives are wrong and the drug companies, the doctors and the insurance companies are all propagating the system, and it is bad for patients. This bold girl went on to explain her plan to build a business that would make the healthcare system work better. She planned to start with a blood test that took very little blood. She called the company Theranos, a combination of the words "therapy" and "diagnosis." I liked her passion so much I committed a $1 million investment at about a $10 million valuation.

Theranos operated in stealth mode for nearly 10 years while she developed the "nanotainer," a microfluidic device that takes two drops of blood for testing; and the "minilab," an integrated device and software platform with the potential capabilities of a full-scale clinical laboratory. People would be able to monitor their own health because the results of the tests would be stored in the cloud, and people could see and determine action based on the changes in their blood. When she finally announced this revolutionary technology, the world was captivated. The business was valued at nearly $10 billion. She made the cover of Forbes and was listed as the first under-30 female self-made billionaire.

For the consumer, this technology was great news. They would save thousands of dollars and gallons of blood. Patients would now have a baseline and an ongoing record of how their blood had changed over time. New data would be available for people to help themselves to make determinations on how their lifestyle and their meds were doing for their health. And all this information would be readily available in the cloud. People could compare their results with previous results as they recorded tests over time. Furthermore,

Theranos could potentially add other data like their DNA, their weight, or the results of a wearable device like a Fitbit or BodyBug. All this data might show that they were taking the wrong medicines or shouldn't be taking them at all. Healthcare was on the precipice of a revolution.

But for the medical status quo establishment, this technology presented a threat. Long term, it could lower the cost of blood tests significantly, while healthcare data could become transparent and abundant. Competitors LabCorp and Quest had enjoyed a duopoly for years, and now they would have to adapt to having this upstart new entrant in blood testing. Revenues would almost certainly go down for them and others. Insurance companies would probably have to lower their premiums. Big Pharma, another oligopoly, might have to reinvent themselves if the data showed that the "one size fits all" prescription drug system was unreliable. And doctors might find themselves with fewer patients, as people would now be able to use data from these results (along with the oncoming advances in artificial intelligence) to self-diagnose.

Healthcare was about to change. Patients could take better control of their own health, and the "status quo" might be adversely affected. But the status quo got relief in the form of an aggressive reporter from the Wall Street Journal who raised concerns about the validity of Theranos's claims about its technology. This one reporter investigated and damned Theranos and Elizabeth with a series of articles, turning public opinion against them, and creating havoc in the company. Elizabeth Holmes spent more than one-third of her life pursuing her mission. She worked tirelessly to build a company that promised to improve our health and our lives. But this series of nearly 40 Wall Street Journal articles turned Theranos from an amazing healthcare transformation to a trial of public opinion. I suspect that competitors were egging on the media, but either way, the effect of the articles was company sabotage. It should be noted that all blood testing companies have varying results, and even have issues with human error (losing or switching vials, misplacing labels, etc.). The writer turned public opinion against Elizabeth so hard that government agencies felt they had to step in, and then lawsuits started to come. She had to close down her lab. Her major partners didn't like the bad publicity, so they backpedaled out of their relationships. Her legal bills stacked up enormously as she worked to comply with the piling on of regulatory agency requests. For the moment consumers have been robbed of what could be a life-saving service.

Meanwhile, the reporter got himself some high-profile stories and, if the rumors are true, a $4 million contract for movie rights.

The thing that strikes me about this tragedy is that the company was just pursuing its noble mission. All startups go through growing pains where their initial products don't perform as well as they hope, and any limitations were blown out of proportion. The reporter damned her with innuendo, and then fanned the flames. The sad irony here is that the Theranos roadmap would have led to much safer, consistent and reliable test results.

After all the articles, Theranos customers were sufficiently scared off, and even doctors were backing away. Negative public opinion became too strong for people to resist. People felt that by using Theranos, they would be getting flawed results that could lead to bad medical decisions.

It is all tragic for the consumer. Patients were loving the service. It was far more convenient than existing solutions and they were excited about the prospect of seeing and monitoring changes in their results over time. Parents were loving it because their children wouldn't cry when their blood was drawn.

Someday, this blood testing technology may prevail, but in the meantime, we are losing blood and paying high prices for blood tests. And hopes for establishing a baseline to watch trends in our blood is still a pipe dream. We are losing data, money and blood!

It is ironic and discouraging that an enterprising founder who ventured out to change healthcare as we know it for the better has been the one to suffer. All her work and effort to build Theranos seems to have gone unappreciated. We should all be thanking her for this breakthrough, but instead we have vilified her.

Similar attacks have happened to entrepreneurs in other industries when they are so successful that they disrupt the status quo. I remember Skype being attacked by the long-distance carriers, who said VoIP (Voice over Internet Protocol) technology was not secure. Skype was able to deflect the attacks, since their technology was peer-to-peer file sharing and was technologically different from the many VoIP businesses coming into the industry. Tesla was attacked by the car companies at almost every juncture. They lobbied the states to not allow cars to be sold unless through registered car dealers. Some states still don't allow Tesla to sell direct to customers there. A New York Times reporter tried to prove that a Tesla battery ran out sooner than the company claimed. After he ran the story, Elon Musk checked the reporter's route, and discovered that the reporter had manufactured the story with a lie. Elon was able to verify that the reporter had driven around in a parking lot for three hours so that he would run out of battery power before he reached his destination. Bitcoin has been constantly under attack by banks (JP Morgan's CEO said it was a fraud), by various governments (China made Bitcoin illegal), and by the media (alleging that Bitcoin was only being used for nefarious purposes), but Bitcoin has proved to be resilient. It helps that the inventor is anonymous, so there is no individual to attack, and that the Bitcoin true believers are so dedicated to the success of the currency. Napster and StreamCast were attacked by the music industry, and although these companies died, the technology lives on in iTunes and Spotify. Uber has been attacked by the cab companies, Airbnb by the hotels, and Amazon by the book stores. The battle between innovation and the status quo continues.

The status quo knows how to squelch innovation. The simple recipe the entrenched oligopolies use is as follows: First, ignore it and hope it will go away. Next, align with other oligopolistic players to gang up against the upstart and manipulate the press to spread fear into the minds of the startup's customers. Then, file lawsuits to try to force the startup out of money. Lawsuits are expensive and big companies can afford to keep them going indefinitely, while startups typically have to settle or run out of money trying to defend themselves. Finally, lobby the government to take action and shut the startup down since they are not playing by the same rules as the status quo, or force them to comply with regulations that were set up for very large businesses.

All this can be tough on an entrepreneur. Entrepreneurs have high suicide rates, high divorce rates, and high substance abuse rates because they aren't all ready for the onslaught that comes from the status quo when they achieve their visions and change an industry.

These problems I have encountered with the health and mental state of the successful entrepreneur, combined with my perception that we need more Startup Heroes to drive progress and change, is what drove me to create Draper University of Heroes. We have made it our mission to prepare the prospective entrepreneur for whatever they may face, so they can make the world a better place.

FUN!!!!!

No billion-dollar business was ever built without the employees having fun doing it. When I visit startups I have backed, there are often ping pong tables, arcades, bars, couches, and VR set ups centrally located in the offices. The entrepreneur is often embarrassed when I see these instruments of fun. They often coyly say something like, "The engineers need to let off steam somehow." But as an investor, I like to see some fun. A job makes up a large portion of life. Humans are not robots. They need fun, love, health and support. They need to be treated fairly. They need to stay healthy.

At Draper Associates, and all the associated firms, everyone has a nerf gun at their desk at the ready for a war that could come on for any reason (a celebration, a financing, an exit, etc.) or for no reason. Over the years, we organized dog shows, fairs, parties, pizza days, birthdays, boating trips, hikes, trips to Las Vegas and Disneyland, anything we could come up with to make sure the employees were happy and emotionally healthy. We created our award "The Ultimate Frisbee" for companies that reached $1 billion in market value, and more recently "The Golden Hero Mask and Cape" for companies that accomplish that milestone with the original founder in place. We threw enormous "schmoozefests" with themes like flying, future, space or science so that we could display our companies in a fun environment. Fun became our trademark in an otherwise stodgy industry with the reputation among its established players for being vultures or misers. Entrepreneurs want to work with us because they want to have a little fun too. They look at the fun side and think that there might be something different or unusual that can come from our relationship.

And for the business, the creative thinking and the network that comes from this kind of work-play is extremely valuable. Our schmoozefests brought in countless deal flow, acquirers, strategic partners, customers, investors, limited partners, suppliers, press and friendships.

At Draper Associates/DFJ, we always thought of ourselves as the mavericks of the venture capital business. We tried many business pursuits that were either unheard of or just frowned upon by the industry. We were the first venture capitalist to advertise, first to build a network of venture capitalist s, first Silicon Valley venture capitalist to set up outside the US, and first to focus on the Internet. When we decided to move our offices to Sand Hill Road, where most of the venture capitalist gravity was, we threw a party. We called it the "There Goes the Neighborhood Party." We invited all our brethren and neighbors from Sand Hill Road. The party had a safari theme and we had monkeys and various other animals in cages. I rode in on an elephant. The landscape was perfectly manicured in our new location. But when I rode in on the elephant, he took a slight detour, wrapped his trunk around a nice-sized elm tree, ripped the tree out of the dirt and ate it. Then he backed up against a window to someone's office, impelling a woman to come out of the building screaming. It was a bit of a calamity. But, on the whole, a very successful party ensued. After I apologized profusely to the woman, we became friendly, and it led to a deal. The party became legend. We all had several laughs about it, and it brought our team (and our neighbors) closer together.

MORE FUN: DANCING WITH CHIEF JUSTICE SANDRA DAY O'CONNER AND FIRST LADY OF CALIFORNIA GAYLE WILSON

I love to dance. It encourages chaos. I don't just waltz or foxtrot either. I make up dances. One I call the fireman's carry is where I pick my partner up on my shoulder and spin like a top. One is where I hold both hands of my partner and we spin against each other until we can't hold on any longer. One I am particularly proud of is where I start with a jitterbug pretzel, and when my partner is totally disoriented, I pull her to me and flip her over my back. I learned it from a jujitsu master. He had flipped me and left me on my back, so I asked him to help me make it into a dance move by pulling up at the end so my partner lands on her feet. Normally, I reserve these moves for wild parties, but sometimes I just need to encourage chaos.

One time, I was at the Chevy Chase Country Club in Maryland at a party my parents threw for the Washington establishment, and at my table was Justice Sandra Day O'Connor amongst other dignitaries. Everyone seemed a little stiff. I thought they had probably been to a hundred parties like this one where they were expected to behave in a certain way. But Justice O'Connor has a real sparkle to her, and I saw it. One nice woman to my left said, "It is customary for the men at the table to dance with each of the women at their table." At that time, the band had already played three songs and the dance floor was empty. I thought, "What the f@#$." I took Sandra Day O'Connor out on the dance floor and flipped her over my back. She was amazing. She didn't miss a step. She seemed to love the flip, but I figured that once was enough. After the dance, I went back to the table and asked the woman who had given me the tip on what is customary to dance. With significant trepidation, she gave me her hand. The flip became the "thing" that snapped the party into overdrive. The dance floor filled up and this room full of self-conscious politicos rocked like they were at the Fillmore. Sometimes you need to instigate to spark success.

I similarly had an opportunity to dance with Gayle Wilson at a Lincoln Club event in Carmel, California. She is delightful and sweet, and I surprised her by flipping her on the dance floor. It happened so fast, that she just kept dancing, and we both got a big laugh out of it. Apparently, her security detail was caught off guard and I realized that if they had seen me flip her, I would have been tackled to the ground. Sometimes fun can be dangerous too. Still, I encourage you to dance with abandon, and love it.

Dance like nobody's watchin'.

My flip came in handy when I was asked to volunteer at a Dancing with The Stars Live Troupe event. I was randomly selected to come up on stage and dance. I flipped my partner and she was dumbfounded. I got huge applause from the audience, but the emcee didn't even notice. Dancing should just be fun.

FRANK

Frank Creer is a good friend of mine. He is some combination of Kato from the Pink Panther and a character out of South Park. He physically attacks me at random to keep me on my toes and keep me laughing. He helps out with survival training at Draper University, and he regularly creates situations that become legendary. He came up with the idea that teams should be tied together for most of their first day of school to get to know each other better, and he made two of the male students paint themselves pink because they missed a class on women in the workforce.

I remember a time when I was very nervous going up an elevator to meet with Arnold Schwarzenegger, and Frank wrapped his arms around me from behind and lifted me off the ground. I didn't appreciate it at the time because I was going over what I was going to discuss with Arnold and I lost my concentration, but I appreciate it now. He cut the tension and made for a more fun connection with Arnold that lasted for years.

THE SAND HILL CHALLENGE STORY

At Draper, we do things differently. When there is an opportunity to show our stripes to the world we rise to the occasion. When Jamis MacNiven from Buck's Restaurant in Woodside came up with a Silicon Valley soap box derby called "The Sand Hill Challenge," we put our heads together to do the outrageous. Where groups like Mohr Davidow would spend nearly $100,000 on a car to win the race, we (not having that kind of money to throw around) did it differently. Each year we had a theme. The first year, we used a surf theme and made the car look like a surf board. Frank was our guinea pig driver, since we had never tried the car, and we joked that he was expendable (and unbreakable). We did well the first year, but the second year it all came together. We were not allowed to use energy sources in our vehicle, so I thought about how to give our car more natural energy. From my physics classes, I knew that height can create potential energy—$PE=\frac{1}{2} mgh$. We built a ramp, a huge ramp. We didn't have much time, so it was a little rickety. We put a hook on the car and used ropes and pulleys to set up for the initial launch of the vehicle. Frank again was volunteered to drive. We hung him upside down from the top of the ramp on the same car we used the previous year, and at the starting gun, Warren Packard and I pulled the ropes and accelerated the vehicle. Frank took off like a rocket, and beat a car that had cost $50,000 to make by 50 yards. We were placed in the winners' bracket, but we couldn't compete for the final because the ramp had fallen apart, and the car steering was torqued. Frank was willing to be the sacrificial lamb again, but I declared victory and took down the 10-foot tall ramp so Frank would not have to die.

After that race, ramps were disallowed in The Sand Hill Challenge. In the years that followed, DFJ won the spirit award every time with a Trojan Horse, a Noah's Ark, and a nanocar.

QUEXERCISES ON FAIRNESS, OPENNESS, HEALTH AND FUN

1. What is fair? Should everyone in the world share equally or should people get more if they produce more?

2. How do you think about getting people to open up emotionally? Do you smile? Nod intently? Listen carefully?

3. How do you think about your health? Do you think it is better to check in with your doctor regularly or to never have to go to the doctor?

4. When did you last have fun?

5. What makes something fun?

6. Is it fun to try something new or do something you are familiar with?

7. Create an original game for you and more than eight friends to play. (If you don't have it in you, use the board game Risk, by Parker Brothers. Lay out all the rules. Then, when the game is heating up, try to force your opponents to change positions with the person on their left. You will learn more about fairness, openness, health and fun than in almost any other scenario.)

FAIRNESS, OPENNESS, HEALTH AND FUN PUZZLES

You are on an alien planet. The aliens are either FRoeBLEs or ScA-boRs. You come to a fork in the road. If you go one direction, you will die from contact with the friendly but hazardous FRoeBLEs. If you go the other direction, you will be grunted at by ScAboRs, who will then lead you to a land where you can build shelter, plant food and make clothing. The FRoeBLEs always lie. The ScAboRs always tell the truth. You are greeted by an alien. You don't know whether he is a FRoeBLE or a ScAboR. He says, "You may ask me one question." Then he sits silently waiting for your question. What do you ask?

Find one counterfeit Bitcoin out of six in two weighings that is lighter than a standard Bitcoin.

Find one counterfeit Bitcoin out of 12 in three weighings and determine whether it is lighter or heavier than a standard Bitcoin.

FAIR, OPEN, HEALTH, FUN

Fair is Fair
Open the door
For health, care
Fun makes lore

I WILL KEEP MY WORD.

We learned about honesty and integrity - that the truth matters...that you don't take shortcuts or play by your own set of rules.. and success doesn't count unless you earn it fair and square.

MICHELLE OBAMA

The supreme quality for leadership is unquestionably integrity. Without it, no real success is possible, no matter whether it is on a section gang, a football field, in an army, or in an office.

DWIGHT D. EISENHOWER

Real integrity is doing the right thing, knowing that nobody's going to know whether you did it or not.

OPRAH WINFREY

Have the courage to say no. Have the courage to face the truth. Do the right thing because it is right. These are the magic keys to living your life with integrity.

W. CLEMENT STONE

Integrity is the essence of everything successful.

R. BUCKMINSTER FULLER

The impossible often has a kind of integrity which the merely improbable lacks.

DOUGLAS ADAMS

Nothing more completely baffles one who is full of trick and duplicity, than straightforward and simple integrity in another.

CHARLES CALEB COLTON

Keeping your word can be extraordinarily painful, especially when people's interests and motivations change.

THE DEFY PRISON STORY

Defy is a non-profit organization that encourages prisoners and ex-prisoners to learn to become entrepreneurs. People who have spent time in prison have a very difficult time getting a job, so Defy wants to help them create their own jobs.

I am a donor and volunteer for Defy. On one effort, I went to a prison facility with some other volunteers to meet and help teach the inmates about entrepreneurship. Catherine Hoke, Defy's founder, told us that like her, we would get to love the prisoners, but not to promise them anything. She said, "Imagine being in prison for 20 years, and the one connection you have had with the outside world is the volunteer you met at Defy. And imagine that that volunteer told you 15 years ago that he would like to hire you when you got out, or put you up in his house while he got back on his feet, or even hinted at either. During those 15 years, you would be visualizing that nice job or that nice house. Don't make any promises, or one of these guys is going to show up at your doorstep at some time, and you may have gotten married to a victim in the meantime, who will have nothing to do with some prisoner you met 15 years ago." Keeping your word can be very difficult, so don't give your word lightly. Always choose your commitments carefully, and thoroughly spell out what you know you are willing to do to fulfill those commitments.

The prison experience was highly emotionally charged. We went to Solano State Prison, an all-male, maximum security prison. The guards were always on alert , especially since there had been a particularly grisly murder at the prison. We went through several gates, a particularly claustrophobic hallway and past the brown dirt yard that served as a field when the prisoners had their outdoor time. We arrived at a large gym, where we held our all-day session.

Catherine led one exercise that was particularly revealing. She put two taped lines down the center of the gym about four feet apart. She asked the 70 prisoners to stand on one side and the 20 or so volunteers to stand on the other. Then she asked a series of questions. If they applied to you, you were asked to step up to the line, and if they didn't, you were asked to step back.

The first question was, "Did you graduate from a four-year college?" Every single prisoner stepped back while every single volunteer stepped forward.

She continued, "Did you have violence at home or did one or both parents die or leave before you were 18?" This time the exact opposite happened. Every prisoner stepped up. Every volunteer stepped back.

"Have you ever taken another life?" About two-thirds of the prisoners stayed on the line. We were dealing with murderers.

"Did you commit your crime when you were younger than 30?" All of the prisoners moved to the line. In fact, almost all the crimes were committed by these people when they were between the ages of 15 and 22. School age.

"How long have you been here?" Two-thirds of the prisoners had been locked up in that cage for more than 20 years. One for 43 years.

Weirdly, I cringe at the idea of leaving my dog in a cage for more than an hour, but for some reason, society in general feels that it is perfectly fine to lock people up for 43 years.

Leaving the prison, I had an epiphany. Maybe we should rethink crime and punishment. Or, if we must keep the current system, maybe we should have a maximum 10-year sentence for murder. If the prisoner gets out and are convicted again, it could be a more serious sentence—maybe the death penalty. This small change would save lives that are being wasted in cages, would save the prisons about 90% of their costs, and as a society we might be more understanding and kinder toward our former prisoners. There is no question that we need more programs like Defy. The prisoners were hungry for knowledge of the world. And we need them to be employable with real skills when they get out.

Keep your word. And stay out of prison.

I recently took a trip to Buenos Aires, Argentina. The country had a severe loss of confidence when the banks and the government couldn't provide the currency demanded by the citizens. The peso collapsed and so did the trust in the country. To this day, Argentina has the least credit of any country in Latin America. When I met with the president of the country, I told him that if he made Bitcoin a parallel national currency, the confidence would return since Bitcoin doesn't rely on banks, politicians and people to be that trusted third party. His eyes lit up. Maybe there is hope for Argentina.

In keeping your word, you might experience difficulties. They can be ethical, complex, or tied to an uncertain future. Take contracts, for example. It is very important to read over everything that you sign carefully. Try to imagine all the implications of the contract. I once signed a contract when I funded a company that I thought was just like the many other venture capitalist contracts I had signed in the past. When the company was sold for a big price, the company sent me a check for my investment plus a small bit of interest. Apparently, the entrepreneur's lawyer had left open a window in the contract that allowed that if he sold the company before there was a round of funding and after our note matured, that I was not allowed to convert the note to stock. Ouch!

At Draper Associates, we have since closed this loophole, and worked hard to build in new terms for entrepreneurs and venture capitalists to have a more aligned and flexible long-term relationship, but the bad feeling persists, and that entrepreneur will never see Draper Associates money again. Keeping your word is more than just doing what you say. It is making sure that the spirit of the contract is held up, that the people around you are treated well, and that even if it is a stretch, doing what is expected of you in every situation.

The entrepreneur from Ukraine took my investment and the money just disappeared. What he didn't know is that incident put a damper on our ever investing in Ukraine again. It is amazing how powerful trust is. A community of distrust is constantly fighting a zero-sum game. There is only enough around for the people who have it, and they constantly steal it from each other. A community of trust, however, can accomplish anything. Incentives are aligned, people don't need to hide things from each other, everyone helps each other succeed. Show me a poor community and I will show you a community of dishonesty where people don't trust each other. Show me a prosperous community, and I will show you a community of trust and honesty.

Keep your word. And make sure everyone around you does too.

QUEXERCISES ON KEEPING YOUR WORD

1. When did you last break a promise to someone? Is there any way you can make it up to them?

2. When did you keep your word even though it was hard? How did that make you feel as opposed to how you feel when break a promise?

3. Have you ever been in a lawsuit? How would you approach it if you had broken your word? How would you approach it if you believed that the other party had broken his word?

4. Make a bet and lose. Then borrow some money and pay it back.

KEEP YOUR WORD PUZZLES

An entrepreneur has three candidates for VP of Marketing. She will only hire one. She decides she will give them a fair test. She brings them together in a room and tells them that she will blindfold them and paint a flower on each of their foreheads. Each flower will be either red or white. The blindfold is removed. They are not allowed to talk or use any tricks to figure out what color flower is on their forehead. The first one to figure out what color flower he has will get the job. She says if there are two red flowers then the third flower must be white.

But in fact, she paints a white flower on all three of them. The candidates stare at each other for a time. After a while, one candidate figures out what color flower is on his forehead and tells her. He has the right explanation and gets the job. How did he know?

Solve Audrey Proulx's song/puzzle. She is a former student at Draper University.

TRIMETER ON CONTRACTS

I will keep my word

To say what you'll do is easy
To do what you'll say is hard

To break your word is sleazy
To keep your word is honored

A short cut usually takes longer
The long road is often the best

A contracted bond is stronger
Puts relationship to the test.

I WILL TRY MY BEST TO MAKE REPARATIONS FOR MY DIGRESSIONS.

Mistakes are always forgivable, if one has the courage to admit them.

BRUCE LEE

In this life, when you deny someone an apology,
you will remember it at time you beg forgiveness.

TOBA BETA

If you want to pay me back one day, that's up to you. I'm not asking for it, and I never will. The best way you can pay me back is by becoming the person you want to be.

C.R. STRAHAN

Payback is a bitch, and the bitch is back.

STEPHEN KING

I'm selfish, impatient, and a little insecure. I make mistakes, I'm out of control, and at times hard to handle. But if you can't handle me at my worst, then you sure as hell don't deserve me at my best.

MARILYN MONROE

This is just common sense. When you know you have done some-one wrong, claim it, own it and try to make it right. There is some-thing to believing in karma. I don't know what happens in the next world, but I know what happens here. The truth always comes out. And when it does, it might be embarrassing or it might even force you into facing a punishment, but it feels good when it is all finally out there. The truth will set you free.

THE SIX CALIFORNIAS STORY

When California passed Proposition 30 that allowed the state to go back and tax people more for their income earned the year before, several of my friends decided to leave the state.

My friends said, "We no longer trust the state." And, "If Califor-nia is taxing me for income they already taxed me for, what is next?" And, "How can a state that charges the most income tax, provide the worst services?"

I looked into what was wrong. I found that California was operat-ing as a monopoly provider and had been for nearly 40 years. During that time, the state had dropped from first to 47th in education, had quadrupled the incarcerated population, had gone from first to 50th to become the worst state to do business in, and had created a pension and healthcare system for their union employees that was making the state nearly bankrupt when the amount the state paid for infrastructure had gone from more than 26% of the budget to less than 3% of the budget.

The state was also forcing nonfunded mandates down to the cities and counties, and some of them were going bankrupt. How healthy can a state be if its cities are starting to go bankrupt?

In effect, the state was being incrementally mismanaged, forcing its citizens into having to pay for an ever-expanding number of perks for its government employees, while state services were reaching an all-time low.

If the state were a restaurant or a clothing store, people wouldn't go there, and the company would go out of business, but people love living in California. The weather is beautiful, it is the home to Hollywood, the Central Valley and Silicon Valley. No matter how badly the state is run, it seems the citizens will continue to live here.

On the East Coast, in the geographic space of California, there are 13 states competing with each other for citizens, businesses, capital, entrepreneurs, etc., so those states have to provide good services to retain their citizens, or citizens can move to a nearby state to get better service for their money.

I thought about this problem. In my world, the venture capital world, when we see a monopoly company that is not providing good service and they seem to be able to charge whatever they want, we start a company to compete with that monopoly company. I reasoned, maybe we need a new state to compete with California. I started researching how that might happen, and discovered that Ohio left Pennsylvania in 1858; that Maine, Massachusetts, and Vermont were once one state; and that North Carolina broke from Carolina, and West Virginia broke from Virginia.

I decided to fix California's problem by creating a new entrepreneurial state. I wanted to offer a small group of counties the option to join a new state, called the state of Silicon Valley. My plan was to later offer the other California counties the option to join the new state, forcing California to become accountable and compete to keep its counties.

But in my discussions with various economic and political experts, I determined that it would be unfair to all the other states for Silicon Valley to be able to create a new state when the rest of the Californians could not, and that for only twice the cost, I could allow Californians to dissolve the existing single government and create six new ones in its place.

This arrangement would allow the new states to upgrade, modernize and digitize their services; avoid being mired in historical pork barrel; and compete, cooperate, and become accountable to their citizens. Citizens could change states if they wanted better education or lower taxes or better infrastructure or better healthcare than they were getting in their existing state, while remaining living in the beautiful land we call California. For those who wanted to remain in their existing location, even their state would be forced to improve or risk losing citizens.

I set out to create Six Californias. Our poll results showed that only 15% of California voters were in favor of dissolving the government and creating six new ones in its place. Reasons stated by those who opposed the initiative were that there was a love and attachment to California, much as we hear about attachments to "Mother Russia" or a favorite baseball team. They also had concerns that this would be a two-step process, whereby Californians could vote it in but would have to wait for the US government to make it law. Finally, they had concerns that some of the states would be rich and some would be poor.

The provincial thinking would be hard to overcome, and like any two-step process, we would need to get step one accomplished first. Some of these were valid concerns, but the weirdest response was that some states would be richer and some poorer, because that analysis was based on what those people were experiencing now. In fact, those people in the poorer regions were much more likely to be in favor of the initiative because the current state was clearly not working for them! They were poor now! If they governed themselves, it is likely that they would be richer.

Even though the polling and the chatter were heavily against Six Californias, I decided that anything can happen in politics and it was too important. I had to make this happen, so all I needed to do was to get the initiative on the ballot and the people could become informed and make their own decision as to whether Six Californias was better for them than the existing union-dominated, bloated, monopolistic bureaucracy.

I went about getting signatures. I hired Mike Arno, the same gatherer that I used for the school voucher initiative. And also went out and gathered some signatures myself.

I went to the Costco parking lot in Redwood City to get signatures and after about 20 interactions with people, I had 15 signatures. Then Costco management came out to shoo me off the lot. Never saying die, I even tried to get them to sign, but they would have none of it.

I moved to outside the Century 20 movie theater, where I ran into other problems. One young man said, "This is from that rich guy I heard about who is trying to take money from the poor parts of the state." One woman said, "Are you registered to collect signatures? Do you have the proper permissions?"

I kept thinking that there is no way that any of the six new states would use this archaic system to drive change in their state government. And I guess the people who would no longer have jobs collecting physical signatures and those who would no longer have jobs counting them for the state understood this.

I needed 808,000 signatures. We collected more than 1.2 million. 1.3 million would have been better, but we were certainly over the top. The various counties have signature counters. They count a sample that should be statistically accurate to the whole batch. On this sample count, the counties determined that we statistically only had 750,000;450,000 of our signatures were not valid.

It seemed unlikely to me that so many signatures were invalid, so I made an appointment to visit the signature counters in San Mateo County to see how we could have so few signatures be declared valid. I sat down with the guy in front of his 1980's green-screen computer and he showed me some of the signatures he had called "invalid." I looked at one and said, "What is wrong with this one?"

He said, "The addresses don't match up." I asked, "What if he just moved?" He shrugged. "That's how we do it."

Then I asked, "What about this one, the addresses are the same." He said, "It looks different than this signature on his driver's license." I said, "Those signatures are identical."

To which he responded, "So sue me."

It was clear that the people who make a living counting physical signatures had a vested interest in Six Californias not making it on to the ballot. I believe they understood only too well that there would be no signature counter jobs in any of the new states. Every one of the six new states would have far more efficient ways to manage their democracy.

To the people of California, I apologize. I was unable to successfully make your state better. You will still have to live under the thumb of the high taxes, bad education system, weak infrastructure and overused prisons that the current government administers. But fear not, I am currently involved in creating 3 Californias, where each of the three new states will have roughly the same population and income and the word California in their name.

In addition to this failure, I have had many digressions. I have not always been the best partner to my partners, the best investor to my limited partners, the best venture capitalist to my entrepreneurs, the best son to my mother and father, the best husband to my wife, the best father to my children, the best brother to my sisters, the best friend to my friends, the best boss to my subordinates or the best subordinate to my bosses. But I will keep trying to be and I will continue to make reparations for my digressions.

QUEXERCISES ON REPARATIONS FOR MY DIGRESSIONS

1. What do you have to apologize for?

2. What can you do to try to make it right?

3. What kinds of things can you imagine that you might have to repair when it comes to people you work with?

4. Go around and apologize to people for all the things you have or might have done to upset them. Alcoholics Anonymous recommends this as a part of the path to getting straight, but it is a powerful activity. In reconnecting, you might make some old or new friends.

REPARATIONS PUZZLE

There is a carpenter. He repairs roofs. He knows he can repair 30 roofs per year, but he only gets called to repair roofs after it rains. Rains come only three months out of the year. What can he do to improve his business? What else?

RAP FOR DIGRESSIONS

You fucked up
Time to fess up
Wanted to live it up
But now you've just messed up

The email that you wrote
Broke laws that got your vote
Made you the bad goat
Left on a bad note

The meeting got screwed up
Blew your top up
Wanting to give up
Trying to move up

Now you want to break up
All that you've built up
End this pain shake up
But you have to make up

Take the hand
Of the man
Who wants to ban
your plan

Save your firm
Come to terms
With the worms
Who make you squirm

Bow down low
Take it slow
Stand up take the blow
Take the slow low blow bro so they know

You'll take the heat
Suffer the beat
Give up the seat
Even hit the street

If that's what they need
You'll do the deed

But after they feed
You'll be freed

Free to bail
Free to sail
Free to fail
Free to send another email

THE SUPERHERO CLAUSE

I will accept the lifelong obligation to hone my superhero powers and apply those superhero powers to the good of the universes.

I want to put a ding in the universe.

STEVE JOBS

THE DEATHBALL STORY

I play a game called "Deathball." It is an ideal game for people in their late teens. It is played in a pool with a basketball hoop and a water polo ball. There are no rules (but we do recommend that you wear goggles). I have been bitten, scratched, slapped, dunked, waterboarded, punched, and physically crushed in this game, but there is no better game for understanding people and how they will respond to a greenfield of competition without rules.

It all started with a gift from my reckless friend Frank Creer. The pool basketball hoop arrived in a big box. My sons, Adam and Billy, and I set it up, and since it was a gift from Frank, I thought I would use it in the spirit it was given. We started shooting baskets, and I thought, "Normally, as a father, I set the ground rules whenever we play a new game together. But this time, I will keep quiet." I just let it rip. We started dunking, and defending against the dunk. Then we started dunking each other. Dunking became waterboarding, and within minutes we were floating nearly dead in the water, exhausted and bloody...it was the greatest!

The game evolved from there. We played it with my daughters, Jesse and Eleanor, who both quickly took it to a new level. Jesse had a tendency to bite and scratch, while Eleanor was a great strategist, pinning back my elbows behind my back, rendering me useless, and staying out of the fray to wait for the ball to pop out to her. One day, we had five of Jesse's girlfriends over and two of her guy friends. We played boys vs. girls. The boys scored over and over at will for about half an hour. The girls scratched, bit and blinded us, to no avail. One girl slapped the back of my head every time I scored a basket, so that I almost had a Pavlovian negative response developing. Finally, the girls scored a basket. There was pandemonium. The game ended with a final claw, a bite and a blow to the head. This was the beginning of the "last basket wins" concept for Deathball.

The next day, one of Jesse's friends sent her the following text during school: "I am sitting here in bio class, looking down at the bruise on my wrist, wondering why I am not back in the Drapers' pool playing Deathball."

We had countless Deathball games. It seemed that I had cracked the code for bonding with my teenagers. I would come home from work and hear, "Hi Daddy, want to play Deathball?" We even played at night, where it got a little more dangerous. Sometimes the games would include as many as 10 people.

Jesse decided to organize a Deathball tournament. We had five teams of five people each. It started out as a round robin. The plan was for the two winning teams to compete in the final playoff round. My team had not won a game up to that point, so we were technically out of the tournament. But this was Deathball. There are no rules in Deathball. I got my team together and plotted to go for the win. We all jumped back into the pool, and the madness began. Seeing us go in, the other teams jumped in too so that all 25 of us were in the pool at once. For nearly a half hour, there was pandemonium. Total chaos! No one could score because there were so many teams defending the goal, and someone shouted, "Last basket wins!" One of our players, Jay Gierak, lost a tooth and was sidelined even though he really wanted to stay in the game.

After a quick call to my dentist friend, and with our team now down a player, we came up with a plan. When one of our players got possession of the ball, I would push against the wall with my legs, arms spread wide, and clear a path for him to dive through and score. Our strategy worked, and we claimed victory even though we were already out of the tournament! There were several mutterings of "No fair!" but everyone was so exhausted that the game ended there, and we were given the Deathball trophy for the win. My message to the Startup Hero is this: As long as you have a business, you are in the game. All is never lost. There is always a way. Keep trying. Keep moving. Stay in the game. Be a Startup Hero.

The tournament became an annual event, and after a successful root canal for our injured teammate, we were all ready for the next tournament, which we branded in his honor, "Deathball, The Return of the Tooth." Jay showed his Startup Hero spirit to me at the Deathball arena, and several years later, I backed him and his partner at a new company called Stik, now called Waymark.

We have incorporated Deathball into the Draper University Startup Hero training. We believe the idea of a game with no rules opens people's minds to new ways of thinking and new strategies. Every game brings out new creative ways and means of play. It is mind opening to allow people to see what they are capable of, where they excel and where they draw their own lines.

Deathball, as well as Melonball, Airball, and a number of other dangerous games we play, have taught my children and the Draper University students some unique skills. Mostly, it prepares people for whatever they may face in the world. Not only do they overcome many of their fears, but it also gives people an edge by providing them with the knowledge of what it is like to be an entrepreneur starting a company with no previous notions, no idea how it will play out, and fundamentally, no rules yet. These games are "life and death" simulations. They train people to plan, to be cautious when necessary, and to be ruthless and reckless when the opportunity presents itself. As a Startup Hero, honing your superhero powers includes overcoming your fears and entering unknown universes. Try Deathball or the equivalent, and you will feel those superhero powers developing.

PRACTICE, PRACTICE, PRACTICE, PRACTICE, PRACTICE

In his autobiography, Arnold Schwarzenegger talks about how important practice is (or in his bodybuilding example, how important repetitions are). He explains that he became the best at everything he did by practicing over and over again, whether it be weightlifting, acting, or giving speeches in politics. Practice makes perfect isn't always true, but practice makes you better and extreme practice can make you the best. Practice!

My sister, Polly, is a well-known actress (and director, and writer). I told her I was going to give a 12-minute Ted-X talk. She said, "OK, give the speech to me." I stumbled through it and thought that would be that. But she said, "Do it again." And realizing that she is an actress and used to doing multiple takes, I humored her and did it again, this time a little smoother, and maybe a little more entertaining. And she said, "Again!" like a taskmaster. And again, and again. I couldn't believe she wanted to hear the speech this many times. When she finally let me stop, I had the speech nailed and the timing down to the second. The speech was by no means perfect, but it was far more entertaining and informative than it had been that first time

I delivered it. I knew it so well that I could make the speech at any time and in any venue. To this day, I can wax eloquently on "Competitive Governance: Its History and its Importance in the World Today," whenever the spirit moves me.

Undoubtedly, in your Startup Hero journey, you will need to pitch venture capitalists or customers with aplomb and eloquence. Your superhero powers will have to include public speaking and pitching. So, practice. Practice. Practice. Practice. Practice. Practice. PRACTICE!!!!!!!

Often, entrepreneurs come to me saying, it took 25 venture capitalists but we finally got a term sheet from one. When they tell me this, they don't really understand what happened. What happened was that each time they were turned down it gave them another chance to improve and practice for the next one. They might have been able to cut that number to 5 or 10 if they had done the hard work upfront and practiced. To be a true Startup Hero, you must practice everything. Practice flying. Practice running through the airport. Practice being invisible. Practice staying up late. Practice teleporting. Practice getting to a podium. Practice mind reading. Practice looking your best. Practice yoga. Practice going without food. Practice eating two meals in a row. Practice strengthening your bicep. Practice being alone. Practice being surrounded by people. Practice reading fast. Practice making your product. Practice selling your product. Practice time travel. Practice telling people about your company. Practice working with people. Practice telekinesis. Practice and you will become a superhero. And you will continue to hone your superhero powers for the good of the universes.

QUEXERCISES ON BEING A SUPERHERO

1. How have you honed your superhero powers?

2. What are your current strengths?

3. What other strengths do you need to help you reach your goals?

4. What other strengths would you like to have just for fun?

5. What is keeping you from doing the learning and honing to

obtain and improve those skills?

6. What do you consider to be "the good of the universes"? How will you achieve that good?

7. Give a speech about your business and its expected effect on your industry five times out loud to a friend. Practicing will help you with your elevator pitch and drive it home. It will also make speaking to a group about your business second nature.

SUPERHERO PUZZLE

If Spiderman took Superman's cape and Superman took Spiderman's mask, and Superman had to fight the Green Goblin and Spiderman had to fight Lex Luthor, and Spiderman wanted to join DC and Superman wanted to join Marvel, and Wonder Woman had three bracelets and just two wrists, and the Fantastic Four lost all their powers, what would the color of Superman's red cape?

THE EVANGELISM CLAUSE

I will promote and add to the ongoing success of Draper University, its students, its faculty, its administration and its facilities. I will help prepare the next generation of superheroes.

And he said to them, Go into all the world and proclaim the gospel to the whole creation.

MARK 16:15

As apostles and prophets, we are concerned not only for our children and grandchildren but for yours as well - and for each of God's children.

RUSSELL M. NELSON

THE DRAPER UNIVERSITY STORY

I always wanted to start a school. I had a top-flight education. The places I studied at were exceptional. Hillview Elementary School in Menlo Park, California, was one of the top public schools in the state at that time. Phillips Academy prep school in Andover, Massachusetts, continues to be the top prep school in the country. Stanford University, where I studied electrical engineering, was the top electrical engineering school, and arguably the best college in the country. Harvard Business School in Boston is usually ranked number one or two in the world for a business education. But as I experienced this top-flight education, I always felt that something was missing.

Not only did I not learn anything about starting a business, but I also noticed that all the schools taught in the same way, by rote. As long as I was able to regurgitate everything the teacher taught, I could get an "A" in the class. With a few exceptions, all the classrooms were set up the same way, with the teacher in the front of the class and the students lined up in rows silently listening and taking notes. The grading system encouraged working alone, not making any mistakes, and not asking any stupid questions for fear that the teacher would think us unworthy of an "A." Further, the teachers generally said the same things to their students year in and year out. Many of them were even showing their boredom with the system—passing that boredom on to unwitting students.

When I got my first job at HP, it was nothing like class. In school, I had learned a lot about circuit design, creative writing, Marxian economics (I find it ridiculous that Stanford teaches this course with the reverence it does instead of the scorn it deserves, where the word capitalism doesn't even appear!), partial differential calculus, and human sexuality (Yes, they had a class in Human Sexuality at Stanford). But through all this training, I only worked alone. I had little idea of how it would be to do work in a group. Since HP encouraged teamwork, I was a little lost in my first job.

Fortunately, I had played a lot of sports (I even played football for Stanford under Coach Bill Walsh, who went on to be the head coach for the San Francisco 49ers and led the team to the Super Bowl several times) or I would not have had any concept of the idea of teamwork. Even so, I was not a great team player and an even worse communicator. I think I may have been HP's worst employee. The company kept me there and even tried to promote me when I left to go to business school, but I was terrible. After all, I had been taught to sit and concentrate on academics alone. There was no training for teamwork. I just did tasks put in front of me as though they were term papers or math problem sets, hoping to turn them in to my boss on time to get my "A."

I muddled through that first job and several more. Even when I started Draper Associates, my assistant, Karen, and later my partners had to pull information out of me as though I was a mouth full of impacted teeth. I was possibly the worst teammate ever. I can only imagine what my longtime partner John Fisher thought of me when I pulled all those unusual stunts without ever explaining my reasoning to him. I give him credit for sticking with me, possibly thinking there was a method to my madness.

I realized how important it was for my team to know what was going on, I just didn't know how to get them the information. And I did far too much individual solo work without periodically checking in to see if I was going off on a tangent.

Teamwork and communications are important, and they are not taught in school. In fact, schools teach the opposite. Most schools have big reprimands for talking and collaborating in class. Schools also seem to discourage aberrant behavior. Breaking from the pack is almost always discouraged. Whenever I tried anything new that might disrupt the status quo, my grade would get docked. But in business, I learned how important it is to be bold and willing to break from the pack to make something important happen. A Start-up Hero has to be proactive in work. You can't wait around for the textbook to guide you. After all, a textbook (even this one) has already been written. You will need to design your own course and lead your own path. Educators have missed some glaring needs!

In 2008, the financial market almost collapsed, and people were looking for direction. I was surprised that no one came out to try to improve the situation for the country and the world. Most financial people were burying their heads in the sand hoping it would all blow over. It made me wonder about our educational system and how it discouraged speaking out, working together and taking risks.

I had challenged the education establishment several times with mixed results, politically through initiatives and working on the California State Board of Education, and philanthropically through my work to create BizWorld and through various school boards, but when I decided to build a school, the stars aligned for me.

I had bought a hotel called the Ben Franklin in San Mateo, California, that had been boarded up for eight years. It used to house the Pan Am flight crew who were on layover between flights at San Francisco International airport. I also bought the building across the street that was an antique collective that couldn't pay market rent. I bought them mostly because, after the financial crisis when the government printed money to bail us out, I figured there would be some serious inflation. Also, San Mateo was in the center of Silicon Valley, but it was a little sleepy and possibly undervalued since it had been passed over by the technology world thus far.

After buying the hotel, as a fun exercise, I asked my kids what I should do with it. I could keep it as a hotel, but clearly demand was no longer high there. I could convert it to apartments or a retirement community, but I would much prefer to do something fun and interesting with it. When my son Adam suggested that I should make it a school, it sparked something in me, and all the thoughts I had on the shortcomings of education came flooding into my head. I had to do it. The world needed a new vision for education, and I was compelled to lead by example.

When I decided that this was my chance to change education as we knew it, I realized that I needed to first check with a lawyer to see what was legal. I called a top education lawyer and asked him what I would need to do to start a school. He answered me with a long litany of rules and regulations that pretty much guaranteed that my school would look exactly like every other school in existence. We needed to have a history department, we needed an individual grading system, we needed three full-time tenured faculty, and we would need to be assessed for two years while the accreditation people would look over our shoulder. He mentioned "accreditation" about six times and my eyes started to glaze over. I was starting to believe that my school would be halted before it ever saw the light of day. Then I asked, "What if we don't want to be accredited?" I recalled in the recesses of my mind that my high school, Phillips Academy, was ranked number one in the country, and it was not accredited.

He responded, "Oh, then you don't need to do any of this stuff." Whoa. None of it? What a relief. The plan to build a school was back on.

Just for fun, and maybe a little to defy the status quo, I decided to use the accreditation rules as a checklist of all the things I would do the opposite of when designing the school. Instead of teaching "history," and fawning over the heroes of the past, we would teach "future," and create superheroes of the future. Instead of an individual grading system that catered to the compliant, we would use a team-based approach with team points awarded for exceptional behavior that forced people to build teamwork and communicate with each other. Instead of tenured and sometimes tired professors, we would make it so nobody spoke for more than an hour to our students at Draper University, and those that did speak would be relevant to the times and the best and brightest in their fields. And instead of running a school that is constantly under the thumb of the accreditation monopoly, forcing us to take the safest path, we would get our students to execute sign-away-your-life waivers and try some things that no school with careful supervision would ever try.

To turn the boarded-up hotel into a school required me to issue a change of use with the City of San Mateo. I won't go into all our challenges with the town (you can see some of this in a documentary that Isaac Pingree produced called *"Draper University of Heroes: The Startup"*), but we had to hold four separate events several months apart where the public could voice their ideas and concerns about us starting a school in their town, pay for a traffic analysis for the city, forego some of our hotel's rights to parking, and be the subject of several city council and building commission meetings, some of which went as late as 1 am.

There were so many commissions that they overlapped. At one point, we were told by the fire inspection people that we needed an outdoor stairway exit, and the historic society said we couldn't change the outside of the building. To get it to work, and to be in compliance, I made them sort it out among themselves. The fire inspectors won, so we built the exit.

Eventually, and mostly because we threatened to abandon the hotel and move our operations to Redwood City, California, we got the school approved to be built. We chose a contractor who ended up being a mismatch, and even more friction ensued. The place was still under construction when we started with our pilot class. It took us several school sessions before construction was finally completed, and even then, although I signed off and the city signed off, I wasn't very happy with the outcome. But we had a school.

In any case, we had a building and the necessary approvals. Now we needed to recruit a class. I went out to my friends, contacts and co-workers to spread the word that we would give our first session for free. We got hundreds of applications from which to choose 40 students willing to give up five weeks of their summer to try us out. Then it dawned on me that we were going to have to figure out what the students were going to do. We needed a curriculum. We needed speakers. We needed activities. We needed assignments. In addition to designing group activities and games, and choosing some interesting reading, I went about recruiting the best speakers I could. Some of them came out of the goodness of their hearts. Others, I offered to pay one Bitcoin to speak. At that time, it was funny money, but they came and spoke anyway. We knew we wanted to train Startup Heroes, so everything we did focused on heroism.

I created a diverse board of directors of people who I just loved. Tina Seelig, an author and professor of entrepreneurship at Stanford University; Heidi Roizen, my many-time business partner, and a partner at DFJ; Andy Tang, a venture capitalist who worked with me when we formed Draper Dragon, the network fund in China; and Cree Edwards, my best friend, who I have known since our mothers dropped us in the same playpen.

Cree suggested that I create a pledge, something that could set the tone for the school and build moral fiber into the students who experienced our program. I was so excited about that idea that the pledge seemed to write itself, and I have never felt the need to change one word of it. I created the pledge for superheroes, for Startup Heroes. The pledge would live on to be the inspiration for many businesses, songs, and challenges as well as for this book.

The curriculum would have to be unique, focusing on the whole person, the team, the vision, the future, and the spirit of change and opportunity. I wanted a lot for the students, so the days would be packed. To become Startup Heroes, students would require some serious training, and in some cases, retraining. I wanted the students to strip away their high school hang ups, so we got them to do embarrassing things in front of their classmates. I wanted them to realize that embarrassment (and failure) was not fatal, and they could recover from the wounds. I wanted them to understand business in their hearts, not just as a pile of numbers, so we worked with BizWorld to develop a simulation that would help them understand business and finance viscerally. I wanted them to be inspired, so we put together a stellar group of speakers including Elon Musk, Ron Johnson, and Tony Hsieh.

I wanted them to be challenged intellectually, physically and emotionally, so I gave them 10 books to read on various subjects (two per week); created survival training that would later be led by a team of Navy Seals, Army Rangers, and Special Forces, and made them cold call people with embarrassing things to sell them. We had extraordinary experts in fields come in and speak about what brought them Nobel Prizes, billion-dollar businesses, or leadership positions, and then we challenged the status quo by bringing in speakers that said that experts might be wrong.

We wanted the students to have an end goal, so we had them give a two-minute presentation to a panel of venture capitalists at the end of the program, and we wanted them to be good team players, so we awarded team points for individual accomplishments.

And it worked! The students loved it, and we got a lot of positive feedback. One student said, "I learned more in four weeks at Draper University than I learned in four years at Stanford." Another said, "I never would have worked this hard if it hadn't been for my team. I didn't want to let my team down." And a third said, "I am so much more confident in myself and what I can accomplish in this life."

Today, the school is still growing strong six years running. We have trained nearly 1000 students from 73 different countries. They have started more than 300 companies, some of which I expect to be household names in the next five or ten years. We already have one "unicorn." And while top schools are struggling to find jobs for their graduates, the average Draper University graduate has created three jobs—already!

So please promote and add to the ongoing success of Draper University, and help prepare the next generation of Superheroes. I think we are on to something.

At Draper University, we try to look for alternatives to a standard education. We teach future instead of history, we have a team-based approach rather than individualistic one, and while other schools fall in line with anything that ensures safety, we proudly declare ourselves to be a dangerous school, complete with survival training and open-ended projects and challenges. We believe that students, put to the task, can perform at a much higher level than ever imagined by other schools, and we believe that a student with a purpose can achieve anything in his or her imagination.

Steve Jobs, Larry Ellison, Mark Zuckerberg, Elizabeth Holmes, Michael Dell, and many others dropped out of school to pursue their dreams. And they were enormously successful -- in some cases, in spite of their formal education. At Draper University, we embrace and support people who have the gumption to break from the pack to start businesses that might transform industries. We attempt to give them the tools they need to help them on their way.

I recently told Michael Dell, founder and CEO of Dell Technologies, about the school. He loved the idea and said, "If there was something like this when I was getting started, I might not have dropped out." I replied tongue-in-cheek, "Yes, if you had attended Draper University, you might have been somebody."

To give you a better feel for the school, I thought I would give you my speeches from the first day and commencement day.

Here is my typical welcome address:

Welcome everybody to Draper University!

I started Draper University of Heroes because I believe the world needs more Startup Heroes. You have been chosen to be those Startup Heroes. Becoming a Startup Hero requires you to go through a process. Some of what you do here will make sense to you, some will not. Some you can start to use immediately. Some will come to you 10 years from now when you are in a critical situation. You will be Heroes in Training, or HITS, for the next seven weeks. By the end of this session, if you survive, you will be prepared to be true Startup Heroes.

You will also be creating a startup company. You will ideate, write a business plan and prepare a presentation for a business that you plan to pursue. Whether you are starting a for-profit enterprise, a non-profit enterprise, an ICO, or even if you are going to create a movement or a revolution, you are expected to make your entity profitable and sustainable. No one did the world a favor by losing money or just taking money from weak rich people.

This school is a startup. Bear with us. We don't have many rules here, but here they are:

- Help each other out. President George H.W. Bush, when asked his secret to success replied, "I try to help people."

- Show up. Woody Allen said, "90% of success is just showing up."

- Throw yourself into every project. Always keep the spirits of your team high.

- Make messes here, but then make it cleaner than you found it. Keep the university pristine. Pick up more than your fair share of messes.

- Have some fun here. No one created any billion-dollar company, revolution or movement without a sense of humor and fun. You are here to try stuff whether you are good at it or not. We only care that you try.

You have been chosen to get Startup Hero training because we saw something special in you. An ambition, a passion, a leader. A spark to be ignited. You are a part of a five- or six-member team. You will live and die by your team. We have carefully chosen your teams based on a number of criteria. We want your team to be diverse and challenging, but if properly cared for, your team will work like a fine oiled machine. Work together. Honors will be bestowed on the winning team.

Your team will be awarded Startup Hero points depending on performance. Performance judging is based on trying extraordinary things, win or lose. At the end of the course you will each do a two-minute presentation to a panel of venture capitalists. Hopefully, by that time you will be well on your way to starting your business. Think of your team members as your board of directors. They are all different enough to provide a wide perspective to your business.

You are going to be challenged academically, physically, mentally, emotionally and socially. Some of the tasks we give you will seem impossible. A Startup Hero always looks at how it can happen, not why it won't. Optimism can take you most of the way to success. It is easy to be a pessimist. But pessimists never accomplished anything. Be the most enthusiastic person in the class.

You are responsible for yourself. Take good care of yourself and the facilities here. If you need to, take responsibility for your classmates to help them out.

During the month, we expect you each to ideate, plan and pitch a business vision. You can write on the whiteboard painted walls. This will help you open up your vision and ideas to the rest of the students. Your seats will be these bean bag chairs. The bean bag chairs are here so that you can lean back and listen the way you listened to your mother read to you. We call this room "The Egg Room." It was named so that you can incubate here, but when you want to start breaking out of your shell, raise your hand. No question is too stupid. Stupid questions might even get your team points.

You will hear very little from academics here. You will hear a lot from people who are out there pursuing careers in the fields they speak about. Since they are not professional teachers but from the real world, be tolerant of their quirks, etc.

We have a green room and a sound room. Feel free to use them to create commercials, Kickstarter or Indiegogo videos, or viral videos. I recommend each of you create a video and a theme song. At times, there will be people videotaping. You will get used to having cameras around. Get comfortable with them. They will try to stay out of your way, but still capture the content they need. We hope you will always think of the reputation of the school while you are here.

We also have a number of mentors you will meet. Be nice to them. They can help you. We will also have some entrepreneurial experts living here for various parts of the program.

Familiarize yourself with the town. Startup Heroes need to understand their environment and what resources are available to them. Read through the curriculum and the schedule, so you know what is coming. But beware, we can and do change things up on you all the time. Some by design. Some by mistake.

Bring your cell phone into the elevator. I once got stuck in there with Frank and Martin, and it wasn't pretty. Martin assures me that it has been fixed, but...

This school is immersive. You will have activities during the day and at night. Game nights are a part of the curriculum. You will have open book, team tests. It will be to your advantage to figure out how best to divide the work with your team.

Now let's get to know each other. When called, jump up and:

- Describe your superhero power.
- Tell us either the first or the last item on your bucket list.
- Tweet about yourself. Do a little dance. Sit down.

Here is this week's homework:

- Write down what you plan to be in 10 years, 20 years, 30 years, 40 years.
- Read all 14 books tonight. There will be a test in the morning.
- Memorize the pledge. It is our superhero credo, a very important part of your training here.

We have sorted you into teams like the Sorting Hat does in Harry Potter. Sorting team assignments are final. Live and die by your team.

And here is how we close on Graduation Day:

The world needs more heroes, so we started this school to create Startup Heroes. We wanted to build something different, something extraordinary. We wanted this school to be a beacon for the future, a place where entrepreneurs can hone their superhero powers. We innovated team learning, teaching future, survival training, and overcoming limitations. We encourage resilience and flexibility in mind and body. We truly believe that this is a place where Startup Heroes can be made, where entrepreneurs can be taught, where the impossible becomes real. And there is so much more we need to do. I hope you will help us in our mission.

What a transformation! You had come to this school as good solid citizens with some potential for a good life, and you are leaving as superheroes. Your life will be more challenging, more risk-taking, and more uncertain. I am proud of this class. You have envisioned the future, an amazing future full of new products and services that will make all our lives better. You have learned how to fail and bounce back.

You have survived survival training. You have learned what it is like to live at a heightened, challenging level. You have learned what it means to create your own job, your own world, your own life. Your energy and creativity will create jobs and better lives for the people around you. You know that you can accomplish more, faster than you ever imagined, and that limits are only there to be overcome. Your lives will be full. Your lives will be rewarding. You will know what it feels like to fail and hopefully, what it is to succeed. You will know what it is to live and to try. You can take what you learned here and try to see your dreams come to form.

Before Draper University of Heroes, you may have been satisfied with the status quo. Perfectly fine to get a job, raise a family, live and die without a wrinkle, avoid trouble, fight fires and not make waves. Now, you are the waves! You will run into the fire to save people. You will create jobs for people. You will do the hard work. You will take on the great challenges the world faces, and you will not just find a solution, you will reinvent the problem.

You will be the one. The one who goes first. The one to make the final call. The one to fire the troubling or listless employee. The one to take out the trash. The one to raise the money. The one to make the critical sale. The one to cut his or her salary first. The one who does the hard thing.

You will be the one. The one to take the heat for a problem in the press. The one to find the team you need to build a success. The one to make sure the business is making money. The one to drive the vision. The one people count on to keep the ship on course.

You will be the one. The one to own up to failure. The one to fight for freedom. The one to take care of your family and friends. The one to pay it forward.

Your life will be challenging, but you are not alone. You will have help. Here, at Draper University of Heroes, you have built a lifelong network of Startup Heroes, and our hope is that this network, including those that precede and follow you, will be among the most influential and positive in the world. They have been through this process too. They have faced the challenges. They have been tested, and they have found their inner strength, their inner optimism. They were also put on the earth for a purpose. These Startup Heroes are here and will always be here to help you on your mission.

We have given you many of the tools you need to keep in your utility belt, but you all still will have challenges ahead, concepts to learn, and things you need to try to fulfill your life mission. Accomplish them all with gusto and enthusiasm. You are now a part of this school. Take it with you and spread the word. I expect that now, when you speak, you will inhale air and exhale our values, our understandings and our credo.

Many new markets are available to you where entrenched monopolists have wallowed for years. Technologies like location-specific marketplaces, crowdsourcing, GPS, drones, big data, Bitcoin, blockchain, ICOs, DNA sequencing, CRISPR, solar and other alternative sources of power, and many others will allow you to pursue new markets in the FinTech, EdTech, GovTech, MedTech, TransporTech, and AgTech worlds. Your businesses can take advantage of platforms that people that started those monopolies only dreamed of back then.

The world needs more Startup Heroes, and we just got 60 more of them. I am now proud to introduce the world to a new class of Startup Heroes. This class has been challenged from all sides. They have been pushed past where they thought they had to stop, and realize that they are capable of much more than they imagined. They have learned from the best and the brightest. They have operated as a class, as a team and on their own. They have had to be creative, resourceful, innovative, and risk-taking. They have been battle tested for endurance, energy, speed, agility, flexibility, ingenuity and thinking on their feet. Please understand if they seem a little disoriented as they reconnect with their worlds. They have been transformed. They are now Startup Heroes, and Startup Heroes see things differently.

We have had an exciting seven weeks. There is so much we have accomplished, and yet we have so far to go. This class was extraordinary and very diverse. They are superheroes!

This class has the potential we only dreamed of when we started Draper University of Heroes. Thank you. You make it worth all the effort.

All graduates will receive a crystal, a cape and a mask. You can use your crystal for strength in trying times, and your cape and mask when it is time for action.

You will all be experiencing reentry. It is similar to detox, or jet lag or culture shock. Mostly like culture shock. Power through it. You are now you. You are your raw essence. You are capable of great things. The world will look gray to you. Your job is to color it…and of course to save it, and change it. Save the world. Change the world.

Live long and prosper. With great power comes great responsibility. Enjoy the journey. Up, up, and away.

QUEXERCISES ON EVANGELISM

1. Have you ever evangelized anything? What were your challenges?

2. What resistance did you face?

3. Who were your rivals? How did you deal with them?

4. How did you build spirit for what you were doing?

5. How will you evangelize your startup?

6. Call someone who seems to have an entrepreneurial spirit and connect them with Draper University. We are about 97% successful in transforming students into Startup Heroes, and you will have a hand in giving that person that chance.

EVANGELISM PUZZLE

If you are one of 100 people playing American Eagle, a game where one person starts alone and has to tackle someone as people run past in order to "recruit" more tacklers for the next run across, and each tackler has an $R*(1/200)$ chance of tackling someone as they cross, where R is the number of remaining runners (those who have not been tackled and recruited yet), how many times on average will they have to cross before everyone has been tackled and has been recruited as a tackler? How long before you have recruited a two-thirds majority?

THE BLACK
SWAN CLAUSE

I am bound to this oath unless in my travels I discover that the oath has somehow missed something important and extraordinary.

Nature provides exceptions to every rule.

MARGARET FULLER

A good teacher must know the rules; a good pupil, the exceptions.

MARTIN H. FISCHER

EXCEPTIONS

Some of the greatest opportunities come when the unexpected happens. Most everyone in the world thought that all swans were white, until someone in Australia discovered a black swan. Black swan has become the term for when an entrepreneur changes the landscape in an industry. I want to make sure you are prepared for when the landscape changes for you.

In my house, we don't watch the news. The news promulgates fear. Fear freezes action. A deer in the headlights is frozen out of fear. We don't want to be frozen only to be hit by a car. I recommend learning about the world through audio or text. Better yet, go out and experience it for yourself. Somehow, the visual images you get from watching the news make your subconscious mind want to freeze.

In a typical day's news, you might see stories about a financial crisis, bomb blasts in India, violence in Congo, an earthquake in Pakistan, Syrians protesting a US raid, police discovering a gun near victim's body.... But in a typical day in your life, you might have met with someone special, sold to a customer, seen a baby do something cute, laid a plan for your business, helped someone with an introduction, walked your dog, cooked, and shopped for a gift. Or even given a speech, closed a contract, run through the sprinklers, or traveled to India, Congo, Pakistan, or Syria. Try to focus on your own news. Richard Edelman, founder of the largest PR company in the world, gave me some great advice. He said, "In this new world of social media, companies have to be their own media companies. They have to promote their own news." Don't worry so much about the stuff the media is scaring you with, go out and make some news of your own.

And when you read the news, read with skepticism. Ask questions like, "What is this writer's angle? Is any business or government manipulating this writer, even subtly? Who benefits from this article?" And read multiple periodicals, ideally from different parts of the world. You might see one story that says, "Evil North Korea threatens Guam," where another one says, "Imperial bastards forcing North Korea's hand."

I think you should decide if you want to spread a culture of fear or one of opportunity. I highly recommend opportunity. We focus on opportunity in our house and in our office, in our school and here in this book.

When the markets collapsed in 2008, a prominent venture capitalist sent out a message to their portfolio CEOs to scare the CEOs into cutting back expenses. The message leaked to the press. It created a panic. People froze out of fear. When all the companies cut back, no one pushes forward, and an economy can go into a vicious downward spiral.

What we told our CEOs was different and more individualistic. I said, "You are entrepreneurs. You have vision. You can make something out of nothing. This panic is one of the greatest opportunities ever. The game has just changed. Change your business. Make it work in the new environment." To some of our CEOs that meant to use this as an excuse to go make the changes you have always wanted to make in your business. Fire the people who have been holding your company back. To some it meant to cut the team back to those who are absolutely mission critical. And to others it meant that now is the time to spend the money to build the business and gain market share while others freeze.

I was on the board at a company called Glam Media (renamed Mode Media). It was a fashion blog. It was making some progress, but the board determined that the company was spending too fast and the progress was slow. The board asked CEO Samir Arora to cut the company's expenses. Recognizing that by cutting expenses Samir would have to change his business model, he went to work imagining a new model. He came up with a black swan--the concept of selling ads across multiple blogs. The new model was brilliant. It helped him develop what became the first ad network. Glam went on to reach $100 million in revenues. Years later, the business closed its doors, but that is another story.

From the various Draper funds I have been associated with, we have been able to back many such black swans. Hotmail was a black swan. It came from nowhere. No one knew it could exist. Bitcoin is a black swan. The Internet itself is a black swan. Twitch.TV is a black swan. So is the Tesla.

Black swans happen. They rock our worlds. They transform industries and ultimately, they transform society. Be prepared to have to adjust, to innovate when you see a black swan.

QUEXERCISES ON BLACK SWANS

1. Have you ever seen a black swan? Did you know they existed?

2. Make a list of innovations that came from people pursuing something unrelated.

3. Is your business prepared to adjust to all the black swan technologies that could enter your business?

4. Are there any technologies or market shifts you could imagine that would make your business vulnerable or even eclipsed?

5. Are you alert to any possible black swans that can help your startup race to the front of the industry?

6. Find a rule that people hold dear. Find an exception to that rule and bring it up in conversation.

SWAN PUZZLE

You have four swans in a bag. One is black. You pull one out and before you can see its color, it flies away. What is the likelihood that the next swan you pull out is white?

THE STARTUP HERO'S WORKBOOK

Book Two is written to help you challenge yourself to build a business. All missions become businesses. I define a business as any endeavor that requires money coming in and has money going out. If you are going to produce a product or a service, it will have to be set up as a business. If you are an artist, you will need to look at your work as a business. If you are a revolutionary, you will need to run your revolution as a business. If you plan to run for President, you will have to build a campaign business. In any case, where there is money coming in and money going out, there is a business. A church, a charity, a rock band, a library, a cartel, a union, a gang, a repair shop, a police force, a bookstore, and a consultant are all businesses. They all have money coming in and money going out.

Now that you have the pledge as your guide, it is important to spend effort planning your business for success. Unlike other books, this is not a step-by-step guide. You can get those anywhere. Book Two challenges you to think bigger, plan better, and work smarter to become a successful Startup Hero.

This book covers the thought process you can go through to make sure you are heading in the right direction, gives advice to avoid some of the problems students and entrepreneurs I have supported have encountered, and makes suggestions for industries that you may want to transform and rethink in case you don't have a business idea to start with.

You will have to think about your plan. Your plan should encompass everything you hope to do and how you hope to do it. No matter what your mission, you will want to write a startup business plan.

BEFORE YOU WRITE YOUR BUSINESS PLAN

Still want to be a Startup Hero? OK, before you go out and start your own Apple or Tesla, and before you start writing a business plan or put a presentation together, I recommend that you do some deep research and thinking. First, you need to make sure the problem you are solving is big enough to matter to you for a long time. Next, you need to brainstorm and come up with an idea for a business. Then, you need to test the idea.

BIG PROBLEM

Introduce a problem you are trying to solve. It needs to be a big problem. Ideally, a global one that many people or businesses want to solve. Some examples might be freedom, convenience, world hunger, bureaucracy, security, cancer, heart disease, education, energy, space travel, communications, waste, transportation, the environment, climate change, human needs, world peace, etc. Make sure the problem you are going after is big enough for you to dedicate your life to. Some of the greatest people in history focused all their attention on one thing, one vision, one mission.

Then think about how the problem you intend to work on is being solved today. Is the industry dominated by just a few oligopolistic entities? Are the entities that dominate the industry providing poor service for the money? Are they getting lazy and bureaucratic? Is there a new technology that has the potential to successfully break into that industry? Will it provide a 10x improvement over what is offered to customers now?

Now think about your edge. Make sure you have an edge before you start up your startup. Are you ideally suited to solve this problem? Have you seen the problem firsthand? Do you feel that your previous employer was missing what the customer really wanted? Have you witnessed or designed some new technology that will make an industry completely transform? Is there some new technology you are aware of that you can use to change this industry?

If the answers to these questions are yes to your satisfaction, you are ready to brainstorm or hack out your idea.

BRAINSTORMING/HACKING

Brainstorming is an art. Some people can just storm their own brains, but most people need sounding boards to really brainstorm.. This mode of brainstorming is called ideation and assumes you are doing it with a group.

Start with a whiteboard, a blackboard, or a video screen that everyone can see. Then, lay out the problem you have identified and ask for suggestions. Use "yes and" instead of "no but," and write every idea on the board.

Now throw a monkey wrench into the works, like the product has to incorporate a Frisbee or a doghouse in some way. At Draper University, we created the Hero-A-Thon, a three-day, no holds barred event, where students had to ideate, design and build a product. To throw a twist into the competition, we told each team they had to in some way incorporate a plunger into their business. All the teams generated unique and interesting products. One group built an organic hydroponic planter out of a plunger. Another group used plungers to identify parking spots.

One of the best brainstorming techniques we ever had happened when Tina Seelig came to teach at Draper University. Tina is a Draper University board member and She who pioneered the DFJ Thought Leaders program, where entrepreneurs come to Stanford to speak to students who are there studying entrepreneurship. She is a bundle of gusto and enthusiasm. She started her class by challenging our student teams. She said, "Come up with your best idea for a restaurant." The teams came back with moderately interesting ideas for restaurants like fusion food with sports on TV and Tex-Mex with mariachis. Then she said, "Teams, now think of the worst possible idea for a restaurant." They did. And there were some doozies.

Then Tina had teams swap and take the bad ideas from other teams and create new ideas with the bad idea as a base. Remarkably, after this exercise, the ideas that the teams came back with were wild and crazy, but in some cases, really interesting, even fundable. They were ideas like restaurants completely run by robots, blind tastings, grow your own seafood, and chef swaps. None of these ideas would have come up by just thinking of what might be a "good idea" for a restaurant, but forcing a wrench into the machine helped students to free their minds to really innovate.

Another brainstorming technique that you can deploy is to apply something new to a product or service that has never had it applied to before. Put together two normally unassociated things and make something new from the two of them. If you put together a refrigerator with an oven, you might come up with a robotic storage and cooking device. Put together a wallet and a cell phone and you might figure out how to eliminate paper or plastic money. Applied to businesses, you might come up with Uber for plumbers or Facebook for circus hands.

When you storm your brain, always think not only of improving what is out there but also reimagine the whole experience from fundamentals. We have washing machines, and dryers, and ironing boards, and folders, and stackers and closets, but what we really want is a system for replacing dirty clothes with clean, dried, pressed and stacked clothes.

Build and spread your ideas. Having an idea can be intimidating and difficult at first, since it can be embarrassing if the idea doesn't make sense to people, but it gets easier, and you will get better at it as you train yourself to innovate. Keep thinking about how you could make something better or how you can put two unassociated things together to form some sort of new or improved product or service. Eventually, as you go through your normal routines, you will find that you will begin to reinvent everything around you. Keep your eyes open for new ideas to pursue, and tell the world about them— your ideas will improve as more people hear about them and you will get more ideas as you talk about them. Note that ideas are only valuable when they spread.

Joon Yun is a brilliant doctor turned investor for Palo Alto Investors. He has a string of patents a mile long from all the medical inventions he has created. (One line of patents covers the opposite use for any given drug, like using blood pressure raising medicine, so that resistance builds up and it lowers blood pressure.) But he noticed that since he has little time to pursue them, his inventions sit dormant. He did something extraordinary. He offered a $2 million longevity challenge to anyone who could hack the genetic code for aging. He figured that if there is an aging gene, someone could hack it and we wouldn't have to age. But he went further. He got the National Academy of Medicine involved, and then he said, "To set an example for the scientific community, since this is more important than any individual's effort, I am donating all my patents around longevity." He (and the rest of us) will probably live longer, healthier lives as a result of this generous display. If other scientists decide to follow suit and we get an open source outflowing of scientific ideas and collaboration, science could go through the same explosion that we have had in entrepreneurship in Silicon Valley, and human progress will again be accelerated.

Look for industries to improve: healthcare, entertainment, real estate, insurance, fashion and banking. Look for new technologies to improve them with: the shared economy, social media, programmable stem cells, CRISPR, microsatellites, virtual reality, Bitcoin, solar economies, self-driving cars, electronic clothes, bioelectronics, robot brains, prosthetic limbs, Pokémon derivatives, offline massively open online courses (MOOCs), enterprise software, and multivariable authenticators. Put them together to approach or even invent new technology industries. Your imagination is unlimited. Use it.

BUSINESS IDEAS

Here are some ideas to get you started. This is a list for those of you who want to do something but can't yet think of an idea that is big enough or exciting enough to warrant dedicating your life to. See if any of these seem interesting to you, and then improvise or add to them and come up with some of your own. Then enter your business plan into our Startup Hero Plan competition. Information is available at www.draper.vc.

- Reimagine the kitchen. Make the refrigerator and cabinet into a sorter that drops food into a cutter that then creates weight ratios, times its drops and cooks it. Or, make a dishwasher that is in a deep sink and you place the plates, etc. on racks in the deep sink and it drops down into a turbulent vat to wash everything.

- Reimagine the hotel. To limit the real estate required and the number of bathrooms needed for a hotel, design multiple "tombs" of beds that people can sleep in that move to connect to a bathroom when the guest needs one. Or to clean up after use, design the building so that the carpets move on a conveyor that vacuums them on the underside.

- Reimagine education. Create VR studios with programmed learning. Students play in large indestructible rooms with various materials, toys, etc. for project-based, team-based training.

- K-12 team-based learning. Students get graded on the strength of their team. Imagine what those tiger moms would do if the As were only given out to teams rather than just individuals. They would train the whole team!

- Reimagine washing, drying and pressing clothes. Users could drop their clothes into a vat. The vat could wash them, and then they could be dropped down into another vat to be dried. After that, they could be identified (pants, shirts, socks, skirts, etc.) and pressed and folded.

- Create a fast food paleo restaurant. Serve only meat, vegetables, potatoes and some fruit. Could be a fast food restaurant where you put meat and veggies inside of a bell pepper and serve.

- Reimagine government. This is wide open. Blockchain redistribution of tax dollars. Networked, Bitcoin accounting on use of funds. Liquid democracy with organic constituencies. A lot of opportunities for technology in government and in replacing government functions.

- Reimagine credit. Currency that is only for "thank yous." Pay it forward currencies.

- Reimagine large item retail. Point and click at products, which are then assembled and directly delivered to your home.

- Reimagine airplanes. Open the entire plane from the side., have people get in the plane through their row, then close entire side of plane. Or rethink the entire model. Make it shaped like a flying saucer or a beach ball.

- Design and build some part of an Ironman suit. My son Adam is determined to fund companies that will get us all using suits that do all the things that Ironman can do in his movies. Everything from thrusters to exoskeleton to artificial assistants to a virtual cursor can be achieved with enough engineering and determination.

- Reimagine borders with virtual governments. Design a business that builds its own virtual government.

- Reimagine war. Totally virtual. Allow leaders to "play" at war, and determine real outcomes with virtual battles.

- Reimagine space. Launch vehicles with electromagnetism rather than rocket fuel.

- Reimagine electricity distribution. Build power through a peer-to-peer grid. Make it decentralized, so we can all buy power from our neighbors without having to deal with the Public Utility Commission (PUC) or the utilities that control the existing grid.

- Reimagine energy. Think about building a new source of energy from waves, people or some other source. Tap into it from anywhere through the air and virtually.

- Reimagine the cosmos. Maybe it is all energy. Maybe it is all spiritual. Maybe it is alive.

- Reimagine religion. What should religion look like in the next century?

- Reimagine medicine. How do you make medicine personal and data driven? Use multiple data sources in the cloud. Imagine drugless, patient-driven medicine in the cloud.

- Reimagine decision making. How can you use artificial intelligence (AI) for targeted marketing, for identifying trends, to program robots, to replace people in repetitive and hazardous jobs?

- Reimagine funerals. How can you better dispose of dead bodies and allow families and friends to remember their loved ones? A Costco for incineration and VR experience for memories.

- Reimagine stock buying. Buy products online then decide whether the experience was good enough to warrant buying stock in the company that created the experience. Just click on a button that says Buy My Stock, and in addition to buying the product, you buy the stock. Additionally, etailers could award stock to customers instead of coupons. This can now be possible with the new Title III of the JOBS act, which allows individual investors to invest in private companies with some limitations.

- Reimagine retail. What will shopping look like? Will products on display be virtual? Will it be more experiential and less targeted shopping? Will people just point at items, click and have them delivered or 3D printed to their house?

- Reimagine boating with an electric boat that runs off energy from the ocean.

- Imagine new uses for Bitcoin or blockchain. You can now raise money for a token through an ICO. Dig in and decide if your vision includes a new token or coin.

- Create a trading platform for private stocks.

- Build out a networked accounting service.

- Do anything that improves or replaces government services.

- Design software that allows the use of big data for healthcare.

- Figure out a better way to educate people.

- Reimagine space travel. How can we get to another planet?

- Reimagine insurance, real estate, concerts or eyeglasses. Go to basic principles. Why does insurance exist? How would a virtual concert work? Should eyeglasses or contacts also be programmable for an augmented reality experience and for zoom and focus?

Use awareness of your surroundings to brainstorm new ideas for potentially heroic startups. Here is an example that is a little yucky, but it makes the point.

I went to the bathroom and only saw blood in the toilet. I went to my friend and internist Dr. Stewart Weisman to get checked out. He asked if I had taken any antibiotics in the past few weeks. I told him I had. He then went on to tell me all about the intestines. He said, "Think of your intestines as a newly mown lawn. Clear and consistent all the way through. Then think of an antibiotic as an herbicide, killing off areas of lawn. Next, think about weeds that grow back in the places where the lawn has been killed." Then he told me, "That is what is going on in your gut and why you are bleeding."

He went on to explain that some people's "lawns" are so totally destroyed by antibiotics that they have to be replanted with what amounts to a "poop transplant." The doctor places new poop in a patient's intestine and the bacteria adjust and "replants" the lawn. He gave an example of a thin woman who decided she would use her overweight daughter's poop for the transplant. The weird thing was that the woman got a clean new lawn, but she also became overweight like her daughter.

I surmised that the bacteria in our intestines is communicating with the rest of our body, telling it how to grow and adapt. Our brains, our hearts, and our limbs may all be affected by instructions from the bacteria in our intestines. I think there may be a whole new biological branch of study that can happen by studying poop and the effects it can have on the body if implanted correctly.

Apparently, my idea was spot on--if not a little late, because there is a whole new field of science being created around bacteria and the effect it has on people's metabolisms and overall health. It got me thinking that Earth might just be a small bacterium in the stomach of some greater celestial body. But that might be a discussion better suited for my sci-fi novel....Watch for it.

Joon Yun is also interested in the idea of transplants as it relates to human longevity. Joon put together a longevity conference, where scientists were talking about fetal cell transplants, and how young stem cells are more effective than older ones. I took that concept and came up with the idea that instead of implanting fetal cells in people, doctors could just implant baby poop to reinvigorate the intestine, which may change the metabolism of the whole body.

Another example of using one's surroundings to come up with a breakthrough came when I was outside watching as bees flew happily into a bee trap. The trap was full of pheromones that would attract the bees into the yellow tube but once they checked in, as the Eagles say in their song Hotel California, "they can never leave."

Around that time, I heard that cancer has "parent cells" that pro-create and drive cancer growth. I thought, "Why couldn't we develop the equivalent pheromones for cancer to attract the cancerous cells out of the body?"

Most cancer treatment is done trying to eradicate the cancer by cutting it out of the body or poisoning it (and the host) with che-motherapy. But what if we could lure cancer out of the body with tempting things like sugar and cancer pheromones?

It is not hard to start thinking this way. You just need not to worry about if it will make you look silly for thinking differently or it will upset the status quo. Only think, "Is it possible that my idea could provide a better way?"

There are so many ideas all around you. Use them. Apply them to a global problem. Make them your own and share them with others. Anytime you see a problem, see if you can come up with a creative solution to that problem that no one has thought about before. Have fun with it. Brainstorming is awesome!

After the initial brainstorm, start paring down ideas and ranking them. This exercise is useful more to hone in on the top few ideas, so you don't get bogged down with random thoughts, but instead focus on those that you might want to pursue. Hold on to the top few and the worst one. The key is to then focus on the best and the worst and see if you can fuse them somehow. I find that putting together seemingly incongruous items often leads to breakthroughs. And you will need breakthroughs if you want to become a Startup Hero.

Note: Throughout history, some of the greatest ideas imagined were so outrageous that no one had ever thought of them before, so there were no guiding regulations around them. Keep in mind, if your industry has a rule book, you might be too late, because if there are rules already posed for you, then someone else got there first and you will always be fighting an uphill battle to keep up with them. Alternatively, if you are really thinking out there, you will be working in open space.

Once the brainstorming process is exhausted, and you think you have a unique, if not crazy, idea for a business, you can start running tests. I have created three tests that I find helpful in evaluating a business: the grandmother test, the 16-year-old test and the fifteen-year test.

THREE TESTS

The Grandmother Test. Once you have the idea, explain it to your grandmother, or someone over 65 years old who cares about you. What happens with the grandmother test is that grandmothers use their wisdom and their love in responding to your idea. They force you to be able to pitch your business in layman's terms. They force you to hone your thinking so that it can be simply explained in a sentence or two. And they tell you if they think you are off your rocker.

This simple concise response will bode well for you when you are running your business because you will have to explain what the business is and describe your business to all types of people in a variety of settings, whether they be in social settings, in elevators, in business conferences, etc. You will have to describe what you do to employees, suppliers and customers. Make the explanation simple and easy to spread. Once you have fully explained the concept and convinced your grandmother that you are on to something, or that you are indeed crazy, you can move on to...

The 16-Year-Old Test (ideal for consumer services). The earliest adopters of many future consumer products tend to be 16 year olds. This may be because 16 year olds are generally challenging the status quo, and they are willing experimenters who are newly exploring their social environment. They will test products in multiple ways regardless of what the instructions say and try to find interesting uses for them, whether intended by the producer or not. Many of the winning consumer businesses are the companies that appeal to 16 year olds, who also tend to love communicating, and can be impatient and cliquey. These young consumers may only be interested in what you are doing if they get the message quickly and easily, and they will likely become users if the rest of their clique is using the product too.

Several well-known companies succeeded by creating early success with 16 year olds. When he announced the first Macintosh computer, Steve Jobs targeted high school students, giving them deep discounts on the revolutionary computers. Facebook started with only students in top colleges, but it didn't really take off until it was opened up to high schoolers. Snapchat was the way high schoolers could share photos and ideas that would disappear after a few seconds, so they wouldn't be held accountable for anything they said or did on the app. All of these companies hit a teenage nerve, and became or may well become multihundred-billion-dollar businesses.

High schoolers set trends that become generational industries if they are properly groomed and cared for. Once you have high schoolers on board, you will need to pass this final test...

The Fifteen-Year Test. Another test is to think about what the world will look like in fifteen years. The best entrepreneurs look at their idea and ask, "Will this be around in 15 years?" If they do not believe that their business will be around in 15 years, they rethink it. Why? Because it takes 15 years to build an overnight success.

Here is what might happen on the path to success:

- Year one: Company gets started. You find a place to work, a co-founder or two, and you start to design your business. You write a plan and get angel funding.

- Year two: You ship your first product. You give it away for free to get people actually trying your product.

- Year three: You face problems, and you rethink your strategy. You pivot, study customer behavior, do surveys, and rewrite the plan.

- Year four: You finally find the product/market fit. You raise a larger round of funding, your "Series A," and you begin to see a small amount of revenue coming in.

- Year five: The media sees your vision and the press coverage makes you famous. You are careful not to believe your own press. Companies are usually overhyped before they become over-successful.

- Year six: You expand the business to exploit the product/market fit. You finally start getting more cash from customers than investors.

- Year seven: You are profitable and growing. You have a business. Your options for the business start to open up. Time and cash consumption are no longer your enemies.

- Year eight: You discover how to go beyond the early adopter customers. Another pivot to take you mainstream. Your early customers are no longer your primary focus. Now your customer base is widespread, and you need to standardize.

- Year nine: You challenge the incumbents. Now you are affecting your competitors. They are quietly seething while your business begins to take real market share and enormous mindshare from the status quo of your industry.

- Year ten: Incumbents fight back with a legal battle, press attacks, and pushes for government regulations. This process takes over your life for quite a while. If you can hold steady through this period, your vision will be unfurled. Don't panic. Lawsuits take forever to be resolved, and the press attacks can be countered and incorporated into your marketing strategy. Avoid fear. Keep your gusto and enthusiasm for the business. Your employees are watching.

- Year eleven: You broaden the market to include the customers you dreamed about reaching when you started the business. You might have been weakened but you are not defeated. Time to put the accelerator down and fly.

- Year twelve: You grow and start reaching those customers. You raise a private equity round.

- Year thirteen: You grow more. You become tradeable, possibly through a public offering.

- Year fourteen: You continue to grow. You have now reached the market position you set out to reach.

- Year fifteen: Your vision is unfurled. The world knows about you. You are the new overnight success. You become the new status quo, and fifty new startups are now gunning for you.

- After year fifteen, your business will likely flatten out as all industries do when they get big. Your product line will go from being innovative to being a commodity that will suffer pricing pressure. If you have designed your business well, your company will become a cash cow where customers are so loyal to you that they will never want to leave, but your growth rate will almost certainly slow.

Will your business be around in 15 years? What will it look like? Will your competitors be better positioned than you are at that time?

Here is a chart of a typical industry that gets to be $1 billion in value over 15-20 years.

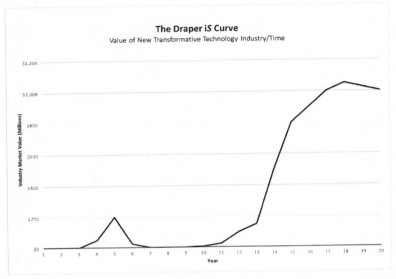

I branded this curve the "Draper iS curve." It reads like a cursive lowercase "i" followed by an italic capital "S." It depicts the value of a new transformative technology industry over time. Notice that the media discovers the industry in year 5, when the industry value goes up and peaks before falling when the media is disappointed that the industry doesn't appeal to the layman yet. But if your industry has real staying power, the true vision is unfurled around year 15, showing real growth before flattening out in later years as the industry matures.

A lot will happen in 15 years. What will the world look like then? Think about what you think might happen and make some projections. Here are some of mine.

There will be over eight billion people on the planet, most of the young ones will be in Africa. The UNDP shows that the expectations are that in 50 years, the population of the world will grow from 7 billion to 11 billion, and Africa will grow from 1 billion to 4 billion in that time. The people of the world will almost certainly be freer. Social media has forced some bad governments to fall and I expect the best ones to rise. In fact, Singapore has grown from a population of 3.5 million to 5.5 million in the last decade, while Sudan, Turkey and Syria continue to lose people. I expect that kind of "government marketplace" to continue forcing governments to be freer, more efficient and more growth oriented.

More of the world population will be able to innovate. More than half of the people in the world today have access to smartphones, and as a result, all of them have access to search engines and media content that educates them and keeps them on top of the state-of-the-art in the field they pursue. The global economy will grow significantly. Every new innovation adds to the wealth of a society, and with all the innovation that comes from a world of people who are educated and up to date on new innovations, our world should grow substantially. The people of the world will have access to global information, global governance, global currency and global markets. They will be mobile and less tied to any single geographic region.

And now for my wilder predictions: People will be traveling in autonomous vehicles and communicating through virtual (or augmented) reality. They will be living very long lives, while cures for cancer and the aging gene are discovered. Their health will be monitored by sensors designed into their clothes, which will be optically programmable to the owner's tastes to match what is required for any occasion. Education will be a competitive, accountable industry, where teachers are regularly ranked with the best becoming enormous media celebrities and the worst no longer teaching. Most trade will be done in Bitcoin and recorded on the blockchain. A computer that fits in a contact lens will be more intelligent than a human, and advice to the user will be displayed in the lens while audio is sent to a wireless earpiece. All actions of all people will be recorded. Crime may be treated differently, where juries are crowd-based and criminals pay their debt to society by working rather than society paying to care for criminals who sit in prison cells. Energy will cost a fraction of what it does now. Robots will be delivering everything to your door, from food to prescriptions to sundries. Travel to any part of the world will take a matter of minutes. Some of us may be on our way to Mars.

So think about your business. What happens to your business in this new world? Does your business even exist anymore? How will it evolve? How does your business stack up against the other businesses of the world with my projections as a backdrop? What will your competitors look like then? And when your business grows large, how will your competitors and those companies that make up the status quo today respond? When you start taking business away from the companies that don't adapt to the new world, and they discover you, how will they respond to your business?

Ask yourself as many questions as you can and do some deep research as you project what the world will look like in 15 years. At that point, is there going to be room for your business in the industry, or will your business (and you) be long gone and on to other pursuits? Answer these questions. Do this work. After all, you are preparing to dedicate your life to this endeavor. You might as well build yourself a clear path first.

MAKING WAVES

It is also useful to think about how new technologies come in waves and transform industries. Some technological waves have come through and disrupted industries with new ways of thinking, providing customers with better, faster, cheaper and more productive ways of living their lives and working in their businesses.

The Internet, marketplace, Bitcoin and AI are examples of some of these technological waves, which it turn have transformed industries and some of the companies associated with them.

Industries transformed by the Internet:

Information (Google), Shopping (Amazon), Communications (Skype), Entertainment (Netflix), Media (iTunes), Gaming (Minecraft), Community (Facebook)

Industries transformed by the marketplace:

Transportation (Uber), Hotels (Airbnb), Startups (AngelList), Workforce (Thumbtack), Lawyers (LawTrades), PR (PRx), Brokerage (Robinhood), Interior Decorating (Laurel and Wolf), Stock Market (Equidate, EquityZen), Cap Tables (eShares, Capshare), Gaming (Twitch)

Industries transformed by Bitcoin:

Currencies (Bitcoin), Government (Tezos), Contracts (Ethereum), Banking (Ripple), Real Estate (BenBen), Insurance (Augur), Finance (Bancor)

Industries transformed by AI:

Automotive (Cruise Automation), Identity (Neurala)

In addition to the industries and transformations listed above, VR/AR promise to challenge education, drones will likely challenge surveillance, and Tesla will challenge utilities

UNDERSTANDING TRENDS

It can also be a good exercise to study trends in and around your industry. Trends are different from being "trendy." While trendy people wear their clothes, facial hair or jewelry the way celebrities do, trends are industry, customer or technological movements that have been moving in one direction for a while and look to continue. Some trends are "exponential," which means that the changes compound over time. Here are some charts that might give you a feel for trends in various industries.

Moore's Law

Moore's Law states that $1000 of computing power doubles every 18 months. This trend has continued since the invention of the transistor, and some would say since the beginning of time.

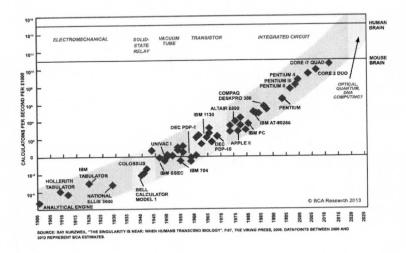

SOURCE: RAY KURZWEIL, "THE SINGULARITY IS NEAR: WHEN HUMANS TRANSCEND BIOLOGY", P.67, *THE VIKING PRESS*, 2006. DATAPOINTS BETWEEN 2000 AND 2012 REPRESENT BCA ESTIMATES.

Suicide Rate

Here is a graph of the suicide rate since 1993. This is interesting. What happened in 1998 to reverse this downward trend in suicides? What do you think the cause might have been? The ADHD drug Adderall was approved for attention deficit disorder by the FDA in 1996 and started to be used as a study aid to help students focus. I wonder if the two are related.

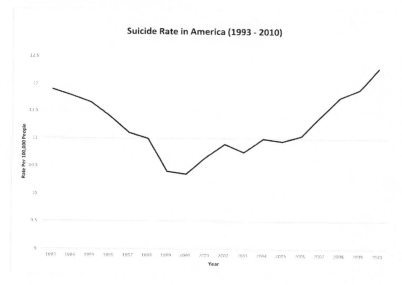

Suicide Rate in America (1993 - 2010)

Bitcoin Price

Here is a chart of Bitcoin market value and the number of Bitcoin wallets. What does it tell you? Is the price of Bitcoin related to the square of the number of wallets? Could this be an example of Metcalfe's Law (see below for an explanation of Metcalfe's Law)?

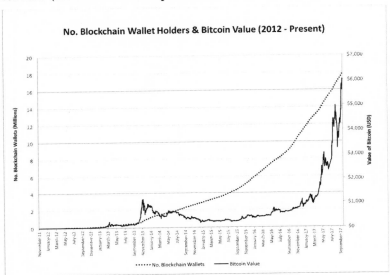

No. Blockchain Wallet Holders & Bitcoin Value (2012 - Present)

Life Expectancy

People continue to live longer lives. If the trend continues, what will the people of Earth look like in 100 years? What happens to the population? Its size? Its makeup?

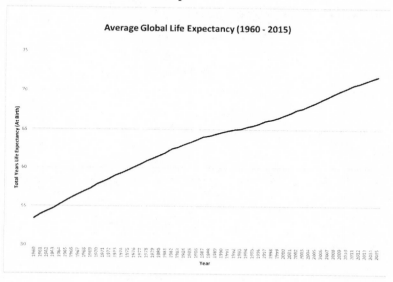

Trends matter. Try to read trends. Go find charts on your own industry. What has happened to the price per unit in your industry? At what rate is the market increasing? What changes have happened in the market shares of the leading companies in your industry?

EVALUATING YOUR BUSINESS IDEA

The world is changing. Entrepreneurship is everywhere. People from all walks of life are seeing that they can create a company to solve a problem that they see in the world. For you as an entrepreneur, this is both good and bad.

The good is that now the process for you to start a business is getting standardized and simpler. It is simple to get incorporated on LegalZoom or Clerky, get legal advice on LawTrades, and apply to Draper University or an accelerator like Boost.vc, Y Combinator or TechStars. It is simple to list your company on AngelList or Crowdfunder and attract people to invest angel money with you. It is easy to list products on ProductHunt, Kickstarter or Indiegogo to see if there are customers interested in what you are doing. Legal terms are getting standardized and easy to research, terms like "SAFE" (Standard Agreement of Future Equity--innovated by Y Combinator) notes, "KISS" (innovated by 500 Startups) and our favorite with Draper Associates, "Series Seed" (with our addition of "TATS [Tradeable Automated Term Sheet]," which you can find at www.lawtrades.com). Shares can be easily managed with products from eShares. Bankers, lawyers, accountants, headhunters, and other consultants are more willing to take a risk on getting a startup on its feet. ICOs or token offerings are starting to be a seed funding alternative, where companies can issue a coin to raise money.

The bad news is that when you come up with a good idea, you can bet that fifty other people are coming up with the same good idea, or they already have. Those other people also have easy access to training, acceleration, funding and advising from experts. And they may already be in business. Maybe they are in Silicon Valley, or maybe in Israel, China, Korea or London. The world has opened up for entrepreneurship and people are going to start businesses that are like yours. What is a Startup Hero to do? Here is what I recommend:

1. Search. Do a Google, Bing or Baidu search (or all three) on your business idea. It will reveal what you are up against. You may see many direct competitors. Maybe you will see some companies that you might be able to work with. Maybe you will find some companies that could be your first customers. It is typical that this search will show that you already have many competitors before you even get started. So how will you differentiate your company from all those other companies? Keep ideating and telling people about your business until your idea evolves and has the potential to eclipse all those companies you found in the search.

2. Pivot. Yes, pivot right now. Immediately. If there are going to be fifty companies doing what you are doing, then let them. Let them succeed. Envision what the world looks like after they succeed. Then determine what customers will need AFTER those companies achieve their visions.

3. Abstract. If you pivot with this in mind, by adding that one more layer of abstraction to your business, you will likely have a better outcome. It seems counterintuitive to say that a business should abstract itself away from today's marketplace, but that is exactly what I am recommending. A more abstract business takes what is out there today and anticipates or even "guesses" what will happen in the future. Seeing Uber's success, you might think of a delivery business, but there are many of them already out there, so you can abstract from there and think of a drone delivery business or an autonomous car delivery business. You might think that those abstract businesses would have a lower chance of success. They do! But I want you to think about success as a Startup Hero. A Startup Hero transforms the world, disrupts the status quo and looks for opportunities that others might think are crazy. The odds of success may be lower, but your expected value is greater if you are a Startup Hero.

Using probability, let's say you enter a startup business that already has fifty competitors. Let's assume you are not too early and not too late, and there will be another forty-nine startups that come after you. And they are all absolutely right about the direction of the market. You have a 1 in 100 chance of being the winner in this industry, and you have absolute certainty of being right. You will only have a 1% chance of winning, but you will be "right."

Now, let's assume you pivot and try to predict the future of what people will want after these companies capture the initial market you are after. They will have educated the market and the consumer will have chosen the winner, so the market may be better defined and larger than when you started. To win in this new market, you will have to guess what the consumer will want next. Your abstract guess will have uncertainty. Let's assume that you have a 1 in 4 chance of an accurate prediction. When you do a search on your abstract, pivoted idea, you discover that there is only one other company thinking about the industry in your new way, and you have to assume there will be at least one more in your timeframe. So now, you have a 1 in 3 chance of being the winner in this more uncertain market, but your business only has a 1 in 4 chance of capturing the consumer. If you put those two together, you have a 1 in 12 chance of winning the market. That is about eight times higher than the 1% of chance of winning with your original idea. Just by being willing to have a good chance of being "wrong," having a willingness to fail, you have a better chance at being a winning Startup Hero.

Yes, it is true that you are much more likely to be ridiculed because you are reaching too far into the future, and people will not understand you. And you will likely be wrong. But overall, your expected outcome is eight times greater if you "abstract" your business and pivot.

Now that you have "ideated" or "hacked" or "brainstormed" your business, it is time to create your business plan. A business plan can be written up in any form: a PowerPoint deck, a Word document, written longhand, even in the form of a pictogram. But if you want funding, your plan must include some in-depth thinking and research. In any case, it is important that you, as Van Wilder says, "write that down."

A STARTUP HERO'S BUSINESS PLAN

Every business plan is different. Write your own. Don't try to copy one that has already been written. And if you use a business plan template, use it to force yourself to think about each issue, but don't let it guide your thinking on what is important to your business. Your business is different. It is being invented on the fly. It is evolving. Know that your business will evolve. It will take on many forms. Make sure your business and the business model (how you will make money) is as innovative as your product, your technology and your service. Business planning should be a creative exercise. Let's think about some innovative business plans:

The business plan for Price Club started with the words, "Americans have garages." The company figured out that Americans could keep more stuff in their garages than they needed immediately on hand, so it made sense to sell them products in bulk. And by doing so, Price Club used Americans' garages as their own warehouses, saving a fortune in storage space. They also figured out that if people became "members," and paid for the privilege, the members would be less likely to steal. Naturally, thieves don't like to pay for things, so thieves didn't become members, and Price Club ended up saving 7% on "spoilage" that its major competitors like Walmart and Target still struggle with.

Amazon's business plan was highly disruptive, overthrowing the status quo. Amazon created the world's biggest bookstore by just listing all the books they could find and allowing customers to place orders before Amazon had the book in stock. Amazon would take the order and the money upfront and then later deliver the book. This model did amazing things for Amazon's cash flow. Cash would come in first, and Amazon's payments would come due later, which was just the opposite of how it works in a "brick and mortar" bookstore. A brick and mortar bookstore pays for books in advance, then stores them on shelves waiting for customers to buy them. And these customers often pay late, creating further cash flow issues. By building a business where the customer pays cash first, and the company pays for the book later, Amazon held no inventory, had no accounts receivable, bad debts, or spoilage.

Hotmail's business plan changed after implementing viral marketing, where people sign up by simply clicking on a link that persisted with every email sent. After we worked out the ability to have our customers become our sales force, Hotmail needed no budget for marketing at all. And since the company saved money on marketing, it was able to spend that extra money on building a better, more scalable product.

By building a communications and logistics platform for suppliers, Uber became the largest cab company in the world without having to buy a single cab, and Airbnb became the largest hotel chain without owning any housing. These business plans directly connected the customer and the service provider and the platforms were paid in advance for "brokering" the most efficient and appropriate connection.

Laurel and Wolf's business plan is to build a platform to allow customers to shop for interior decorators online and for interior decorators to be able to show off their skills and compete for the customers. What was unique about Laurel and Wolf's business model was it was able to work with the furniture suppliers to get a commission on all the furniture ordered on the platform.

Write your own business plan. If it is a good one, it will have no peer and it can be the basis to transform an industry.

Note that a business plan should not be a thesis or a novel, but it should be comprehensive. A good business plan is both a sales document for the outside world and a guide for you to help run your company.

A HERO'S STARTUP PLAN

Below is a list of the things that should be included in your business plan.

The company vision – a statement of what the world will look like when your idea becomes reality. A good vision might be "to make data ubiquitous" or "to bring better housing to the masses."

The company mission – show how your company will be a force for good. A good mission might be "we make better cars" or "we make travel easy" or "our furniture is light and indestructible."

The problem – lay out the problem that you see and why it matters to people. You might say, "fast food is unhealthy" or "we need cleaner energy."

The solution – what is your business going to do? Here you lay out your business. This is your "elevator pitch." A good elevator pitch is no more than three sentences and it gives people the gist of what your business will provide.

The market – figure out how big the market is that you are pursuing. This will help you show the potential of your business to venture capitalists and bankers, and it will also help you understand whether the business you are pursuing is large enough to warrant spending your life building it. You can determine the size the market by doing a "top down" assessment or a "bottoms up" assessment, ideally do both.

To calculate a top down market estimate, you try to determine how large the market you are going after is today, and how it will grow (or shrink) over the next 15 years as you grow your business. To find this number, you can search public and private market data to find out the relevant revenues of all the companies that participate in your market and determine the total.

To calculate a bottoms up market estimate, you simply determine how many people can possibly buy your product or service each year and multiply that number by how much you plan to charge for the product or service each year. You might have to break out this assessment into smaller market segments to get to a closer approximation of the figure representing the actual market you plan to reach. Also, be sure to comment on what you expect the market to do once your product or service is a part of the mix. Will your product be cheaper and thereby shrink the market, or will your product be additive and grow the market you are approaching?

How it works – tell how the product or service works. Don't hold back. Tell it all. Often engineers try to describe what their business does without letting out any of their trade secrets. This paranoia (warranted or not) sets a relationship of distrust in motion that almost never works, and in selling your product or your business, it is not effective. You need to get comfortable with the fact that you are the best and most knowledgeable in your business and even if someone knew everything you were planning to do, they would never be able to do it as well as you could. Open up in your business plan. Show the world what you are doing. Trust is an important part of business and by trusting people, you encourage them to live up to that trust. And for the most part, they will.

How you will build it – who are the people and what is the process involved in building your product or service. Do you have multiple suppliers? Having multiple suppliers gives your customers assurance that you will always have a steady supply and allows you to negotiate stronger contracts since there are more than one of them and they will compete for your business. Are you reliant on any one supplier? How will you adapt if that supplier goes out of business or becomes too difficult to deal with? Do you have any concerns with the construction of your product? What technologies must work to make your product or service successful? What risks are involved? What might not work the first time? What will you do to mitigate the risk or respond quickly to early failure?

No buttons – In building the first iPod, Steve Jobs said, "one button." He wanted the iPod to be so easy to use that a customer could find, choose and hear their music with one button. He apparently kept sending engineers away with a wave as they kept coming to him with solutions that required multiple buttons. He finally got what he wanted, a music player that had one button with a touch ring around the button, and the iPod was made.

Now, when you design your product or service, you can think, "no buttons." There is so much information about people available now that products can anticipate needs of their customers. Uber is a one button experience, but I can imagine a time when Uber is hooked into my calendar and, knowing that I have to be at Hero City at 3 pm, an Uber arrives at 2:20 pm to pick me up from Buck's Restaurant in Woodside to make what it calculates is a 40-minute drive. Figure out how your business can anticipate the needs of your customer. No buttons.

How you will market it – how do you get your customers to become your greatest sales force. The best businesses delight their customers so much that their customers become, in effect, their sales force. I know I am always more likely to buy something if a friend tells me how great it is. How do you delight your customers? How do you keep your customers? This is perhaps the most important part of business planning. Marketing can be the largest expense item for most companies, and if you can figure out how to get your customers to sell for you, you could significantly reduce this expense. Some of the best companies in the world have made their product a part of common language. How do you get your customers to use your company name as a verb, like "Skype me," or "Google it"?

Who is on your team – who is working with you and why are they relevant to the business. Do their bios match the companies needs and their job description? How will you motivate your employees? Think hard about your team. How will you train them? How will you pay them? How will you motivate them?

And finally:

How you will make money – this seems like the simplest part of a business on the outset, but making money requires some of the most innovative thinking and creative executing. Here are some of the questions you will have to struggle with.

How much does it cost for you to provide the product or service to the customer? Sometimes this can be difficult to answer. The first Teslas off the production line cost the company more than $1 million each, but the factory was built to be able to make so many cars that the costs would soon go well below the purchase price. You will need to think through the long-term and short-term costs as well as the variable and fixed costs. Variable costs are usually tied to the specific product, the cost of the wiper blades or the battery, for example. Fixed costs are constant whatever the quantity of goods or services are produced, like the costs of the robots that paint the cars or the salaries of the people who run the business.

How much will you charge for the product or service?

Will the pricing be dynamic or rigid? Will you charge a different rate at different times of the day, like movie theaters charge a discount for matinees, or will you charge a rigid price like $2 per soda? Is the pricing part of your overall marketing strategy? Steve Jobs transformed the music industry by fixing the price of a song at 99 cents. Before that, pricing was variable. Some songs were more, some were less. On the other hand, most enterprise software companies price to the value they believe they are providing to their customers. In fact, certain software companies and consultants like Anderson Consulting and Deloitte will charge different prices for the same software for its use in different industries. Some startups use something called "flinch pricing." That is when you keep adding costs and features until your customer flinches. You will have to figure out which pricing model works best for your product or service.

Are there multiple revenue streams? Can you get paid for advertising AND circulation as most media companies are? If you are a marketplace company, can you get money from both buyer and seller? Many investment bankers get money from both the buyer and the seller of the transaction.

How about loyalty? Will your customers continue to pay forever? Is the product mission critical for them to succeed? In other words, once your product is embedded in your customer's business, how difficult would it be for them to remove it. Once a house has cable TV embedded in it, people are reluctant to have it ripped out of their wall, no matter how much the cable company charges them every month. Or do you have to continue to find new customers? A used car salesman makes the one sale and knows it is unlikely for that customer to return to his lot for a long time, so his incentive is to just make as much as he can on each customer. What is the churn? How often do you lose customers? How painful is it? Another number to try to estimate is your CAC, or cost to add a new customer. Often startups are judged by how low its CAC is against how high its LTV, the lifetime value of a customer, is.

How will the cash flow? Who will pay you and when? When will you have to pay and to whom? Customers who pay in advance can make your company enormously successful, while customers who pay late can cripple you.

One example of cash flow business modeling comes from my interaction with Pebble. I met Eric Migicovsky at an early Y Combinator event. A tall lanky European, Eric distinguished himself as being the only presenter who dared to create a hardware company. Venture capitalists at the time were wary of hardware companies because those companies had to buy inventory in order to sell products and that required a lot of cash. But I backed him because I saw something heroic, earnest, determined and visionary in him. He was going to build a smart watch company, which he eventually called Pebble.

It was an inauspicious beginning. Almost immediately after I invested in Pebble, Eric tried to build up his inventory and he ran out of cash. But then, like a Hail Mary pass in the last seconds of a football game, he tried something outrageous. He put a video together for a Kickstarter campaign (one of the first), and within three weeks, he had $10 million in pre-orders. He got the cash up front. In those three weeks, he went from near bankruptcy to a darling of the industry and he had cash with which he could build the inventory and ship the watches. The company sold over two million watches, reaching over $100 million in sales. But then, the company got so big, it seemed to forget where it came from. Instead of sticking with selling over the Internet to people who would pay for their watches in advance, Pebble had an opportunity to sell its watches through retailers. Retailers would give Pebble the opportunity to sell many more watches, but Pebble would have to build up the inventory of watches before the retailers would carry the watch. And retailers notoriously pay late. Pebble started selling the watches through these retailers and ran into a cash crunch. The company became insolvent and was forced into a fire sale. This is the story of cash timing in business planning. At what point your startup's cash comes in to the business is often more important than how much the startup gets for each product.

THE PERFECT FINANCIAL BUSINESS MODEL: ZERO ASSETS AND ZERO EXPENSES

If a financial expert evaluates a Startup Hero's business model, he is often befuddled. After all, Startup Heroes break the mold. A financial expert is used to the status quo, and if you have planned your business well, your business will not fit with the status quo. You must be comfortable with changing the nature of your industry. Accountants, advisors, consultants, bankers and government workers will try to make sense of your business, but if the model doesn't fit, they will advise you to change your model to fit the rest of the businesses in your industry. DON'T DO THIS! Resist the temptation to go along with the experts. If you are doing it right, your business will not fit, and you will have to get comfortable with that discomfort.

Most businesses have a standard balance sheet. Under assets, they have accounts receivable (money people owe the business), inventory (stuff in the warehouse or on the display floor), a physical plant, and some cash in the bank.

Amazon's business had no assets. It didn't hold any books in inventory, and it was paid right up front. There was no brick and mortar facility required to keep an inventory of books, and yet it became the largest bookstore in the world.

Uber has no cars, Airbnb holds no real estate, Thumbtack does not own plumbing tools or paintbrushes in bringing handymen to your house, and my daughter Eleanor's company, Bulletin, owns no real estate or artisan work, but it sells both through its platform.

Most businesses have a standard income statement. For expenses, they have cost of goods sold, research and development expenses, marketing and sales expenses, and general and administration expenses.

Microsoft initially had zero cost of goods sold. It was simply software (bits of information) that was installed in systems. Hotmail, Skype and now many other companies have zero marketing expenses because they use viral marketing. eBay had zero sales expenses. In fact, its entire product line was user generated. Parametric Technology operated on a 3% research and development budget when their competitors were operating at 19%, leaving Parametric 16% of revenue to out-market its competition.

Put some zeroes in your financial statements and you might just need more zeroes when describing the value of your extraordinary business!

Bottom line: do some real business model thinking about how you can turn a business or even an industry upside down by making some lines of your financial statements zero, and you can potentially transform an industry.

Once you have put together your startup plan, think about how you will grow and finance your Startup Hero mission.

GROWING YOUR STARTUP

Startups are hard, but the journey is worth it. It's important to keep in mind that behind all successes are countless failures. Work on something that you can see yourself doing for the next 10 or more years and don't underestimate the benefits working with a strong co-founder can bring to your business. Whether you succeed or not, know that you are moving progress forward with every step you take, and know that you must make sure your own company is healthy before trying to save the world. First, get your own house in order.

As an entrepreneur, don't try to get there too fast. Companies grow in fits and starts. Sometimes they are seasonal, sometimes they grow and then plateau, and sometimes they grow and shrink until a new product is launched and they can grow again. Most semiconductor businesses design a chip, build some samples, and then have to get the chips designed into other companies' products who then ship end products. Those customers are likely to continue to use the chips since the semiconductor is built into their product, so the semiconductor company doesn't really take off for years, but once their products are embedded in the customers, they live on for a long time. At some point, the customer demand will flatten out as technology moves forward. The semiconductor company will need to do new designs to keep growing, so their revenues are often cyclical.

Many companies that I have backed have run into similar pitfalls. By some measures, they were tremendous successes, but when they got to be a certain size, they tripped. Sometimes it was from losing control of their businesses, sometimes it was from not watching their cash flow and sometimes it was from hiring too many people too fast.

Some founders see the money from early success in the marketplace (or worse just in fundraising) and they extrapolate to hiring more employees to grow faster. Some use the term "ramp up" when they are only talking about how many people they have hired, and not how much revenue or earnings they have achieved. This employee expansion can be a huge mistake! Only hire when you absolutely have to. This is especially important early on while you are developing your product or service. Only after your company has created a repeatable, predictable product/market fit does it make sense to hire a lot of people.

Companies are like plants. They have a natural organic rate of growth, and if they get the right amount of fertilizer, they grow a little faster, but if they get too much, they die. Entrepreneurs who get too much venture capital money too soon often spend it, and build up an expense burden that is unsustainable.

Money can be wasted in startups at the very beginning. The best startups raise as much money as they can and spend it only when they have to. This frugality is particularly important while the product is being developed. Many companies overhire and overspend during the development phase, not realizing that the best products and services were created by teams of two or three great engineers. When the CEO overhires, all those extra employees can become a time suck as well as a money drain on the company, and they often slow down the progress of the development.

Successful companies often lose the controls that made them successful. Often at a critical point, usually when the company passes 150 employees, but sometimes much sooner, the business gets past the stage where the CEO knows everyone and then even past the point where the CEO does all the hiring. At that point, the CEO loses his intuitive grasp on the company. He often delegates hiring decisions and the team starts growing too fast. It becomes too easy to hire more people, so the company gets too big too fast, and by the time some CEOs discover that they are overweight, it is too late. Hiring can happen in a day or two, but layoffs always come too late and cost companies months of pay. What all companies need to know is when they get beyond 20 employees, they need to put in serious controls.

A strong CFO who will keep your company apprised in real time about the short-term and long-term effects of hiring can be an invaluable resource. Being able to anticipate a downturn in the business, being adroit at collecting receivables, and understanding the ramifications of cash flow timing will serve as mission critical for companies as they move past this vulnerable growth stage. People cost money. Make sure you hire organically.

A few rules of thumb here might help you continue to run your company like a Startup Hero. A company should spend as little money as possible creating the product and getting it evaluated by its first three customers. A company should not build up a marketing team before it has identified a product/market fit with at least three customers. And hire a CFO, but not before the company is generating revenue from at least three customers.

Startup Heroes need to prioritize their time, which is sometimes tricky to do because heroes want to do it all. But being in a startup requires focus. Startups should always qualify their leads, whether they are raising money or selling product. Much time is wasted on unqualified leads. A Startup Hero should do his or her homework to understand who he or she is about to sell to, and should decide ahead of time which customers or investors are their top priorities. In general, smaller customers and investors should be approached first. They typically decide faster, and give the entrepreneur practice before approaching larger, more complicated customers who can be slower to decide.

Once the company finds a few customers and it is satisfied with the product, and the product/market fit is a lock, the Startup Hero may start spending money on marketing. When the product hits the market, a Startup Hero needs to push hard and get in front of as many customers as possible as fast as possible, so the competition doesn't have time to catch up. Once customers are excited about the product, it is time to throw gas on the fire. While the company always needs to remain frugal and not over hire, the company should put some real marketing money behind its business when it has its first open market window.

FINANCING YOUR STARTUP

A venture capitalist looks for three things in evaluating a startup: technology, market, and you.

The technology must be unique so that you can have an edge over your competition, justify premium pricing and allow your company to wedge into an existing market. The market must be large with incumbents who are vulnerable, and your business model must be able to show that you can generate enough cash soon enough so that the return will be good for the investor if all goes as planned. And you need to be awesome. You need to know your customer and your competition well. You need to know everything about your technology. You need to be on top of your business model, you need to be open to new ways of thinking, and you need to be enthusiastic and optimistic about your business.

A note about venture capitalists. They make their money by generating profits for their investors. Their main source of income is a "carried interest" that only gets large if they take big risks on companies they invest in. They are willing to lose a few of their investments as long as their winners become extraordinarily large. They do that by pushing potentially great companies through their investment committees and finding a few companies that will provide outsized returns for their investors. venture capitalists know only too well that many, in fact most, startups don't succeed, so venture capitalists have to count on the few that do succeed to become very large so they can make many times their money from investments in the successful companies.

Here is an example that might make the motivation clearer. A venture capital firm might raise $100 million in a "blind pool," which means that its investors are not allowed to be involved in the decision making. That $100 million might be invested across 20 companies at $5 million each. If 12 of those companies go out of business and six more are just able to return the invested money, the venture capitalist's returns are all contingent on the success of the top two investments. A venture capital fund is usually a 10-year fund, so to receive a market return, investors are hoping to double or triple their money over that period of time. The last two companies have to bring something like $250 million into the partnership for the fund to be successful, which means that each of them must turn the invested $5 million into $125 million or 25 times its investment.

The venture capitalist is looking for a true Startup Hero, one that has a 10% chance of returning 25 times on the money. He or she will be looking at you to evaluate whether you have the guts and skills to accomplish this unlikely heroic outcome.

Since venture capitalists have this incentive structure, most of the time they are on the side of the Startup Hero. But there are times when the interests of the venture capitalist diverge with the interests of the Startup Hero. The venture capitalist might encourage some reckless behavior that might have long odds at success, but they want to see if they can make the company huge even if the likely outcome is terrible. The Startup Hero occasionally needs to push back on these suggestions out of self-preservation, since the likely outcome of some of the more reckless activities are total disaster.

But the true Startup Hero is willing to take on some of those reckless activities to see if they can make them successful, knowing that the huge success outcome outweighs the likely failure by many times.

Once a company has cleared all the market size and unique technology hurdles, a venture capitalist relies on the focus, enthusiasm and tenacity of the founding team. The one mitigating factor for a setback, no matter how significant, is a strong team that has the ability to navigate past it. As a venture capitalist, I look for a depth of understanding, but also drive and perseverance. In a market that changes as rapidly and unexpectedly as the technology market, founders have to be creative and flexible too.

MARKETING YOUR STARTUP

Marketing a hero's startup is an art form. Every startup will experiment before they find a winning formula for marketing. Here are some things to consider when you think about your marketing plan.

PR

Richard Edelman, the founder and CEO of Edelman, the largest PR firm in the world, told me that with the new world of social media, companies will have to become their own media company.

Take his advice. Become your own media company. Do what you are doing, but build your base organically and through crossover interests to topical issues, like writing a blog about how a certain presidential candidate's victory would have an effect on Bitcoin prices, or one about how schools will better perform with VR.

You should get to know all the writers that write about your industry. If they have written once, they will tend to continue to cover your industry. Understand what they need. They are always on deadline and always looking for new stories to write. Always stay positive. Always get back to them as soon as you can. Always give them a quote. And when you can, create a story for them.

To create a story they want to write, make people think without being incendiary. Stick your neck out for issues that you think are controversial, but you know you are on the right side of them, for example, "Why do we trust fiat currency now?" or "Who needs a teacher when you have VR?"

Be a continued source of stories. "I bought it on eBay" was the best example of this. The press kept writing stories every time someone sold something interesting on eBay. Stories went out about everything from Pez dispensers to nuclear power plants to houses to cars and eBay kept the stories coming.

I remember when I was running the school voucher initiative, an education writer pulled me aside and said, "We can't really write you a balanced piece because we need the stream of stories that we get from teachers' unions, and they are clearly opposed to what you are doing. We know that while your story is a good one, the coverage will end after the election, whereas the teachers' union will keep giving us stories after the election as long as we play ball." While this was horrifying to hear, it helped me think about PR and how a business should continue to have stories to provide to its writers, not just a single "launch" announcement.

Always take the positive side for the press, even when talking about your competition. Ideally, I think it is better to never mention your competition, unless it is a specific marketing strategy like "Coke vs. Pepsi" or "Box replaces SharePoint." Coke and Pepsi realized that by performing the taste tests on TV, they could each double the effect of their own advertising, since both company's products would be featured in every ad that BOTH of them ran. Box's strategy was to take down a dinosaur. Many of its target customers were on Share-Point already, so Box decided that mentioning the competition was worth it, knowing that Box would size up well in a head-to-head battle.

I have gotten some great advice on how to talk to the press from my former marketing communications manager, Barry Hutchison. He sent me to a press trainer and together they worked me over. Here are some of the things I learned from them and from the various interviews I have experienced. If you are interviewing for TV, go check yourself in the mirror before you go in front of the camera. Your look of confidence and happiness is more important than what you say. Speak in complete (and short) sentences. A good rule of thumb is that your sentences should end when you run out of breath. For radio or podcasts, remember that the listeners can't see you, so you can read notes while you talk. Ideally, with both radio and TV, you will need to keep your energy level high. It has helped me to do a few jumping jacks before going on air and when I am on, I try to sit upright in my chair and never get too comfortable.

While TV is all about how you look, and on radio about how eloquent you are, when you are going to be quoted in print, you should take a different approach. When talking to writers, you must be clear, but you also need to take the writer through your entire thinking. The writer is looking for a slant on the story, and how positive or negative that is will be purely dependent on how you are able to get the writer to empathize with you. It is also good to make suggestions to the press, like "Would you like me to send you a table of the data?" or "Would you like a picture of our logo?" These additions might help you market your business no matter what the story says about you. Some great marketers I know write the entire article that they want to see put in print, and the reporters often just make a few edits and print it.

Watch what you say on your way out the door. You might think your interview is over, but the reporter is still a reporter, and the microphone is probably still on, and whatever you say may be put in the story. This happened to me when, after giving a formal interview, I got up, walked the reporter to the door and then mentioned a fund I was considering raising. The fund became the headline, and because in our business we are not allowed to use general solicitation, it created problems for us.

Many reporters now take video and audio of their interviews. Beware that they can use these in any way they want when they tell their story. My father was working for the US Export-Import Bank, and the famous interview show 60 Minutes offered to interview him about how he was handling some specific loans that had gone out. At the time, there was some speculation that 60 Minutes would sometimes take a "yes" answer given on video and replace it with a different time when the interviewee said "no." My father suspected that the story they would tell would not show the US Export-Import Bank in its finest light, so his response to the offer was, "Yes, we are happy to do the interview, but we will also be videotaping the interview." Hearing this, 60 Minutes cancelled the interview. Dad dodged a bullet.

PR can be air cover for fund raising and direct sales. Investors and customers all read. You can think of PR as one way you can do pre-sales. Make sure that when you get on air to say your company name, what your company does, and how customers can reach you. If you don't, you may have lost a major opportunity.

Finally, make sure to mention your company name, what your company does, and how customers can reach when talking to the media in any format. If you don't, you may have lost a major sales opportunity.

OTHER MARKETING TIPS

Use the latest technology to market your product or service. You want to be identified with winners, new platforms and what is hot. It is far better to have built your business on a new platform like Instagram rather than on one that is weak or even obsolete like Friendster.

Also, the marketing tools available now are much better than any tools created five years ago, so use those. A marketing edge in technology can make all the difference to a startup going after an established market. Get everyone you know to be your proponents on social media. Retweeters and Facebook friends are incredibly valuable to most startup missions. Since it will generally be difficult to get a lot of media attention when you are just getting started, your friends can help you spread your message.

Measure everything in marketing. Marketing is an art, but the best marketers are scientists too. You should try to measure the effects of each of your marketing efforts to determine what worked and what didn't. You should know how many customer leads you got from your Facebook ads, how many came from your viral campaign, how many came from the blog post you wrote, how many came from the billboard you rented, everything. And then you should know the quality of those leads. You might find that the best marketing you do is totally counterintuitive.

Many entrepreneurs I have backed thought they would get most of their leads from their big original equipment manufacturer (OEM) or resale partner, but they found that it was hard to get the big OEM or resale partner to do anything for them, while their Facebook ads were generating an ongoing flow of customers they could serve. And don't just measure, act! When you see something working in marketing, double down on it. Don't wait around for more results. You have a limited amount of marketing resources, so put them to their highest and best use.

Compose a theme song. Taylor Swift had 1.4 million likes on one Instagram photo. A song that sticks in people's heads can be super powerful and can drive customers to you.

Write a book. After you have written a book, and get it out there, you will be the natural expert that the press will refer to and promote. If you don't have time to write a book, start a blog and become the expert.

Speak in public. Public speaking on a subject can be a powerful way to move customers to your way of thinking. When you speak in public, you have the attendees' full attention for the time you are speaking. Make the most of it. Promote yourself and your business. Guide the audience toward doing what you want them to do, and always have an "ask." If you don't ask, you won't get what you are looking for, but if you do, you might.

VIRAL MARKETING

Viral marketing is an art form. When I came up with the idea of viral marketing as a way to spread web-based email organically from customer to customer, I realized that the technique could be applied to any company, and any industry. The concept is that if you have something of value to provide, a customer is willing to spread the message if it is easy, frictionless and if he or she benefits in some way. In the case of Hotmail, customers had the incentive to get other people to communicate with them through the web, so they were more than happy to spread the word, and promote the company.

The Viral Top 10:

Here are the 10 most important things you will need to have a successful viral marketing campaign for your company:

1. A value proposition. You have to have something the customer will want to use, even buy.

2. An implied endorsement. People who use the product must be willing to tell others about it, or at least be neutral enough to allow the message to proliferate.

3. Minimal effort for the user. The word has to spread without the user having to do anything they wouldn't normally do.

4. A "cool" product or service. It helps if the product has some sizzle to it. Sizzle comes with controversy. Be comfortable with that, and let the word spread.

5. A clear message. The product should be simple, intuitive, and natural to use.

6. Computer inoculation. The customer's computer must not be susceptible to error after using the product. Even the threat of a problem can kill the demand for your product.

7. Network vaccine. The network cannot suffer delays resulting from the product.

8. No contact. The product should be able to spread without contact.

9. Fractal spread. A viral marketing product spreads like a fractal. The product reaches a new community and spreads throughout that community, and then that community makes contact with (or creates a bridge to) a new community where it then spreads through that community. You should try to see how to accelerate both the product's spread inside a community and from community to community.

10. Complete freedom of movement. A virus is cured (or spoiled) if it is limited or controlled by an external source. You want the virus to live!

See if you can turn your customers into your sales force. See if you can get your customers to say your company's name when they discuss your product or service. The friends and family incentives that you may have seen on TV encourage customers to sell their friends and family on a service in exchange for payment or free service. Tupperware actually forced its customers to be its sales force. People could only get Tupperware products if they became sales reps for the product. As sales reps, they were encouraged to throw Tupperware parties to better sell the product. There are many other recent examples of customers becoming the sales force of companies. Every time you take a photo and put it up on Instagram or Facebook or Snapchat, you are spreading their service to your followers. Every time you write a tweet, you are spreading the use of Twitter. Kik and Tango are two services that allow people to get free video calls, but any call that is made on those platforms adds a new customer to Kik or Tango. If you provide these companies with your contacts, their user base spreads, but you can more easily reach your friends.

These viral marketing approaches induce "network effects." One of the greatest network effects is described through Bitcoin. Bitcoin is nothing if no one uses it or values it (as is true with any currency), but as more people adopt Bitcoin as a way of transmitting funds, the more people recognize its value and its value rises.

Metcalfe's Law states that the value of a communications network is proportional to the square of the number of connected users of the system (n^2). The value increases exponentially according to the number of nodes in the network.

METCALFE'S LAW

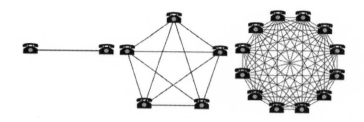

THE MATH WORKS THIS WAY:

The value of the network (relationships) = sum of all numerals from 1 to N-1, where N is the number of nodes.

THE SIMPLIFIED EQUATION LOOKS LIKE THIS:

If R is relationships, and N is the number of nodes, let's make X = N-1 to simplify the equation. It becomes: $R=(X^2+X)/2$

Metcalfe is mathematically correct. If we define the number of relationships as how much value a network has, that value increases with the square of the number of nodes.

A network compounds in value as it grows. With a network of 1, you have no relationships. With 2, you have 1 relationship. With 3, you have three relationships. With 4, you have 6 relationships. With 5, you have 10 relationships. And so on. See the table below:

Nodes	Relationships
1	0
2	1
3	3
4	6
5	10
6	15
7	21
8	28
9	36
10	45

Every additional node (or person) that joins a network adds the number of nodes minus one to the value of the network. The second person adds only one relationship, but the 1000th person adds 999 relationships.

Here is an interesting thought experiment. Apply Metcalfe's Law to Bitcoin. If Bitcoin price is at $5000 today with 15 million people in the network, what will be the price of Bitcoin be when it has 150 million people in the network?

What is interesting about viral marketing is that each time a person is added, that person brings on their own network of people, so viral marketing accelerates the penetration of a market so that the network effects can grow the number of relationships quicker and hence grow the value of the entity. As more people are added in a viral marketing scenario, there becomes an overlap, and each additional person is marginally less valuable, so as we approach the population limit, they are only adding themselves (and the relationships they can connect to) to the value of the network.

In an infinite population where one new customer has 10 friends and they each have 10 friends and none of them overlap, the customer acquisition process can be accelerated immensely.

Let's say a company alone, without viral marketing, takes one week to add 10 new customers, while with viral marketing the customers themselves reach 10 new customers each week, and they spread from there. You would have:

	Week 1	Week 2	Week 3	Week 4	Week 5
Company Alone	10	20	30	40	50
With Viral Marketing	10	100	1000	10,000	100,000

So viral marketing saves you time, and it might just lead to the success of your company.

But the process doesn't continue indefinitely, because of course, there is overlap. Some of my friends and family might intersect with your friends and family. And as the number of users grow to approach the total number of customers you are trying to reach, viral marketing becomes less effective.

Here is the table that assumes every user adds 10 people with a total population of 100 (numbers rounded):

Customer #	Network	Likely Overlap	Network Add	Customers Acquired
1	10	0	10	10
2	10	1	9	19
3	10	2	8	27
4	10	3	7	34
5	10	3	7	41
6	10	5	5	46
7	10	4	6	52
8	10	5	5	57
9	10	3	7	64
10	10	3	7	71

There are a couple of ways to look at this data. One is that as you add people in a limited population of customers, it gets harder and harder to add new customers. And if the network is a network of people, there are diminishing returns as you reach the size of the population of the world or the population of target customers.

Puzzle: What is the curve of viral marketing? How fast can the product spread over time and how does the curve change as more people are added? Is it linear or exponential or something else? Is there an asymptote that caps how many customers a service can reach?

The viral marketing equation (for those of you who are really into the math behind viral marketing as I am) describing the rate of change of customers over time is:

$$dp/dt=kp(1-p/P)$$

P = population of total users in your marketplace

p = number of users at any one time

t = time

so dp/dt = change in the number of users over a change in time

k is rate of change (how often people sign each other up)

Moving on from math back to your native language...

BECOME A VERB

Marketing is the art and science of getting into people's consciousness. A few, but very few, companies have been able to do this. If you can, you have a terrific marketing opportunity. "Skype me" and "Google it" were carefully planned marketing campaigns. People don't say, "Hotmail me" or "Bing it," but they could have if the marketing departments at those companies had done some thinking about making their companies' services into a verb. As you go through your daily routine, try to think about all the companies that touch you and whether they are verbs.

Marketing is 20% hard facts and 80% human brain. When Steve Jobs introduced the iPod, there were 40 other music storage devices on the market and some with four times as much memory. But Apple dominated the market. Why? Because Steve Jobs understood the human side of commerce. He understood that by creating a story behind the product, by making it "cool" or "hip" to have an iPod and making it fun and easy to use, it didn't matter if the product was not quite as powerful or as fast or as cheap as the competition, because he knew that he could capture the customer's emotion, mind, spirit and ego. If you can capture the spirit of the customer, you will benefit well beyond those companies that are just giving them features, advantages and benefits. Humans are aspirational, jealous, ambitious, consumptive, and communicative creatures and selling product to them should take into consideration their human side.

THE HERO STARTUP PITCH

Notice that this book places the pitch after all the thinking has gone into the business plan, the marketing, the product, even the pledge. There is a good reason for that. Many companies start with the pitch, but the entrepreneur hasn't put the work in to building out the plan. It is important for you to make sure you have a clear plan BEFORE you try to pitch anything. It will be hard enough to describe a well thought out, fully developed plan where you are going to change the world and transform an industry. But trying to do it without all the forethought will waste investors' time.

I recently got an email from someone who said, "I have an idea and I need 80 million euros." That was it. I thought it was ridiculous that she would ask for so much money before laying out her idea, so I just deleted the email. It is possible that she was really onto something, but she hadn't led with her best foot. If she had started with, "I have figured out how to cure cancer," or "I have discovered how to travel in time," I would have read on.

When you have built out your plan to the best of your current knowledge, it is time to hone your pitch. Here is some advice you might want to incorporate into the development of your pitch.

If you are going to be a Startup Hero, you will have to stand for something, and as an entrepreneur, you will have to give your elevator pitch many times. It should be passionate, and clear and convincing, but it also should be something important. We do pitch training at Draper University. Some of the advice we give is about the mission and the business model, and some of the advice we give is about the person and what they need to do better. Below is advice I have given to my students at Draper University. Some of the advice was general for business planning purposes, some of it was specific to individual students, and all of it is potentially useful for you if you plan to be a Startup Hero. I recommend that you apply the various pieces of advice to your own business.

Here is some of the general advice I give to the whole class:

- **Think bigger.** Many of you are going after markets that are too small. Even if you feel you need to walk before you run, there should be a long-term vision that is big.

- *Make money.* Very few of you have yet developed a business model where you will make money from real customers buying your service. Do this. Include market sizing and how you will go to the market. Figure out how much you will charge and what your costs will be. See if you can get paid upfront. See if you can make your customers into a sales force for you.

- *Know your market. Know the competition.* Do a simple Google search on your business. Many of your businesses already exist out there. To win in the market as a startup requires something new, even if it is just doing it faster or cheaper.

- *Don't read it.* You should know your topic well enough so that the presentation should be natural. Practice, practice, practice.

- *Show enthusiasm.* When you pitch, do it with feeling. Electrify the stage. You have something they need to hear.

- *Be alert.* I find it helps to go to a sink and splash water on your face. A wake-up splash! It has the added benefit of forcing you to look in the mirror and see if you need to comb your hair or brush your teeth.

Here is some specific advice I have given to individual students:

- Know your numbers cold. No investor will back someone if they don't understand their own financials.

- Make sure your personal passion blends well with your business plan.

- Think global when you plan. Your business will not be big enough if it doesn't scale.

- Think about how you can best reach your market. Is it direct to consumer? Is it leveraged through another business? Are there network effects that you can capitalize on?

- Avoid being trendy. If the press is writing about it, it is too late, or it is not a trend. I have had students that focused on bullying one day, global warming the second, and wealth distribution the third. The trendy news is your window into today, not your window into 15 years from now.

- Make sure you have a product that accomplishes your vision and one that will sell for more than you make it for.

- Think about how your product/service/business is different. How is it better than what is already out there?

- Run some trials with customers.

- Make sure your customers have money.

- Make sure your customer is with you for life or figure out how to spread the word about your business from person to person easily. Diapers and wedding dresses are tough businesses because your customer leaves when she is no longer in that part of her life.

- Know who is on your team. Do they match up well with the work they will have to do to get you to success?

- If you can't easily explain what your product does with words, make sure you can with pictures, video or simulations. Often a mock up is important for selling the product to customers and to investors.

- Make sure your business isn't just a feature on another platform. If Google or Tesla can just copy your service and add it as a feature with their search tool, you probably are not transforming an industry.

- Determine if you have an edge. Is this something you know better than anyone? Do you have a geographic or technological advantage?

- Come up with a story. Stories sell products. Stories sell companies.

- Search for competitors on Google, Bing, Safari, Yandex or Baidu. Find out what they are doing. Are you still unique?

- Consider how easy it would it be for someone who heard your idea to copy it and beat you because they have more money or more people than you do.

- Don't rely on government changing a law to get your business to work. Don't rely on government to buy your product. Don't rely on government.

- Try to create a movement where people will rally around your product. Is there an emotional reaction to your product that you can encourage?

- Think about how your competition will respond, both the big companies and the small companies. How will you defend yourself? Who will support you when you have the onslaught. Make sure your customers can't do without you.

- Charging for something that is free is a challenge, but not impossible.

- Plan the business so that your margins expand as you expand your offering. Does your competition drive the pricing down? Who has the power long term? You or your customer?

- If the product requires working capital, presell it to customers and see how many you will have to make, ideally, getting paid upfront to cover costs. Tesla required a 90% upfront payment for its Founder Series, and it was able to bankroll its production. Many other new products are raising money on Indiegogo and Kickstarter.

- Think about whether this company is more appropriate as a token. ICOs are a new form of entity that allows entrepreneurs to raise money for tokens or coins on the promise that they will spread. If you can envision a token, design the token to be useful. Make sure you complete the marketplace cycle, where there will be demand and supply and movement of the tokens.

- Find out about all the companies that have tried something similar and find out why they failed or succeeded.

- Make sure the person who pays for your service is the

same one who benefits from the service.

- Ask advice of experts, but don't assume they know what they are talking about. The world is different for you than it was for the expert.

- Don't dance with elephants. As a startup, you might have an opportunity to work with a big company. People often call this dancing with elephants. Most startups that pursue this strategy get crushed. They think that the big company will do all their work for them, but instead the big company studies them and takes a long time to decide on anything while the startup loses time and money trying to bag the big one.

Some companies have succeeded in dancing with the elephant. Here are some steps to properly perform the choreography.

Make sure you are paid enough in advance and ensure your margins are high enough to justify working out the contract. The contract will take you much longer than you anticipated. Many elephant contracts take as long as a year to put together. Draw out a spreadsheet to show how your cash will flow before and after the contract kicks in. Then add 90 days to the contract signing, and add an additional 90 days because the elephant will pay late. If you do this exercise, you will understand why so many companies go out of business when they dance with elephants.

Startups can be successful if they ask for a non-recurring engineering (NRE) fee, a break-up fee, and an advance to mollify their cash flow needs in trying to work inside a large bureaucracy. Beyond understanding the payments, it is good to understand the dynamics of an elephant. Once an elephant starts moving in your direction, the momentum inside the business increases, and the big company will have a hard time changing its direction, so make sure when you start dancing with the elephant that it is the dance you want to dance.

IPOS

Why would any company want to go public today? It used to be a goal, even a dream, to build your company up to about $50 million in value and then have an initial public offering (IPO). Now it doesn't even make sense. It currently costs companies $5 million a year to comply with all the new regulations put forth under Sarbanes Oxley. The Sarbanes Oxley Act of 2002 was originally set up by Congress as a reaction to corporate scandals like Enron and WorldCom that occurred in 2001. But the new and additional requirements of the act were overreaching in retrospect. Accounting, legal and insurance costs pile up to make it impractical for a company to be public. To be able to pay the required $5 million a year without causing serious damage to the bottom line, a company would have to be extremely large, where most of the growth had been squeezed out of it. The unintended consequence of Sarbanes Oxley is that the people the government is trying to protect are not allowed to invest in high return, high growth companies.

Compliance requires expensive lawyers who can take the company through the process and keep the company from tripping over any obscure regulation. To add insult to injury, every public company starts off with risk of a class action lawsuit from lawyers (so called trawlers because they trawl for lawsuits) who buy one share of every IPO so they can lead a class action lawsuit against the company if its shares go down or the company doesn't perform as expected.

The way a class action works is that investors become plaintiffs unless they specifically read through copious amounts of legal-eze and fill out a form that says that they do not wish to be a plaintiff—and the lawyer usually gets one-third of the settlement plus whatever is not specifically collected by investors who have to read through additional text to figure out how to collect. Since there is a risk of class action lawsuit, the company has to pay more for insurance. Moreover, since the rules are so complex, more calculations must be made, so accounting costs are extremely high, and it makes reading financial statements that much more complicated and nebulous.

Further, if a government pension like CalPERS is an investor, they influence the company to change the nature of its board to comply with political winds. And public investors want to see quarter to quarter progress, without regard for the long term, so companies are not as aligned with their investors as they were when they were private. Public investors can also short sell your stock, which in some cases is enough to drive the company out of business. A public company has to show its customers (and its competitors) how high its profit margins are, and after seeing them, the customers might try to renegotiate their contracts. Salaries and incentive pay are scrutinized by the public. Competitors who stay private, saving the $5 million per year compliance fees, can use the extra money for marketing their product or designing a more advanced product to compete with the public company. Ever since these Sarbanes Oxley regulations were imposed on public companies, going public is more of a gauntlet than a celebration.

Because of the downsides to going public, most bright entrepreneurs decide to avoid the public markets and keep their companies private, and as a result, employees, investors and founders have completely illiquid shares. Airbnb and Uber, at this writing, have created hundreds of paper millionaires who can't sell their shares, even though there are plenty of willing buyers. You could have a billion dollars' worth of Uber stock today and not be able to buy a cup of coffee with it.

These regulations built around trying to protect people from losing their investment money have stymied the wealth in America and around the world. A wealthy society is a liquid society, and any limitation to that liquidity puts a serious damper on the jobs, wealth and prosperity of the people in that society.

Our government allows, even encourages, people to play the lottery while they carefully control, monitor and restrict those same people from investing in private companies that could become major engines of progress. It is time our regulations let private companies trade.

The value of a company is determined by what the investors believe the discounted cash flows of a given company will be over time. Investors do tend to suffer groupthink in that they celebrate together and panic together. When investors are optimistic about the future, short-term cash flows and short-term profitability don't matter as much to them as future prospects. When investors become more pessimistic, they fly to 'quality.' which means that they focus purely on historic numbers to determine company value. Often unwary investors can lose money in the process. But, on average, they are more likely to make money. The Dow Jones Industrial Average has grown on average 12% per year over the last 100 years.

This is a weird time. Heavy-handed regulations have made it unattractive for companies to go public, even to be public. And private markets are more illiquid than they have been at any time since I have been in the business. I think there is an opportunity for entrepreneurs to create a more liquid market for private companies (even if they have to be limited to a walled garden of qualified investors), and there is an opportunity for politicians and statesmen to build a new platform around ownership liquidity. Governments are in competition with each other now, so expect to see a race to light touch government regulations by businesses as they choose their locales based on who provides the friendliest neighborhood.

The word is getting out. There needs to be a new way to build liquidity for shareholders. The government has regulated IPOs so much that IPOs are no longer palatable for companies or investors.

Here are some alternatives for liquidity in the private markets that I have come across. eShares (now called Carta) is reinventing the capitalization table, which keeps track of who owns what in a company, and long term could help companies become more efficiently tradeable stock without the need for a lot of accounting or legal work. AngelList, Crowdfunder, and FundersClub are connecting companies directly to their investors and could ultimately become exchanges. My partner, Aamer Sarfraz, at Draper Oakwood created a new form of special purpose acquisition company (SPAC) that does all the legal work to create a public shell so that companies can do a simple merger into that public shell company to bring a new company public. Bitcoin and smart contracts on the blockchain could become a simpler means to pay a dividend or distribute proceeds. ICOs might circumvent the entire process by allowing entrepreneurs to raise money for projects through a token offering.

In any case, heavy-handed regulation leads to fewer IPOs and a sinking economy, but hopefully new solutions will arise that will allow more liquidity into the system to improve the economy.

CONCLUSION

Becoming a Startup Hero is not easy. There are challenges everywhere. But if you have the passion in your heart and the drive in your head, and you are willing to do whatever it takes, you can be a Startup Hero. Your life will be difficult, challenging, exciting, unique, and constantly changing. You could be the next Gates, Zuckerberg, Bezos, Brin, Page, Hewlett, Packard, Ford, Procter, Gamble, Disney, or Nakamoto. But remember, failing is important too. Whether you run your own business or shake up someone else's, the people who make waves move progress forward.

Anything is possible.

FINAL NOTE: THE RISKMASTER

One of my first experiences with a true entrepreneur brought something to light for me. Bob Russ had created Unity Systems, a home management system that controlled all your creature comforts at home. I was impressed with Bob because he was clear, focused and determined and had taken out 30 different credit cards from different states to keep his business alive. He was the most passionate entrepreneur I have ever met.

Bob hired Tom Riley, a solid Harvard MBA, who knew how to run a business. Tom became frustrated with Bob, who kept odd hours, made absurd declarations, and wasn't managing his people. Tom came to the board and asked to replace Bob as CEO and to throw Bob out. It was a tough decision at the time. I was new to the business and deferred to the more senior investors in making the call. The board has one job—to hire and fire the CEO. And given the ultimatum, we went with Tom, the wise Harvard MBA. What we should have done was somehow keep both of them. Bob was the heart of the business and Tom was the mind.

Bob left the company with the same passion he came into it with. He was bitter, angry, and although still a large shareholder, he almost didn't want the company to succeed without him. To this day, I believe that the spirit of the company left with Bob. Tom worked tirelessly for years to make the company work, but without Bob and his vision, passion and willingness to do whatever it took, the company struggled and ultimately died.

Tom has gone on to be a very successful diplomat and served as ambassador to Morocco. I have not heard again from Bob.

Because of my failure as a Unity board member, I have come to believe that both passion and business sense are necessary to make a business successful. All the qualities necessary to succeed are rarely contained in any one individual. I believe that every company needs a heart (like Bob) and a mind (like Tom). If the heart leaves the company, the company dies. If the mind leaves the company, it might live on indefinitely, but it won't achieve the success it deserves.

As much as I have tried to support the entrepreneur, I found that

I often am yelling into the wind. Businesses have a life of their own, and sometimes entrepreneurs become collateral damage as issues of practicality come into play, overriding the urge to build the vision. I have found that the businesses who lose their founders become hollow without them.

The experiences I have had with Bob and other Startup Heroes helped define me as a venture capitalist. My mission has been to support them; to support these people who may be misunderstood, may be willing to take the company further to the edge of the cliff than their boards do, but still have the heart and vision that may change the world. They need the respect and protection to overcome nervous boards like ours that might not have the same vision or risk tolerance that they do.

This one is for you, Bob, and for all of those entrepreneurs like you out there who make extraordinary sacrifices for their businesses, some coming up short and some going the distance.

THE RISKMASTER (ALL RIGHTS RESERVED. LYRICS BY TIM DRAPER)

Invested all his mattress money
Divorced his prom queen hometown honey
Scraping up his alimony
Friends think he's a little funny

Needs a "world class CEO."
And just another million or so
Get him to some real cash flow
So tears and sweat can IPO

For 15 years he's been out gunned
Bankers demanding blood refund
Company's looking moribund
Even Draper will not fund!

Chorus:

He is the Riskmaster
Lives fast, drives faster

Skates on the edge of disaster
He is the Riskmaster

He's got a mission
Company vision
An artist's ambition
Gut intuition

Fearless and free employee
No guarantee
for the corporate escapee

Team fights on against the trend
Had to lay off his best friend
Called a "recession" seems like "depression."
Chapter seven. Is this the end?

But then a salesman shouts, "We got it!"
The company's gonna show a profit
To think the papers rang, "quixotic"
The sky has opened astronautic.

Chorus:

He is on top, on top of the world
At last they see it. Vision unfurled!
Cashflow landslide!
Now everybody wants a piece of his hide.
Press wants him fried. Court wants him tried.
Anyone this rich must have lied.

The Riskmaster became my theme song, something I sang for the Startup Heroes that drive progress, employ people, create wealth and make our lives better. I recommend that you write your own theme song to your customers. It will highlight the respect you have for them, and when you sing it, they will all know that you are a true Startup Hero.

BENEDICTION

It seems to be the case that some new technologies are replacing the need for many workers. AI, marketplaces and the blockchain promise to make life better for us as consumers, make our society wealthier as a whole, and free up working people to do more abstract and higher-level things with their lives. The jobs that computers can potentially do better are the monotonous jobs, like driving us or our things from one place to another, analyzing data patterns of customers, and administering regulations. These monotonous jobs will give way to jobs that are more abstract (and frankly more interesting) like monitoring autonomous vehicles, enhancing customer experiences, and improving banking, legal, accounting or even government service.

While some may have difficulty adjusting to the new world, the jobs in the new world will be more interesting and more fulfilling. After all, before the industrial revolution, most people had to be out working on the farms, but with automation, a lot of those manual jobs were replaced with more interesting abstract jobs, and we adjusted. Technological progress is taking us through a similar transformation. People of the future may look back at us and say, "Those poor people used to have to drive themselves around spending as much as two wasted hours each day trapped in a car."

Technology drives human progress forward. Workers will have to adapt to these technological changes and reinvent themselves to find new jobs. If the world remained stagnant, these technologies would leave many people idle. But humans are adaptable and creative, so I am optimistic about how this new technological future will look.

And technology is progressing faster than it has at any time in history. Moore's Law states that compute power doubles every 18 months. And there are new sets of breakthroughs as computers become smarter and smarter. Each new generation can do more for us than the last one. Compounding Moore's Law is Metcalfe's Law that states a network becomes more powerful with the number of nodes on the network. And that has become more apparent as more of us get smartphones to communicate with, and those phones build out information about who we are, where we are, when we will be somewhere, who our friends are, what we eat, how much money we can earn for doing what for whom, what our most efficient use of time would be and other patterns of behavior.

And progress is not linear. Progress is accelerating. Whereas last year, we could do about two-thirds of what we can do today with equivalently priced equipment, 15 years ago we could do about one-one thousandth of what we can do today.

We have to anticipate progress. For job seekers, or for those who will be disintermediated in the coming wave of technological change, I recommend projecting out and imagining what the world will look like 2, 3, 4, or more years into the future and decide what will be your highest and best use to society then. If we are to think about what kind of job to get (or to create) today, we have to think about what trends are relevant and what might be an important market-place in the future.

Beyond that, we need visionaries. People who might create trans-formations in industries, who will catch the exponential curve of technology and ride it to success, create the new jobs, and improve the outlook for humans and humanity. These people will be the Startup Heroes of tomorrow. Maybe one of them is you!

ADDITIONAL CONTENT

The Startup Hero podcast and video available on iTunes and YouTube

Watch luminary Startup Heroes: drapertv.com

Watch Startup Heroes pitch, then invest: meetthedrapers.com

Check out our global venture network: drapernetwork.com

Teach children to be a Startup Hero: bizworld.org

Become a Startup Hero: draperuniversity.com

Pitch your startup, hero: draper.vc

STARTUP HERO ASSESSMENT

Do You Have What It Takes to Be a Startup Hero Entrepreneur?

What is your Startup Hero potential? Take this assessment to find out. (Note: This assessment is completely subjective and unscientific.) Answer the following questions at your own risk. This is mostly for fun, so don't rely on this test to determine your true potential. Only you know if you are capable of becoming a Startup Hero.

If you don't score well, have no fear. Draper University is here to reshape your thinking.

1. Which of these three people do you admire most (choose at least one woman and one man)?

   a. George Washington.

   b. Henry Ford.

   c. Arnold Schwarzenegger.

   d. Hillary Clinton.

   e. Sheryl Sandberg.

   f. Oprah Winfrey.

2. Do you drink alcohol?

   a. Yes

   b. No.

3. Which of these do you consider to be the best use of money?

   a. Giving society liquidity.

   b. Building my vision.

   c. Buying a nice house or car

   d. My customer to show how much they appreciate my product.

4. Do you believe that the college admissions process worked for you?

    a. Yes

    b. No.

5. Have you had any trouble with authorities?

    a. Yes.

    b. No

6. Have you ever saved anyone from drowning or a fire or other life-threatening situation?

    a. Yes.

    b. No

7. Are you female?

    a. Yes.

    b. No

8. Do you like red or green better?

    a. Green.

    b. Red

9. Are you a second, third or later child?

    a. Yes.

    b. No

10. Do you get emotional when things are not going according to your plan?

    a. Yes

    b. No.

11. Do you enjoy creative pursuits?

    a. Yes.

    b. No

12. Are either of your parents entrepreneurs?

    a.   Yes.

    b.   No

13. Are you particularly short or particularly tall?

    a.   Yes.

    b.   No

14. Do you have any sort of sixth sense?

    a.   Yes.

    b.   No

15. Do you look for ways to improve things?

    a.   Yes.

    b.   No

16. Do you get satisfaction from repairing mechanical products?

    a.   Yes.

    b.   No

17. Are you either an engineer or a marketer?

    a.   Yes.

    b.   No

18. Do you like to tell people what to do?

    a.   Yes

    b.   No.

19. Do you want to build an empire?

    a.   Yes

    b.   No.

20. Are you particularly ugly or particularly beautiful?

    a.   Yes.

    b.   No

21. Do you like it when the underdog wins the game?

    a. Yes.

    b. No

22. What inspires you to travel?

    a. Learn about history

    b. Understand the culture.

    c. Learn the language

    d. Meet new people.

    e. Have new experiences.

23. Is status important to you?

    a. Yes

    b. No.

24. Do you keep up with the trends?

    a. Yes

    b. No.

25. Do you change your look regularly?

    a. Yes

    b. No.

26. Have you obsessed over anything beyond what others think is normal?

    a. Yes.

    b. No

27. Do you judge people who are acting out?

    a. Yes

    b. No.

28. Do you ever say, "There should be a law"?

    a. Yes

b. No.

29. Do you ever say, "Let's be reasonable"?

    a. Yes

    b. No.

30. Do you use the word "impossible"?

    a. Yes

    b. No.

31. Do you ever say, "What if you," or "What if I," or "What if we"?

    a. Yes.

    b. No

32. Do you ever say, "What goes around comes around"?

    a. Yes

    b. No.

33. Do you ever say, "Get to work"?

    a. Yes.

    b. No

34. Do you know how much money you have?

    a. Yes

    b. No.

35. What would you rather do (choose two)?

    a. Change people's minds.

    b. Improve the lives of the poor.

    c. Build something with your name on it

    d. Make money-

    e. Help with progress.

    f. Have something to do

Some answers have dots after them. Count your dots. If you have more than 15 dots, there may be a greater purpose for you. Come to Draper University. If you have fewer than 15, there may still be a greater purpose for you, and Draper University might help you fulfill that purpose.

ACKNOWLEDGEMENTS

Special thanks to everyone who helped me with this book. To my wife, Melissa, for reading it and subtly telling me to throw it out and start over. To Wendy McArdle and her sister Shannon Topalovich for adding their special touches and sweating the details. To Gil Lubetsky for saving this book several times when I deleted it or the computer crashed. To Megan Kurohara for getting this out on social media. To Andy Tang for encouraging me to continue. To Siri Srinivas for trying to make it politically correct. To Rohan Gupta for his fast turnaround help. To all my partners at all the Draper Funds for their involvement in all these experiences. To Steve Jobs who created the iPhone that I wrote most of this book on. To United Airlines who provided me with countless hours of time sitting in their planes to recall stories. To all the entrepreneurs I have met who have driven me to write this book for future entrepreneurs. To Dad for being the first to read and comment on it. To all the people I have written about in this book, and to you who are reading it. I love you all.

Made in the USA
San Bernardino, CA
07 May 2018